DECEMBER 2003

Larry Kane's
Philadelphia

Larry Kane's
Philadelphia

Larry Kane

Foreword by Dan Rather

Temple University Press
Philadelphia

Temple University Press, Philadelphia 19122
Copyright © 2000 by Larry Kane
All rights reserved
Published 2000
Printed in the United States of America

⊗ The paper used in this publication meets the requirements of the American National Standard for Information Sciences—Permanence of Paper for Printed Library Materials, ANSI Z39.48-1984

Library of Congress Cataloging-in-Publication Data

Kane, Larry, 1942–
  Larry Kane's Philadelphia / Larry Kane ; foreword by Dan Rather.
    p. cm.
  Includes index.
  ISBN 1-56639-806-1 (cloth : alk. paper)
    1. Philadelphia (Pa.)—Politics and government—20th century. 2. Press—Pennsylvania—Philadelphia. 3. Kane, Larry, 1942– . I. Title: Philadelphia.
II. Title.
F158.52.K36 2000
974.8'11—dc21   00-028649

For Donna, Michael, and Alexandra

Contents

Foreword

How do you go from young upstart to dean of Philadelphia newsmen in thirty-four years? Larry Kane knows. And therein hangs a tale. Larry Kane is, as he puts it, an unapologetic "homer." He eats, sleeps, and breathes his chosen city. His work on and off screen and his words between these covers speak eloquently of a deep and abiding love for Philadelphia. And for this, Philadelphia has loved him back.

It's something they don't teach you in anchor school, but it's an invaluable lesson: You can't just live in the town you cover; you must weave yourself into the very fabric of city life. You need to go to the PTA bake sales; walk the streets of neighborhoods rich, poor, and struggling to get by; and relish taking part in the cherished traditions and idiosyncrasies that distinguish your place on the map from the next. Larry Kane not only understands this, but he has embodied it heart and soul throughout his career.

Larry stands as a notable exception to broadcast journalists who all too often regard their cities as just another stopover on a market-to-market tour. Evident in his coverage are both his hard-won experience and the bottom-line value he places on local news. You may not know that Larry has been on the Philadelphia political beat since the turmoil of the 1960s, that he's done frontline reporting on everything from busing riots to papal visits in four decades in the city's history. But you can certainly feel it in the insight he brings to each story, can see it in the many firsts and exclusives his deep roots and hard work in Philadelphia have brought him.

What's more, he has always kept an eye on the larger picture of world affairs. It is regrettable but true that these days even certain national news operations turn up their noses at foreign stories, and there are local news broadcasts that consider their complete lack of international coverage a point of honor. Such an attitude is anathema to this reporter. And with dispatches and datelines from Paris to Jerusalem, Larry has shown an abiding awareness of how the local and the far-flung interact to produce what we call the news.

This is his story. In these pages are the ups and downs of a life well spent in broadcast journalism—gritty tales of city politics, of meetings with popes and presidents, of painful lessons and close calls. It's a story told with candor and suffused with affection for the city he calls home. Here Larry Kane shows you his world and his Philadelphia, and I can't think of a better guide.

DAN RATHER

Prologue

My Philadelphia, or I Am a Marked Car

Gathering information and relaying it to my viewers is what I do for a living. I sit in a chair, look at a glass lens, and talk to someone I can't see. I think, "What are they saying?" or perhaps "Do they like me?" It is an unusual way to make a living, giving information to nameless and faceless people. But, except for one brief fling in New York, it's what I've been doing here in Philadelphia for thirty-four years now.

Those thirty-four years have been a learning experience for both of us—the city and me. Philadelphia has had to learn a number of painful lessons about class, about race, about confrontation and entitlement. As for me, the job that lured me to this city and the job I got were in different worlds. In three years, my job description changed. The world of the microphone was replaced by the world of the camera, and I had to face down my personal insecurities quickly and painfully. I also had to learn some hard lessons about being well known and negotiating the networks of power. I've been flattered, threatened, humiliated, and honored, all in pursuit of a story. What keeps me at it is the big story, the one that continues to obsess me—the relationship between power and politics and how those forces come together in one of the world's most beautiful cities.

But I haven't always been an eyewitness to history in Philadelphia. For the Brooklyn-born son of an electrician, it was a strange fate that set me down in the soft pretzel capital of the world, talking to a camera.

From 1957 to 1966, starting at the age of fifteen, I was a radio reporter in Miami, where I chased ambulances for news stories, covered politics, and hung around police stations. I made a brief stop in St. Louis, returned to Miami as a news executive, and spent three unbelievable summers traveling with the Beatles on their North American tours, reporting to fifty radio stations. (No, that's not in this book, though John Lennon does turn up later on.) Then, in the summer of 1966, I was offered a position as anchor-reporter at WFIL Radio in Philadelphia. The nation's fourth largest metropolis was a mystery to me, but I figured the job would provide a juicy item for my developing resume.

In 1966, three stations were doing news in Philadelphia. WCAU TV, with anchorman John Facenda, and KYW TV, with anchor Vince Leonard, were the leaders of the pack. Facenda, the dean of Philadelphia broadcasters, was a native son who was also the voice of the National Football League's dramatic weekend documentaries. Leonard, who came from the Midwest, was the consummate broadcaster, a good journalist with all-American looks. WFIL TV, located in the same building as the radio station I came to work for, was a distant third. Eventually, I would work for all three stations, but on that foggy night when I arrived in town, that all lay in the future.

My first view of Philadelphia was of a fire. I was crossing the Walt Whitman Bridge late at night. The date was September 12, 1966, and at the age of twenty-three, I was arriving to begin a job as radio newscaster for WFIL Radio. I saw the flames roaring at several locations to the south. I paid my toll, immediately drove to a phone booth, dialed up, and asked for the fire emergency line, where I promptly and vigorously reported these flashes of fire. There was a pause on the line. Then the fire radio dispatcher said, "Whateryoutawkin about? Them there's oil refineries. You crazy?"

Nevertheless, he thanked me. Feeling like a fool, I drove on, looking back at the patches of fire and the skyline of a city that would offer wonderful opportunities and trap doors of jeopardy.

In the months that followed, I moved cautiously through this metropolis of city and suburb, encompassing three states and bounded by an ocean to the east, rivers to the west, luscious green mountains to the north, and smaller cities to the south. I was exploring, trying to get a feel for the area. So this is Philadelphia, I began to understand, a city where they put mustard on soft pretzels, devour the lowest of meat products called scrapple, and consume more cheese steaks than any community in the world. This is Philadelphia, where politics is a blood sport and going to jail has become a badge of honor. This is Philadelphia, where power is concentrated in two professions joined at the hip—politics and law. This is Philadelphia, where race is used as a political weapon on both sides of the racial divide, where blacks—chased out of their neighborhoods by gentrification and singed with economic hardship—emerged in the sixties in a wave of protest followed by electoral power. This is a community where crime is an obsession, safety a priority. It's a region of livable homes and unbearable poverty. It's a treasure chest of arts and culture, ranging from the art museum on the Benjamin Franklin Parkway to the opera house in Wilmington. Visually, the area blends urban sophistication with a small-town flair and suburban beauty in a way unmatched in America. But most of all, this is a town more than a city, a conglomeration of neighborhoods with separate identities and a collection of villages in outlying counties, and its greatest strength is not in the concrete canyons of Market Street but in the soul and hearts of the millions of people who make it the most livable big-little city in America.

Over the years, through success and failure, I became addicted to Philadelphia, like its other citizens complaining about everyday problems but reveling in the joy of just being here. I came here to get some big-city reporting experience, and I wound up experiencing thirty-four years of the best and worst of human behavior in the corridors of power and on the streets. I have worked for three major news operations in Philadelphia. In between, I spent sixteen months in a city to the north named New York. But that Philadelphia addiction drove me back.

All cities, small and large, lay claim to being the greatest, the best, and the most livable. Philadelphia and its surrounding counties have never made those grandiose boasts. In reality, it took professional sports victories to make people of the region feel good about themselves. When the Flyers won the Stanley Cup in 1974, people declared, "Philadelphia is back." Who's kidding whom here? Philadelphia is back from what? The fact is that this community never needed a comeback. It has always been a great American city; good looks can obscure the true meaning of greatness.

My Philadelphia has the good looks, the big buildings, and the small row homes. But to this reporter, Philadelphia stands out for two reasons—the people who live here and the way they are.

Chances are that, as you read this book, you will get an impression of Philadelphia that's different from the one you have now. That doesn't invalidate your Philadelphia. But this book is about *my* Philadelphia. My Philadelphia is a burgeoning suburban superpower, a community with a countryside of smaller communities, a city of pomp and hopeless poverty, a region where people never take yes for an answer. In this town, you either put up or shut up, and if you don't have the goods, please don't come to market. There are no pushovers. Philadelphians can spot a phony a mile away. As they say in South Philadelphia, money talks, bullshit walks.

Perhaps this book will also serve to illuminate the perils of being well known. Being well known doesn't mean you're a better person. It does get you a better table at a restaurant, a good seat at a concert, but with it comes a price—the pained expression on a child's face, the total lack of privacy, and, sadly, the fear of walking into a crowd of strangers.

It has been said that I am an icon in Philadelphia. Frankly, anyone who could last this long would be a candidate for icon—or relic. On the way to a mayor's reception at Lemon Hill Mansion in Fairmount Park, a production assistant noted that we were taking a car with no station logo on the side to avoid notice. I retorted, "Are you kidding? I *am* a marked car."

That comment became a source of constant ribbing in the newsrooms I have worked in, but it is a fact of my life. A television journalist, bringing his face and perspective nightly, becomes as familiar as a favorite lamp, a member of the family. Being recognized is a product of just being here. One of my greatest pleasures is to walk the streets of a faraway town, where my peripheral vision isn't telling me that someone is watching. At times, I've needed a vacation from myself. But being a marked car, accepting adulation and sometimes contempt, is not as important as being respected. Respect, to this reporter, is being recognized for your work, not your facial features.

My Philadelphia is not the town that Bill Cosby and Oprah Winfrey sell in TV commercials. The people who visit never see it all. Tourism is great for the cash register, but day trippers will never feel the grit of the street, the lure of the people.

There is no pretense or superficiality in my Philadelphia, none of that Southern California "gosh and gee whiz and have a great day," those moronic, utopian, feel-good expressions of the perfect life. Philadelphia is not *The Truman Show.* Cherry Hill is not the San Fernando Valley. But its people and its diner crowds are much more interesting. If you want to know more about my Philadelphia, sit yourself down at Ponzio's or the Melrose or Oak Lane Diners. The tables may be small, the stools a bit undersized, but there you will meet the people, observe their manners, hear their accents, eat their foods.

In my Philadelphia, race relations are far from subtle. People are loath to hide their prejudices. It's ugly, but it's real, and preferable to the phony baloney racial harmony of the new South. And despite the tensions, a simple fact remains: more blacks and whites work and live together peacefully in this city than in any other in America.

In my Philadelphia, people debate the issues till they are red in the face and dry in the mouth. There was never any middle ground, for instance, about former mayor Frank Rizzo. You either loved him or hated him. But the big man embodied the spirit of individual Philadelphians. To Rizzo and to most Philadelphians, everything is black and white. There are friends and enemies, and there is no in-between. The best and worst of Rizzo will stand out in this book, and not just when I'm talking about hizzonner.

It is true that my Philadelphia contains some of the worst drivers in America. Road rage is the rage of Philadelphia, and unfortunately I have become one of those drivers, complaining about people who tailgate at high speeds and then, in a hurry, doing it myself. Yet find yourself stuck on any street in any neighborhood, and someone will stop and help, without trepidation.

In my Philadelphia, crime is a major issue and is not swept under the rug. Because of good politics and public relations, a dramatic shift has occurred: people seem less afraid, and because of that, Center City has resumed its lock as the city center. Then, in 1996, the murder of jogger Kimberly Ernest in Center City frayed the myth of the safety net, even though federal statistics show that, in general, crime is down in the area.

In my Philadelphia, habits die hard. In 1902, for example, the nation's first Horn and Hardart automat opened at Eighth and Chestnut. And on April 4, 1967, it was one of the last to close. Tradition and endurance go hand in hand in Philadelphia.

In my Philadelphia, people may feel unloved by the rest of the nation, but they still live up to the advertising slogan—"Philadelphia . . . the City That Loves You Back." They disdain those who take cheap shots at their town. Witness Phillies great Mike Schmidt, respected as the finest third baseman in baseball history but despised by thousands of fans for his negative vibes about the city. He seemed ill at ease here and complained about the fans. No wonder Schmidt decided to live in Florida.

But they are also the most generous people in America. When trouble breaks, they break in with aid, monetary and personal. In the business of TV news, you just mention someone in need and the phone rings off the hook. On June 6, 1967, when a power failure affected thirteen million people, some for up to ten hours, neighbors and strangers delivered thousands of flashlights and candles in the Greater Northeast, South Philadelphia, and Montgomery County.

In my Philadelphia, performance counts. For years, the national press has made chopped liver of Philadelphia fans for booing and throwing things onto the field. What's the problem here? The difference between Philadelphia fans and their counterparts across the country is simple: Philadelphians will pay big bucks to watch millionaire athletes, but if they don't perform, they are usually fired—by the fans. Eagles quarterback Randall Cunningham soared, sank, and sought new employment, though when he made a 1998 comeback with Minnesota, he was cheered on by Eagles fans who remembered his greatness. Another Cunningham, Billy, of basketball fame, is still revered, along with Julius Erving and ex-Eagles coach Dick Vermeil, for his hard work. These men all work in other cities, but the love for them here has never stopped.

In Philadelphia the welcomes are generally shaky for new people on the block, even in TV news. In my Philadelphia, good looks don't count as much as good reporting. The names of failed TV personalities are written on pink slips. Some of the most beautiful and handsome anchors in America have had brief stops in Philadelphia. They dazzled with their glamour, but Philadelphians want more than that. That's why I will forever be grateful for the opportunities viewers have given me here.

In my Philadelphia, the people want their public figures to be vulnerable and therefore acceptable candidates for forgiveness. Ed Rendell can lose his temper, and Philadelphians mark it down to hard work and stress. Frank Rizzo could invariably say the wrong thing, but he never paid at the voting booth on his first two bids for election. Two events in my career illustrate this point—my brief stint in New York and the libel lawsuit filed by another former Philadelphia mayor, Bill Green. Either one might have jeopardized my career. But the people in my Philadelphia were forgiving, although never forgetting. Today, viewers still walk up to me and say, "Welcome back, Lar," a reference to my return to Philadelphia TV in late 1978; lots of others still bawl me out for having left in the first place.

A flag of caution here. In this book I will refer to "the people of Philadelphia." They may actually come from Cherry Hill, Dover, or Upper Merion. They may come from Kensington or Kingsessing. I don't intend these interpretations as a form of stereotyping. Not all people fit a general mold, but many do, or they fit it in one or more particular ways. There are similarities that simply can't be ignored. This is a family town, a town with a stable way of life encouraged by postwar construction that gave hundreds of thousands affordable housing.

The people of my Philadelphia take pride in living here but are proprietary in their allegiance. Where you live is much more important than where you work. Where you live also means how much you will know. Delaware, for example, is a tight-knit community where there are few secrets and even fewer mysteries. The Anne Marie Fahey murder changed that, but even in the layers of intrigue, this murder case highlighted the simple reality that everybody knows everyone and everything about them in that little diamond of a state. Tom Capano, convicted of dumping her at sea, was so well known that it was almost impossible to pick a jury. The people of one of Pennsylvania's two Springfields want to make sure you know which county they live in, since one is in Delaware County, the other in Montgomery. The residents of Mount Laurel, New Jersey, are careful to separate their fortunes from those of Cherry Hill or Moorestown residents. On the fashionable Main Line, the people of Gladwynne, which is part of Lower Merion Township, clearly delineate between their plush neighborhood and the middle-class neighborhood of Narberth in the same township. If you live in Overbrook, is that the town of Overbrook or the neighborhood of Overbrook Park? In Nicetown (what a wonderful name), the block captains don't want you to confuse the neighborhood with Olney or Feltonville, two nearby neighborhoods with their own personalities. In Northeast Philadelphia, an area called Mayfair, the jewel of the Frankford area corridor, is just a few miles from Oxford Circle, but it could well be a thousand miles.

My Philadelphia includes areas that have been grossly neglected. Camden and Chester come to mind, and the leadership of the remainder of the region should be sued for nonsupport. The great Philadelphia councilman Thacher Longstreth, a twenty-five-year veteran, has been urging regional cooperation for years, but in my Philadelphia, turf is turf, and individual interest reigns supreme. The power of personal interest often collides with much more dire human needs.

In my Philadelphia, geography is paramount. You're either from Fishtown, with its ethnic diversity, or Kensington, its immediate neighbor, with its narrow row homes in the shadow of the Frankford El. The street map defines the diagonal boundaries. East of the Boulevard and west of the Boulevard are separated by one street, Roosevelt Boulevard, but they are miles apart. In my Philadelphia, your credibility lives or dies on your mastery of geography.

Beyond these geographical boundaries lies another world, the landscape of the mind, sometimes called the human spirit. For a reporter navigating this mapless landscape and learning to cover this area, the effort seems equal to pursuing a graduate degree—a degree in understanding humans. With this study come some real mysteries. Why, for example, do many Philadelphia men wear bow ties? There are more here than almost anywhere. Is gasoline gas, or is it gazz (heavy on the z's), as Philadelphians and South Jerseyans like to call it? In the neighborhoods, why does everyone shop on a street they call the avenue? Who mapped the city's streets, and why is it impossible to figure out how to get to any neighborhood outside of the carefully planned grid of Center City? Why are there are two downtowns—Center City and South Philadelphia, which is affectionately called downtown by the people who live there? In the suburbs there is also a hub—the King of Prussia Mall, one of the world's largest shopping centers. It certainly doesn't offer the charm of Manayunk, a neighborhood of steep hills and hip bistros, or of Center City, but it is without question a suburban center of significance. More mysteries.

My Philadelphia contains some unforgettable personalities, many of whom you'll meet in this book. But the most fascinating personality is that of the people—solid, honest, very challenging, not easily impressed, and persistent in their ways. They have their shortcomings and bad habits, their frustrations and their prejudices, but they are also, on the bottom line, fair and reasonable. What other group of people would have given a twenty-three-year-old newsman the opportunity to anchor the news and would hang with him through thirty-four years of joy and gloom, success and despair, sharing the events that shaped their community and his career? Philadelphia has changed in the last thirty-four years, and I've grown with it, but there is one constant—the unrivaled passion of the region's people to demand the best and settle for nothing less.

This book is my view of Philadelphia and its surrounding regions. This is not a history; it is a journal of the most important events of this community from the perspective of a reporter who lived that history up close. It is also a chronicle of power in government and in journalism. I hope you take from this a sense of the textures of the people and the place—and that it offers you a new and more controversial look at some of the people who made news, for better or worse.

I have done it all in Philadelphia—helped raise two wonderful kids with a dynamic and loving woman, tried to help people in the community, and covered more news than I can remember. That news took me from Paris to Pennsauken, from Tel Aviv to Torresdale, from Mount St. Helen's to Mount Laurel. I've encountered presidents, senators, mayors, and kings, movie stars, superstars, fanatics, phonies, and ordinary people who've made extraordinary achievements. In my business, I've met some wonderful people and some real jerks. I have been honored, chastised, respected, and sued. My career has been rich in challenges. And now I've faced another challenge—to tell the story of my life in Philadelphia, candidly and with nothing to hide.

Part One

The Road to the Anchor Chair

When my high-school graduation took place in 1960, the teachers told the graduating class of an exciting decade to come, with peace, prosperity, and opportunity for all. We were headed to the moon, but here on earth there was some troubling and unfinished business ahead. Those problems had not yet surfaced five months later, when I covered the press conference of a future president. I sat on the sunny porch of a South Florida hotel, watching a tall man with auburn hair gracefully walk in. He talked of a new frontier, a land energized by young people with fresh ideas. The man was president-elect John Kennedy, and at that press conference he offered us a vision of a rose-colored world. Who could know in 1960 that America's cities would be shattered by violence and fire; that another fire, annihilation by napalm, would symbolize a faraway war that would divide the nation; that law would evaporate and order would become more difficult to find; and that assassins' bullets would kill three national leaders, including the new president, all in the space of eight years? The sixties were not so fabulous, but the heat of the protest and the fire of the battles would shape our destiny for years to come.

And I certainly couldn't know that, in one single decade, I would find myself at the Berlin wall, in the middle of a violent protest at a political convention, mired in anarchy on the streets of Paris, and trapped in volleys of gunfire on the streets of Wilmington, Delaware. Life in the sixties was full of surprises, not the least of which was Philadelphia.

Good Evening and Almost Goodnight

The year 1966 was a decent one, although I didn't believe that at the time. After eight years in radio news in Miami and St. Louis, I was coming to the fourth largest media market in America to spend a year, learn the ropes, and head on to a radio network. That one year turned to thirty-four, and the anonymity I had enjoyed as a radio personality would end in a television career and a life without any privacy.

My first year in Philadelphia was sheer hell. I didn't know anybody, and I kept getting lost. It is easy to get lost in this region, especially in suburban areas, and I was a lost soul, searching for the right street sign and an identity at the same time. But I was fascinated with the physical beauty of the city and suburbs and even more so with the spirit of the people. I'd walk the streets of Center City and marvel: this was a downtown area where people actually lived. The river drives fascinated me, as did the suburban areas. As a child in New York and Miami, it had seemed to me that you had to travel very far from the city to reach country green, but in Philadelphia that green was right before my eyes.

For the first few years, I lived in South Jersey and toured its countryside, surprised to find a major farming industry. I learned little things about my new town—including the language of South and Northeast Philadelphia ("yo" comes to mind), the rich gospel culture of North and West Philadelphia, and the influence and power of the Main Line elite. That power would eventually wane, but in 1966 the fashionable and posh Main Line mafia was well entrenched in banking, law, and the arts. I was fascinated by the region's blend of cultures and devoured it, along with the food, with gusto and anticipation.

I was a month into the new job when loneliness began to overtake me, that feeling of being by yourself and far from home. Although I savored my new experiences, I felt nagging doubts. Like a kid at summer camp, I found the adjustment period painful. At one point my former employer flew me back to Miami to talk about returning, urging me to make a fast escape from Philadelphia. My cousin Jeannie stopped all that.

Jeanne Medoff Spitz is my father's first cousin. Jeanne and her late husband, Joe, were marvelous hosts when I first came to town, eager to show me around. One Sunday night in the fall of 1966, the Medoffs did a selling job in the warm kitchen of their Cherry Hill home that would have awed the Chamber of Commerce. The talk centered around the joys of living in the region, with the Medoffs sharing their love for Philadelphia and its impact on their lives. Their message was direct: give it a chance. Years later, when the area was attached to me like a second skin, I would remind and thank them for their campaign to keep me around. So Miami was history, and Philadelphia was home.

WFIL Radio was launching a new contemporary music format to compete with the reigning radio kings, Hy Lit and Joe Niagra, at WIBG, a station affectionately known as Wibbage. WFIL, first on the AM dial, was considered no match for WIBG, but our new format caught on. My job was every radio newsman's dream—anchoring the late afternoon newscasts, then hitting the street at night, an attractive combination of delivering the news and—the best part—getting it. WFIL Radio won the ratings war, and my eyes were drawn to the television station, Channel 6, that was in the same building. One thing I pass on to future broadcasters: go where people need you. In early 1967, the news department at WFIL TV, Channel 6, was in desperate need of good reporting on the streets. They gave me the opportunity to help fill the vacuum. Within a year, my job description had changed to radio anchor in the daytime, TV reporter when the sun went down.

It was the sixties, when skirts were short, as were the tempers flaring over the war in Vietnam. Race relations in Philadelphia were tense. Civil rights activist and lawyer Cecil B. Moore was fighting housing, education, and employment barriers. Moore was determined to end the all-white policy at Girard College, an institution funded by the early nineteenth-century merchant capitalist Stephen Girard, whose will named "poor white males" as beneficiaries of a portion of his estate. Moore eventually won, but not without a struggle. The city's mayor throughout most of the sixties was James Tate. Tate looked distinguished, his silver hair and spectacles highlighting a great Irish-American face. His smile was infectious, his power absolute. The City Council president during Tate's reign was Paul D'Ortona, a crafty politician who had no diplomatic skills. D'Ortona was the man who introduced the ambassador of an African country to City Council as "the Ambassador from Niggeria." The correct pronunciation was lost on the council president. The acting police commissioner at that time was a rugged individualist named Frank L. Rizzo, who took it personally that cops were often targets of frustration in Philadelphia.

Against that backdrop, I began my career in Philadelphia. Free love was in the sixties' air, but not for me. Miserable and lonely, I chose to dive into my work. In my field, information is power, and gathering it was my primary goal in the fall of 1966. Pursuing crime and city politics was more exciting than feeling sorry for myself for being alone on the weekend.

WFIL Radio and TV were owned by Walter Annenberg, who also laid claim to the *Inquirer,* the *Daily News, Racing Form,* and *TV Guide.* His radio and newspapers were successful. The TV station was a different story. Despite its blockbuster success with a show produced there, Dick Clark's *American Bandstand,* WFIL TV was a loser in the most lucrative game in town—the evening newscast. The TV news operation was poorly staffed and lacked focus and commitment. Not only that, but in 1966, WFIL TV was the only station not broadcasting news in color, and the late news was only fifteen minutes long. But until I joined the news team, that wasn't my concern. I was hired to do radio news, and that's what I did.

In the fall of 1966 radio was my life, my pastime. Since the early days of my career as a teenage newsman in Miami, I had been an insufferable news junkie. My favorite activity of the day was making the rounds of the police departments, looking for tidbits of information. I loved news and the joy of broadcasting it on the radio. For Philadelphia news teams, there were three states to cover and plenty of crimes, which I had always paid attention to. Yet I found another sort of news that was even more compelling, and I found it at the place where the bats controlled the hallways at night—City Hall.

The annual budget hearings of City Council are often conducted at night, and it was during such a session that I discovered two things. Like politicians, bats frequent the corridors of power. But unlike Philadelphia politicians, bats do not thrive on verbal bloodshed. The city commissioners, the ones who supervise elections, were locking horns on the budget. One evening, an especially harsh exchange took place between two Democrats, Marge Tartaglione and Gene Maier. Tartaglione and Maier were yelling back and forth when Tartaglione asked, "Are you finished,

Gene?" Maier replied, "Yes, Marge, I am." Tartaglione responded, in a moment that defined the special and unique nature of Philadelphia politics, "Okay, Gene, if you're finished, then wipe yourself." It was at that moment, stoked with laughter, that I came to relish political coverage. I ran out to the hall, tape in hand, to find the nearest phone when I heard a swoosh, and there they were, an air force of silent fliers flying through the long corridor of City Hall, moving at breakneck speed and totally in control. That was quite a night—my first encounter with both street-level politics and the ceiling-level populace. Bats were living a quality life after dark in Philadelphia's City Hall. The bats have since been chased to another venue, but they haven't been forgotten by this reporter.

City Hall was also the home of the mayor, or as Philadelphians would pronounce it, "the mare." James H. J. Tate ruled his empire with twenty-four thousand patronage jobs. That is power at the purest level, and he exercised it. Much has been said about Boss Richard Daley in Chicago, but he was no more powerful than Jim Tate, who ruled the roost and doled out the political favors, without leaving fingerprints. Loyal Democratic Ward leaders and committee men and women were rewarded with one of two gifts—a job or the power to fill a few jobs. Tate was a man of the streets, a walking symbol of hardball politics. He also strengthened the Irish-Catholic hold on the city's power structure. This shift had been a long time in coming. The city's Protestant elite had been calling the shots for centuries.

Jim Tate loved Philadelphia, and Philadelphians feared him back. Privately, he had a profane temper and little tolerance for the growing power of the minority community. And Tate had another shortcoming: he hated the press.

My first encounter with the mayor was at a formal news conference about court-ordered desegregation in late 1967. By this time I was also reporting for television, and my deadlines were very short. Tate called the news conference for 4:00 P.M., and his staff wouldn't open the doors to the meeting room till he got there. Since there were no chairs in the hallway, most of us sat on the floor, which was where news people belonged, as far as Tate was concerned. When he passed us by on the way in, the mayor looked at me and said, "Oh look, the new kid on the block is sitting on his ass." I replied indignantly, "Is this any way to treat the press?" He retorted, "Yes," and moved on.

Tate's demeanor was tart, cool, and collected, but ready to break into sarcasm. In the question and answer session that followed our exchange, I asked him why he was sitting on his posterior in pushing desegregation of the schools, although I didn't use those exact words. He replied, "Next question." My face turned red; the veteran reporters around me smirked. I yelled out, "Mayor Tate, will you answer the question?" He said, "No."

Tate was a world-class strong-arm artist, but he had one great talent: he knew how to run a city. Tate ruled City Hall like a medieval landowner, doling out patronage jobs and contracts. But he managed to hire some extraordinary department heads, including City Representative Abe Rosen, a master in public relations. It was Tate who promoted Frank Rizzo, a decision he would later regret when Rizzo became a force to reckon with and Tate resented Rizzo's success and notoriety. Tate also set standards for his workers so that, under him, city government ran smoothly. And Jim Tate set a record for service—two terms elected to office after his initial two years of filling the unexpired term of Mayor Richardson Dilworth, who had left office to run for governor.

Years after Tate left office, I found myself seated next to him at a Chamber of Commerce luncheon at the Bellevue Hotel. I leaned over and said, "Do you miss it?" He said, "Damn right I do." I persisted, "What is it you miss the most?" He replied, "Making people in the media crazy, and one other thing—power. Nothing is better than power."

Power, I learned in my many years of covering politics, is the name of the game.

Still Ahead, Rude Awakenings

I was blessed in my early years in Philadelphia. When I hit the streets for WFIL Radio and TV, my reporting took me all over the area, including to the doorsteps of powerful men like Joe Clark and Richardson Dilworth. Clark was a liberal U.S. senator who had been Philadelphia's mayor from 1952 to 1956. Dilworth succeeded Clark as mayor and then became school board president in the sixties. Both men were obsessed with a project—the Society Hill renovation, a move to create upscale housing in a historic area of the city. With their aggressive push, blighted blocks and shoddy homes were replaced by colonial-era brick and mortar. With lamplights in place, freshened sidewalks, and new playgrounds, Society Hill was a jewel. This transformation of Society Hill was applauded, but it also created major problems for other sections of the city. The neighborhood glistened for its new and well-heeled occupants, but not for thousands of blacks and Hispanics who were forced to move uptown to even more miserable and rundown housing than they had left, housing abandoned by whites fleeing to the suburbs. Society Hill made for a wonderful photo opportunity, but its resurrection assured decades of poverty for many Philadelphians. Clark and Dilworth were considered the dynamic Democratic duo in the early and mid-sixties, but they boosted the dreams of the upper class in Society Hill without a concerted plan to deal with the needs of those they had displaced.

Joe Clark was a patrician, a man who carried himself with southern charm and sophistication. Clark was thin, graying, and intense, a man of unbridled passion who didn't mince his words, especially when it came to Lyndon Johnson. Joe Clark was one of the major antiwar forces in the U.S. Senate. In the heat of the tumultuous 1968 Democratic Convention in Chicago he told me, "Lyndon Johnson is a sonofabitch. He's an asshole. This war is killing the country, goddamit." His public break with the White House cost him critical votes. Three months later and with support waning from his own party, he lost his Senate seat to Republican Dick Schweicker. Clark retreated to a life of obscurity, appearing briefly in 1978 to oppose the charter reform that would have eliminated the two-term limit for mayors, giving Frank Rizzo a chance to be mayor for life. The reform measure was defeated, and Clark was rarely heard from again.

Richardson Dilworth was a giant among leaders, a man who said in public what many merely think in private. Sometimes he said too much, as he did when he almost became governor in 1962. Tall, tanned, and handsome in his double-breasted pinstripes, Dilworth was the favorite to beat Bill Scranton for governor, but he injected two issues into the race that doomed him. First, he endorsed recognition of Communist China. Then, in one of the great screwups of political history, he opposed parking on the medial strips in South Philadelphia. Neither issue had anything to do with state government, but the China issue embarrassed him, and the parking issue caused a backlash from the row-house Democrats in South Philadelphia. In November, Bill Scranton had him for lunch.

Interviews with Dilworth were straightforward and dynamic. During one conversation with me, Dilworth waxed poetic about his personal experiences, especially the coincidence of his presence during his mayoral term on the cruise liner *Andrea Doria* as it sank on its final voyage to the deep sea. Dilworth rescued scores of passengers, escorting them to lifeboats, exercising courage and chivalry befitting the mayor from Philadelphia.

When it came to politics, he became even more passionate. In an interview with me after he had left politics, he admitted that his policies had caused racial tension and that he could have been more responsive. I was shocked when he told me his view of John Kennedy's Philadelphia campaign in 1960. "He was a phony then, and he was always a phony," Dilworth said. "I sat in the car with him in a motorcade up Broad Street, and he said to me, 'So how much longer do we have to do this?'" Dilworth continued, "I couldn't believe it. . . . JFK was superficial. What a bunch of crap."

If Dilworth disliked JFK, his comments paled by comparison to his feelings about Frank Rizzo, whom he described as a "pompous right-wing bully who is a danger to Philadelphia." The feeling was mutual. Rizzo bragged to me that, as a police captain during Dilworth's years as mayor, he worked overtime plucking Dilworth out of late-night trysts and depositing him at his front door. Ironically, Rizzo and Dilworth were very much alike: shoot-from-the-hip, trash-and-burn politicians for whom the world was black and white: you were either an enemy or a friend, and there was no room for anyone in the middle.

If I were to pick out one event as emblematic of the career of Richardson Dilworth, it would be the 1967 school board hearings on a court-ordered plan to bus minority students to schools in Northeast Philadelphia. That was the night when Richardson Dilworth lost his shirt.

Thousands of parents from the far Northeast, a neighborhood of clean streets, affordable homes, and schools a notch above those in the rest of the city, arrived at school headquarters at Twenty-first Street and Ben Franklin Parkway to rally against forced busing. Dilworth, who was then school board president, looked as dignified and affable as ever as he emerged from his car. Before he could take two steps, however, some angry women started yelling into his face. He tried to push his way through the crowd, but a woman grabbed his suit coat. The material tore around his shoulder. She grabbed some more and a piece of his shirt was ripped open, exposing a well-tanned chest. Dilworth looked ready to explode—which he did, quite fabulously, about an hour later.

For an hour, he sat at the school board table as, one by one, parents testified for and against busing. One of the final speakers was a mother from Fox Chase, a working-class neighborhood in the Northeast. She complained about the inclusion of new people in her schools and neighborhood and chastised the partially shirtless Dilworth for supporting integration. Dilworth sat there, staring at the woman. Then he got up, looked her in the eye, and said, "I get where you're coming from. You like white and don't like black. You tell your kids to hate. You pass on prejudice to a whole new generation. What are you afraid of? Tell me that. Of course, I'm sure you'll reply by saying, 'Well, Mr. Dilworth, some of my best friends are niggers.'"

It was a powerful moment from a man loaded with high-octane conviction. The room was still as people pondered his remarks and a realization spread through the board room that you can't legislate understanding. People may never change, but those with the courage to challenge them and make them think may provoke a first step. Dilworth had that courage. When he left the building, I raced after him, along with the station's camera crew.

"What a night, Mr. Dilworth," I exclaimed. "Any reflections?" He looked at me and said, "Not really, Larry, I'm just tired." His voice was cracking with emotion, and I saw tears well up in his eyes. Richardson Dilworth had just faced the enemy of the 1960s, and the enemy was hate.

Our Next Report Comes from Police Barricades

The tribulations of Richardson Dilworth were an ominous precursor to events in the late sixties. My arrival, orientation, and trial under fire at WFIL came at a time when race relations were helping to define the immediate future of greater Philadelphia.

As mentioned, the city's school headquarters is located on Twenty-first Street. It's across from the Franklin Institute, a venerable place that—among other things—spreads the love of science to children, and within view of what I believe to be the most enthralling and lavish parkway in America. When you look up or down the Benjamin Franklin Parkway, you see a grandeur matched only by the Champs Elysées in Paris. In fact, the street, built in the early 1920s, was purposely designed to look like the Paris boulevard. The *Rocky* movie immortalized Ben's parkway when Rocky ran down it and climbed the steps of the Philadelphia Museum of Art as a part of his training regimen, but Philadelphians knew the beauty was there years before Hollywood did. It is a magnificent sight—and an odd place for a riot.

School was in session on the morning of November 17, 1967, but not for the thirty-five hundred or so public school students who left their classrooms to descend on the school administration building. Minutes after the news assignment desk called me at my apartment in Haddon Township, New Jersey, I hooked up with a camera crew. What I saw when I got to the scene was the potential for trouble.

The students, mostly high-school age and mostly African American, had gathered to protest the school board curriculum and to push for a black studies program. But by the time I arrived, the march had turned into madness, and the madness transformed into a sixties-style hysteria. On their way downtown, some of the students had trashed a few stores, physically attacked some women, and appeared to onlookers as a physically threatening force. At the time, the school system had no formal security unit, so the Philadelphia Police Department responded, under the command of Frank Rizzo.

When the police arrived just before noon, I was standing on Twenty-first Street, with the Franklin Institute to my left and school headquarters to my right. It was a bone-chilling November day, and everyone was bundled up in jackets and topcoats. Rizzo was flanked by the new school superintendent, Dr. Mark Shedd. Rizzo and Shedd had no love for each other. Rizzo believed Shedd was an extremist liberal who wanted to turn the schools into one mammoth classroom without walls. Shedd had privately called Rizzo a bully. Meanwhile, the kids were running amok.

At first, Rizzo demonstrated considerable patience. Although his police officers were taking verbal abuse from the young people, they had been told to hold their ground. Most of the students were milling around peacefully, but some troublemakers were being intentionally provocative. One student, for example, ran up to a highway patrolman (Philadelphia's elite mobile force) and spit at him. Suddenly, in a burst of emotion, Rizzo yelled, "Get their asses." That quote would have a considerable impact on the subsequent mood in Philadelphia, much more than the protest itself, even though Rizzo's comment was hardly the reason for the riot. In fact, I observed Rizzo showing enormous restraint until his patience ran out. By the time that happened, the riot was already underway, with police barricades collapsing. Even the

A high-school student by day, a radio news reporter by night, I broadcast in 1959 from WQAM Radio in Miami. (Photo from the author's collection)

My high-school graduation picture. (Photo from the author's collection)

As news director for Miami radio station WFUN, I chat with John Lennon and Paul McCartney on their charter plane during their whirlwind 1964 tour. I traveled on the Beatle tours of 1964, 1965, and 1966. (Photo from the author's collection)

Here I am as anchor, subdued and ready for broadcast, at WPVI TV, Channel 6, September 28, 1973. (Photo courtesy of the Urban Archives, Temple University Libraries, and WPVI TV)

Anchor John Facenda of WCAU TV in 1979. (Photo courtesy of the Urban Archives, Temple University Libraries)

Mayor Frank L. Rizzo offers me a gift for my work in the community. (Photo courtesy of the City of Philadelphia, Office of the City Representative)

Ron Tindiglia, legendary broadcaster and my best friend. (Photo courtesy of Mrs. Bar-bara Tindiglia)

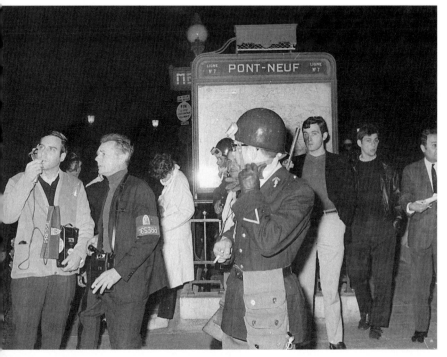

With tear gas in the air and riot troops on the ground, I prepare a radio report during the 1968 student rebellion in Paris. (Photo courtesy of Corbis/Bettmann)

Days before his 1968 loss to Richard Nixon, Hubert Humphrey joins Anchorman Gunnar Back and me at the WFIL TV studios. (Photo courtesy of WPVI TV)

famed civil disobedience chief, Lt. George Fencl, was concerned about what would follow.

What followed was a nightstick-swinging, punching brawl that caused twenty-two injuries and fifty-seven arrests. The fight was not particularly brutal, but it was an unsightly and despicable event for Philadelphia that showed two things: a lack of discipline in the city's schools and a failure of the authorities to comprehend the fervor of the protest in the late sixties. A few days later, on November 21, eight students were injured and sixteen arrested during a racial clash at South Philadelphia High School. An estimated 125 people marched on the Police Administration Building, demanding that Frank Rizzo be fired.

For Rizzo, this period of tumult was a political win. The Philadelphia row-house voter, even in predominantly minority neighborhoods, viewed him as a force of order in a society breaking down on many fronts. In the face of chaos, he was a symbol of discipline, and that image became a paving stone on his fast track to City Hall.

A Tear-Gas Cocktail

If you've never experienced tear gas, you are among the fortunate. The word "tear" is a misnomer, because the gas brings more than tears. Liquid comes pouring out of your eyes, but the gas also debilitates and disorients you, and it can cause uncontrollable nausea. It's not the way to feel while trying to do your job.

On February 17, 1969, tear gas was in the air as violent criminal suspects awaited trial in the halls on the top floors of the Camden County Courthouse. It was, in a word, a riot. When I parked at the courthouse doors to cover the story, I saw smoke coming from the upper floors. Since the elevators were not running, I headed for the emergency stairwell. Nearly out of breath, I emerged through the fire door into an office corridor. There I got my first clue that this was going to be a vile night. Immediately in front of me was a man dressed in prison garb, wielding a metal letter opener with blood on the edge of it. He swung hard at my face.

Any newsperson who tells you nothing affects their ability to cover a story is feeding you a barrel of cow chips. We have all feigned courage, only to be left in a state of nervous, tongue-tied paralysis at the sound of gunfire or the purplish tint of fresh blood. On that night I was scared, because although the police were there, they had limited control. Some prisoners were running through the halls, some beating on guards and sheriff's deputies.

One man was leading the charge against them. His name was Harold Melleby, and he was Camden's police chief. Melleby's credo was "Talk first, pay later." His rhetoric bordered on inflammatory, especially when it came to the polarizing issue of the sixties—race. There were three racial problems in Camden—black and white, black and Latino, and white and Latino. Camden was a town without shame when it came to crude, unrefined hate. Melleby intensified that division with his campaign for law and order and his "take no prisoners" attitude.

Whatever his faults, however, the man had courage. That night, the prisoners were doing the taking, and it became a game of hide and seek, punch and run, tear gas and take cover. The blood was running, and so were many of the cops, who decided to let the rampage continue with no counterattack. Melleby was chasing down prisoners by his lonesome. He approached one prisoner, screamed, "You bastard," and struck him across the bridge of his nose with a nightstick. In such a situation, my presence was not welcome. In fact, at times it appeared that some of Melleby's marauders and the prisoners might turn their crude weapons on me and those other newspeople who had ventured onto the floor. Considering my earlier close call, I exercised caution, retreating to the safety of offices whenever possible. For me, bravery is admirable but stupidity in the line of fire is unacceptable.

Eventually, the chief realized that the best solution was to seal off the floor, let the prisoners run wild, and flood the vents with tear gas. It worked, although the gas became an equal opportunity attacker, which is why I am able to talk with such authority about its effects. Afterward, Melleby declared victory, though he was embarrassed by the news coverage showing that he had lost some control.

The city of Camden was already a war zone of vacant and boarded-up buildings, a place where urban renewal often came in the form of arson. Camden was also becoming a symbol of hate and despair, which often go hand in hand for people who have little hope. The prison riot magnified that image.

Harold Melleby remained Camden's police chief for fourteen years, until his resignation in September 1981. A year earlier, he had been accused of firearms violations, rude or insulting language, and disgraceful conduct. He got no formal criminal conviction, but a Superior Court judge, while not recommending his dismissal, found him guilty of misconduct for displaying a shotgun while demonstrators protested outside his home.

Discoveries

In the business of news coverage, you're always in the process of discovering. Whether it's a street festival, a homicide, or a protest march, the job brings you to intersections and interesting people that you never quite forget.

Take a walk me with me on any busy street—on Kings Highway in Haddonfield, New Jersey; on Broad Street in Center City; on Passyunk Avenue in South Philadelphia; or in any area mall—and you will get a feel for the people who call the Delaware Valley their home. Every community in America has its fables, foibles, habits, and unique pieces of culture. Ours is no exception.

As a newcomer, my first impressions included close-up encounters with row-house Philadelphia. These are the neighborhoods that pumped up the iron of Philadelphia after World War II. Their people, then and now, treasure the sanctity of their neighborhoods, and those who have moved out celebrate their memories and return regularly. Some time ago, an *Inquirer* columnist, Bob Lancaster, referred to the people of the neighborhoods as "the great unwashed." It was a sad day for the columnist—he hardly knew Philadelphia.

The people of Philadelphia carry the torch of the city proudly. When TV news crews look for a "typical" Philadelphia neighborhood, they routinely go to the Italian Market, a colorful display of old-time marketing, complete with the smells of fish and fresh produce. But they could also go to Battersby Street in the Northeast, Rhawn in Fox Chase, the Bustleton Avenue Corridor, Drexel Hill, or Kennett Square. If you want to really see Philadelphia, stand at Broad and Olney at five in the afternoon and watch the stream of people heading to public transit, with Broad Street sloping down and City Hall, visible a few miles to the south, standing out in its classic grandeur. Or take a ride across Haverford Avenue. Start in Haverford Township, cross City Line Avenue, and in the space of a few miles, you'll observe quiet suburbia, the Jewish-Irish neighborhoods of Overbrook Park, and the African-American neighborhood of Overbrook, followed by the old Italian-American enclave, known simply as just plain Overbrook. The mix of ethnic urban and suburban has never been more plentiful.

The city's culture is deeply rooted in its neighborhoods, and people tend to identify with those neighborhoods. Some rarely leave. Years ago, during a taping of my feature on adoption, "Sunday's Child," I asked a young man from Camden, "Have you traveled anywhere?" "Yeah," he replied. "I went to Philadelphia once."

The neighborhoods are cities within the city—or, in the case of outlying areas, minisuburbs in the suburban sprawl. With the cultural roots of each neighborhood comes an unfortunate trend: stereotyping. Let me shake off some of the myths.

In many ways, for instance, North Philadelphia looks the same as it did when I arrived in 1966. But while despair lives on the streets, the attitudes have changed. Many young people refuse to be bound by the financial handcuffs of society. Years ago, courage in North Philadelphia meant confronting the drug dealers on the streets, dodging the traffic at Broad and Erie, and taking a minimum-wage job in hopes of finding a better life. Today, those choices remain, but there is also a higher degree of upward mobility, a deeper sense of neighborhood pride, and a twinge of hope because of small windows of opportunity.

Ironically, the city's challenges have moved to the suburbs. Communities like Abington, Bensalem, Sharon Hill, Norristown, and Upper Dublin mirror the city and share in the vestiges of pride. When you travel in a big crowd in this region, you'll see as many sports jackets with high-school logos as you'll see with logos of the Philadelphia Eagles or Phillies. North Philadelphia is a neighborhood, but so are the individual suburbs. Each has a personality all its own, with small-town charm and big-town sophistication.

Perhaps the city's most interesting neighborhood is the Northeast. Covering both sides of Roosevelt Boulevard, Northeast Philadelphia was once considered a suburb. Its wide-bodied streets and comfortable row homes make a statement: Philadelphia is a great equalizer. There are rich and poor, but most Philadelphians are somewhere in the middle, empowered by the postwar building boom that made buying a house more affordable. The Northeast symbolizes the opportunity to live the good life: to have a family, a nice home, a decent job. There are few social strata in the Northeast or, for that matter, in South, Central, and

Northwest Philadelphia. In the Northeast, blacks and whites, Jews and Catholics, merge in a fairly peaceful melting pot of life.

Then, of course, there is the Main Line. Many people visualize the Main Line establishment as it was portrayed in the movie *The Philadelphia Story:* big houses, horses, tea at four, dinner at six, and black tie every night—a virtual smorgasbord of upper-crust Americana. That was then. This is now. True, the horses are still there, as are the big houses, but you will also see foreign cars, Gap slacks, tennis, golf, gourmet restaurants, a copy of the *Main Line Times,* and, goodness gracious, a bevy of people who have actually moved there from the city. The Main Line today is more mainstream than the old imagery of haughtiness and elitism would suggest.

Many people's images of beautiful Bucks County are crystallized in New Hope, with its storybook houses and chic stores. But the heart of Bucks County in fact lies in Feasterville, Newtown, Yardley, Richboro, Doylestown, Upper Black Eddy, Chalfont, and hundreds of other communities. Theirs is the personality of small-town America, linked by rail and highway to the big city and its air of sophistication. Here you get the best of both worlds.

South Jersey, also a conglomeration of small towns, has a different terrain, but the people speak Philly-talk. After all, Cherry Hill is closer to Center City than to King of Prussia or Cheltenham, and the South Jersey town of Palmyra is a short bridge hop to Tacony.

Compact and lovely Wilmington is only twenty-five minutes from the Liberty Bell and a few miles from Chester County. Again, the people of rural and spacious Chester County can enjoy the culture of Wilmington, and the people of Wilmington can celebrate nature on the banks of Chester County's Brandywine River.

Think of the possibilities of a single day in Philadelphia. In one day, you can travel from the skyscrapers of Center City to the sprawling and romantic wine and mushroom country of Chester County. If you wish, a car can take you to the ocean or the mountains. You can take in a play and, in the same day, drive twenty minutes to walk through a flower garden in one of the world's great arboretums, like Longwood Gardens or the Morris Arboretum in Chestnut Hill. On the budget plan, the regional rail system will take you from the textured, historical culture of Old City to the rolling fields of Valley Forge.

And education is never far away. The library system that Ben Franklin began is alive and well, along with educational opportunities that are low in cost and high in quality. Community colleges have produced great leaders in this area. Restaurants abound, including a surfeit of top-notch ones and plenty more with less fancy fare. Cheese steaks, grinders, subs, and soft pretzels will never lower your cholesterol, but they are guaranteed to raise your spirits. If this isn't quality of life, what is?

So we live in communities diverse and divided, but one common thread runs through the Delaware Valley quilt. Some people call it a spirit of giving. I call it the courage to come forward and help, the ultimate shared experience, the Philadelphia way.

> 1999, crisis in Kosovo: So many cartons of clothing came from the Philadelphia area that the Red Cross had to send some back.

> 1970s to the present day: Deborah Heart and Lung Center in Browns Mills, New Jersey, saves young people's lives and doesn't charge a cent. Volunteers and individuals make up the difference.

> 1975 to the present day: Soviet Jews, facing oppression and suppression, begin trickling out of the Soviet Union. A letter-writing campaign to Soviet leaders by thousands in the area's Jewish community and their friends begins to show results. In fact, most early arrivals came to Philadelphia first.

> Blizzard of 1996: After thirty inches of snowfall in March, the region is paralyzed, with trucks unable to plow side streets. Block captains, mostly in North, Northeast, and Southwest Philadelphia, launched volunteer brigades to clean up the city.

Those are a few shared experiences that illustrate my point. The individual and organizational efforts would take a full-length book to chronicle. The Jewish Federation of Philadelphia sets national standards in its support for Jewish causes. Ditto for Catholic Charities. In an age of government cutbacks, people's campaigns have made up the difference. The Children's Hospital and St. Christopher's never turn away children without insurance, because thousands of volunteers collect the money year round.

Tension may be a commodity in Philadelphia. Division may be a legacy of generations. But love and giving are priceless legacies handed down to all Philadelphians.

In December 1980, southern Italy was ravaged by earthquakes, and aid poured forth like a river of salvation. Philadelphians from all backgrounds raised over two million dollars to rebuild several communities near Naples. In my coverage of the earthquake, I focused on the town of Montella. Three years later, I was invited to a dinner in the borough of Norristown. The young mayor of Montella was there, and in beautiful Italian, he addressed the people, thanking them on behalf of his beleaguered municipality. The interpreter read it this way: "With heavy hearts and a strong will, the people of Montella have rebuilt their lives, with the help of thousands of people they've never met. On behalf of them, I offer thanks, with love, from the Italian people to the warmest people of America, the citizens of Philadelphia."

If you believe that my take on the people of Philadelphia is biased, that I'm just a cheerleader for the people and the region, you've hit the mark. In sports, they use the term "homer" for a broadcaster who is overly biased toward the hometown team. When it comes to this region, I am a homer, with no apologies.

Love Letters to the Media

Rittenhouse Square in Center City is elegant, but not haughty. Seeing it and walking it are delightful experiences. Watching the sun set behind the highrise apartment towers that surround the square, its glow turning the trees golden, is a visual feast. Bounded by Walnut and Locust Streets, the square is a Philadelphia highlight, reminiscent of the Philadelphia stories that John O'Hara penned. In the far southwest corner of Rittenhouse Square is the building housing the Ethical Society.

The Ethical Societies in America were founded in 1876 to promote an alternative view to established religious institutions, a view based on ethical values. During the sixties, the Ethical Society and Rittenhouse Square itself were favorite spots for antiwar speeches and rallies. There were many, and I covered a lot of them. This was an eye-opener for me. I was always startled, for one thing, by the labels people were laying on other people. In 1969, for example, people took it for granted that if you were against the war, you had to be against cops. If you supported the war, then surely you supported the police. People who had long hair were drug users; those with crew cuts were right-wing fanatics. If you were black, you were a follower of H. Rap Brown, and if you were a blue-collar union member, you were against integration. Those were the stereotypes that dominated the debates surrounding war, peace, and law and order in the divisive years during the war in Vietnam.

Members of the news media were not immune to the labeling process. We were either liberal and permissive, no doubt siding with the Commies, or we were controlled by the establishment, whoever that might be. These labels set up some truly hideous moments. In the sixties, news people were at great risk on the streets of America. And Philadelphia was no exception.

Activist Ira Einhorn was a minor icon in the late sixties and early seventies, so much so that when celebrity protesters came to town, Ira was usually their host. Ira was a great user and abuser of the media and, as we would learn later, was not the man he appeared to be.

One afternoon in 1969, Ira Einhorn issued me a "special invitation" to cover an antiwar rally being held at the Ethical Society. The guests of honor were two poster boys for protest in America, Jerry Rubin and Abbie Hoffman.

I arrived with two camera-crew members at 8:00 P.M. The hall was packed—standing room only. As we walked into the room, looking for a good camera spot, Einhorn mounted the stage, hurried over to the microphone, and screamed, "The fascist pigs have arrived. The bullshit right-wing press is here. Look. They're in the back." In a few moments, the assembled crowd, mostly students, started screaming, "Pigs, pigs, pigs!" I was dumbfounded, and then I realized I was being used to stir up the crowd. These rallies had become old news by late 1969, and Einhorn had come up with a new gimmick to get attention. I was the only newsman there. At one point, a couple of the would-be hippies started grabbing at the camera. A member of the police department's civil disobedience squad suggested we leave. We did.

The next morning, outraged, I called Einhorn. All he had to say was, "Great shit, wasn't it? That crowd was really turned on. Man, thanks for coming."

A side note: Einhorn, who had been a favorite of the city's movers and shakers, was charged with murdering his girlfriend, Holly Maddux, and stuffing her mummified body in a trunk. He fled justice and was tried in absentia and convicted. Einhorn was later arrested in France, but he continues to fight extradition.

Ira Einhorn is a perfect example of how Philadelphians fell in love with labels and imagery in the sixties. Many of us considered him an activist, a fighter for justice, and a man who stirred the pot with public protest. Who could have guessed that someday he would be a murderer on the run?

From the sixties through the eighties, the media was under fire by people who used us. During the disorder at Bok Vocational High School in South Philadelphia in 1969, I learned the hard way that the media could become a target of violence for those hoping for empowerment and those already holding power. Bok is a fine high school located in the heart of mostly white South Philadelphia, east of Broad Street. Fueled by the rhetoric of State Representative Leland Beloff (who later spent time in jail for corruption), the Bok situation was explosive. Blacks walking to school were regularly insulted by white residents, who in turn charged that their neighborhoods were being vandalized by the students. The war of words developed into a war of rocks and other objects, like trash can covers and broken bottles. During one of the confrontations, I drove down to the scene in my 1966 Chevy Bel Air and parked close to the school. There was a press sticker on the windshield, and therein lay my problem. Several young men, standing on the stoops of a row house, began hurling stones and wood at the windshield, which shattered immediately, hurling glass into my cheeks. Blood trickled down my face, but there was no pain, and I wasn't too frightened. Then a second barrage of garbage landed on the side of the car, smashing in the door and busting a side window. Behind me I heard a station cameraman yelling as he swung the lens of his sixteen-millimeter camera toward the faces of the attackers, who scattered quickly. It was the first time I had been cut in the line of duty.

It would happen again, especially after the assassination of Martin Luther King, Jr., and always for the same reason: the media is perceived as a part of the power structure. The media is the problem. Attack the media: it feels good. After a while, we got savvy to the anger against us and rarely used lights when using cameras at night in areas experiencing racial tension. We worked hard to exercise restraint in stories involving potential trouble. But sometimes, because of inexperience or a lapse in judgment, we did become the reason for trouble. And sometimes, as in the case of Ira Einhorn, we were used.

We Call This Story "The Mirror Never Lies"

We all remember what makes us feel tall and proud of our lives, and we all try to forget the rest. But although I try to forget it, the case of L. Kane v. the Gremlins is branded in my mind.

Radio is an imaginative medium of communication. Sound can soothe, inform, and entertain. Sound can also be deceptive; the voice on the other end can conjure up imagery of what the broadcaster looks like, but it is rare for the face to "look like" the voice. Television is a different story. You can run, but you can't hide from the camera. When it comes to appearance, the camera never lies, and that's why my entry into television brought years of anxiety and insecurity.

During my formative years in Philadelphia, from 1966 to 1969, I lived in fear of two things—television and my new hometown. The TV part still lingers with me. I came to town bearing an incredible insecurity about my appearance, an insecurity etched in my mind by teenaged Florida rednecks who thought it was fun to pick on Jews (among others). My nose was big. My contemporaries in Miami during my junior high years would call me "the nose with the curl on top," referring to a popular advertising campaign for Dairy Queen. Couple that abuse with the fact that I did not have the looks of a teen idol, and you can understand why the thought, "Oh, my God, they're looking at me," kept echoing through my head.

Despite this aura of ugliness, perhaps self-imposed, I made the decision—no nose jobs for this character, thank you. I would adjust. When I began my television reporting career, I was so conscious of the size of my nose that I tried not to turn sideways, although that's pretty hard to do without completely ignoring your fellow newscasters. In April 1967, while editing a report, I grimaced at the view of me from the side angle, but what could I do? I also had the sense that my face didn't fit the all-American model of TV imagery. Let's face it, this mug will never have the movie-star qualities of John Wayne, Tom Cruise, or Steve McQueen. I clung to the knowledge that John Facenda had been accepted here. If an Italian could make it, so could a Jew, I thought.

Fear of Philadelphia is not like fear of flying. What scared me about the city and its environs was its bigness and the take-no-prisoners, show-me attitude of its people. Sinatra sang about the Big Apple, "If you make it here, you can make it anywhere," but he was singing for the wrong city. Philadelphia is the all-time, no-bullshit American city. Prove it to me, Philadelphians say—and if you do, the love never stops. But if you fail the test, whether you're an actor, a ballplayer, a politician, or a reporter, you are basically dead on arrival.

Like TV viewers, newsroom staffers can be a tough audience, especially when they're sizing up a twenty-four-year-old journalist. Fear and loathing are favorite pastimes. In 1967, I was universally respected and rejected by my colleagues at WFIL TV. Information is power, and within a year I had established news sources and contacts that guaranteed exclusives for me and the station. That aggressiveness made others jealous. That jealousy, the unfriendliness, and my own doubts about my appearance turned me into a most insecure human being. Fortunately, that lack of confidence made me work harder. Unfortunately, working longer hours did not endear me to the staff. In fact, my long hours irritated many old timers. Much of the staff was hostile toward me, and they only came around after the station became a success.

It was hard to cope. Before Donna came along in late 1969, my primary supporter was Ron Tindiglia, a twenty-four-year-old production assistant, writer, and show producer at WFIL TV. This remarkable man, who had the best flair with people I've ever witnessed, was my best friend. Late at night, we would sit in one of our cars in the Channel 6 parking lot and talk about our futures—his goal to run a news department, mine to anchor newscasts. We were dreamers, and we fantasized so much about our futures that they just had to come true. Ron went on to have a brilliant career—as news director for *Action News* in Philadelphia and WABC in New York, as a powerful CBS executive, as the founder of the first morning business program in America, and finally as the most respected consultant in the business. Ron and I remained best friends until his death from lung cancer in 1997 at the age of fifty-one—a life too short, a life well lived.

The Glue That Holds the News Team Together

Dreams live in people, but they never come true without dedication and some luck. This adage was proved for me on the night of an uncanny and funny break that changed my career.

I've always enjoyed the view heading in and out of town on the Schuylkill Expressway. It relaxes me and buoys me for the work ahead. But late one night in the fall of 1968, I didn't even notice the view. My stomach was cramping, my body ached, and I didn't know if I would make it home before I got sicker. My stomach felt like I was on a roller coaster and couldn't get off, and the roller coaster was my career.

My difficulties had begun quite innocently. I had returned to WFIL from covering an event at City Hall. As was the custom, I checked in with our anchorman, Al McDowell, a veteran broadcaster from Pittsburgh who had two sharp talents. Al was a world-class ad libber who could talk his way through a tornado, and he was one of the newsroom's great jokers. Al was notorious for studio pranks and for loosening up any tight emotional environment. On the other hand, he could make me feel nervous just before air time with a nod or a comment. A typical Al exchange: "Lar, do you have a mirror?" "No." "Find one, 'cause you got a headlight, and it's shining bright." "Headlight" was his expression for a big pimple. Of course, I was much too close to broadcast time to check it out, meaning that while I was talking, my mind had visions of a quarter-million people looking at a bulbous growth on my right temple. This vision also made me laugh, and laughing during the broadcasting of an apartment fire or a terrorist attack is no way to develop a career. When I finally made it to the mirror, I saw no blemish. The only mark was the one left on my mind.

Al was unstoppable and unflappable. We had a ritual. Before each newscast, he and I would apply our makeup in the third-floor men's room. Al walked into the men's room, script in one hand and glue in another. The glue was how Al kept his red toupee in place. While I applied some powder over my makeup, the anchorman twisted off the cap of the glue bottle and said, "Oh shit, no more glue left. Damn!" Turning to me, he added, "It's your show, kid. I'm going home. Here's the script." I said, "Are you nuts?" Al replied, "No, I just won't have my hair falling down," and he pointed to his head, where the glue-less hairpiece was sliding down his forehead. From the look on his face, I realized that he was telling the truth.

I raced into the newsroom, my heart pounding. I had never delivered a full half-hour newscast. My previous experiences had been short studio appearances to introduce my field reports. The producer, discovering that Al had left the building, was in a state of horrified panic. After I reached the studio, I delivered a half hour of news, standing alone at our news podium, my heart beating hard and sweat slithering down my chest. When the program was over, I was sweating bullets. In the bathroom, I took off my makeup, hyperventilated, and threw up.

That was my first full-length television newscast, and, incredibly, management was happy with it. But I will never forget the terror—and the aftermath.

A Profile in Courage

Even to a seasoned newsman, there are some events that stick in your mind because of their intensity and, sometimes, their severity. On the cold morning of January 8, 1968, the Normandie Retirement Club at Thirty-sixth and Chestnut was being ravaged by a fast-moving blaze. It was a time for fast action and a courage that few reporters had ever seen.

When I arrived at the scene, the Normandie, not a club but a retirement home, was enveloped in heavy smoke. Three hundred sixty people lived there, and when all the smoke was cleared, two people were dead and forty more injured. But the outcome could have been much worse. In the morning cold, brave Philadelphia firefighters had joined with a helicopter traffic team to prevent a deeper tragedy.

Philadelphia firefighters, many gasping for breath, ran through the floors, waking people and directing them out. Time was of the essence: the building's structure was cascading. There was great fear for the safety of the people on the upper floors. Then a helicopter landed on the roof bearing John Carlton.

John Carlton was a household name in the sixties, the gung-ho traffic reporter in the Go-Patrol helicopter. Carlton had been broadcasting traffic news when he witnessed the smoke billowing in the West Philadelphia sky. Without hesitation, pilot Dick Scholfield landed the chopper on the roof of the burning Normandie. From the street, I could only hear the helicopter. But it stayed there for a long time, and I wondered what was happening. Not long after, I found out.

Carlton and Scholfield had rescue on their minds. After landing, they found a fire door and traveled to the seventh, sixth, and fifth floors, rousing residents and directing them to fire corridors and safety. When the residents were safely out, without missing a beat, they boarded their helicopter, took off, and began broadcasting traffic reports, urging motorists to stay away from the area.

On the ground, I watched in amazement as Philadelphia firefighters courteously escorted frightened residents of the Normandie, some of them barely clothed, others shivering in the morning air. The fire department was brilliant in its rescue, aided by a mercy flight from the Go-Patrol helicopter.

This had been a textbook rescue, with everything going as well as it could have, and that was a good thing. Sixty minutes after the fire had started, brick and mortar exploded around us. The Normandie collapsed to the ground.

A Year of Infamy, 1968: Let Me Tell You the Story

The miracle of the Normandie in 1968 was one of the bright spots in a year of major news and considerable pain for the region and the country. Turbulence was the marching order for the sixties, and the flash-point year was 1968. The problems seemed never to end—Vietnam, the race conflicts, the political murders, and the wave of youth protest.

The spring of that year brought us the Memphis assassination of Dr. Martin Luther King, Jr. The report on his condition was inconclusive at first. In our 9:00 P.M. radio newscast, we simply reported that Dr. King had been shot on the balcony of his hotel. But within forty-five minutes, the assassination had been confirmed. At the moment the teletype report arrived, I was sitting in the joint radio-TV newsroom of WFIL. Grabbing the wire copy, I ran to the glass-walled radio booth that overlooked the newsroom and broke into deejay George Michael's popular music show with the news.

As often happens to me while part of my mind is dealing with breaking news, another part flashed back to a quiet morning in Cincinnati three years earlier. The suite at the Sherry Netherlands Hotel was filled with people sipping from paper cups of wake-up coffee, smoking incessantly, chatting about the recent civil rights protest at the New York World's Fair. I was nervous, a condition common to reporters meeting someone for the first time. Then a bathroom door opened, and a short man, sleeves rolled up, walked over to the sofa and shook my hand. "Martin Luther King," he said. I replied, "Larry Kane."

The interview was scheduled as a part of my coverage of the African Methodist Episcopal (A.M.E.) church national convention. The company I was working for, Rounsaville Radio, owned one general music station, WFUN in Miami, and six stations that appealed to black audiences. There were no news directors at those stations, a troubling sign of the times, and as the only one, the news chief in Miami, I was assigned to cover the convention for all of the stations. Dr. King asked why I was there to cover him, not a representative of the stations that programmed to blacks. I said, "I'm the only news director in the group." He retorted, "We'll change that."

That interview with Martin Luther King was a close encounter with history. The man was the best interview subject I had ever met, smooth and clear, with the ability to form his words into direct messages. King was a master of words and a messenger of peaceful protest in a decade when hatreds were boiling all over the country. Unlike many mainstream reporters, I had previous experience in and around the civil rights movement. In my 1963 days in St. Louis, during the earliest protests advocating minority hiring by banks and other businesses, I had interviewed Malcolm X and Dick Gregory. And now, sitting across from me, was the man whose life and death would change so many lives.

So as word of his death lit up America's cities, I reflected on the man and the mission. There wasn't much time for thinking, though. Gunfights and riots were beginning across the nation. Philadelphia remained relatively quiet under a limited emergency edict announced by Mayor Tate and top cop Frank Rizzo. The emergency edict restricted gatherings on street corners. It was clearly unconstitutional, but Philadelphia didn't burn. How could it? In the dark of the night, Car One was on patrol. Car One was Frank Rizzo's car, and he employed tactics that were copied for years to come. Busses were loaded in Center City with riot-trained police, remaining in place unless they were needed. Rizzo's strategy was flawless: show up in strength, but avoid using police cars with lights and sirens that might incite.

Our news team could have learned from Frank Rizzo. On the night after the King murder, I was on the streets in North Philadelphia with a cameraman. The area was 8th and Diamond, and the news car was clearly marked—mistake number one. The cameraman was fearless, deciding that, to get great film of the peaceful atmosphere, he should use a portable light—mistake number two. The light drew people out of their homes and into the street, where, noticing our car, some of the stronger folks lobbed beer cans and rocks at the car, ripping the windshield to shreds. "Let's get the hell out of here," I screamed. There were two lessons in that hail of hatred. First, the death of Dr. King was a devastating setback to dreams that had lived with him; second, never underestimate the force and power of angry people. I also learned that shining a light on a street in a period of mourning and potential violence is a recipe for trouble.

Philadelphia, as I've mentioned, had the clear-thinking and—in a pinch—indestructible Frank Rizzo, so this city experienced little of the violence of other cities. The state of Delaware had Governor Charles L. Terry, Jr., and that is the reason I spent the night of April 9 crouched under the body of a car, fearing that I would become a meaningless journalistic footnote to a bloody night in Delaware history.

The King death triggered an extraordinary development: Delaware, a proud state with usually moderate leaders, witnessed some of the worst violence in the country. Delaware is a small and physically beautiful state. In the north, New Castle County adjoins Pennsylvania. It is a suburban county with a cosmopolitan flair and the home of the city of Wilmington. To the south, Sussex and Kent Counties take you to another world, where the attitude is southern in hospitality and in politics.

Many residents in Wilmington reacted with violence to the Memphis murder. Most cities in the United States dealt with the trouble by deploying police, some of them trained to deal with civil disorder. But the Wilmington crisis was treated with scorn by Governor Terry. Mayor John Babiarz had requested National Guard forces to supplement his 250-man police department. Governor Terry responded by mobilizing most of the 4,800-member Army and Air Guard of Delaware. Without a firm strategic plan, hundreds of guardsmen were deployed on the streets of Wilmington. In taking a hard line against violence, Terry was almost certainly overreacting, sometimes blurring the line between anticrime and racial rhetoric. So in Wilmington, mob rule prevailed, giving me an opportunity to learn the fine art of dodging gunfire.

The banner headline in the *Wilmington News Journal* of April 10, 1968, read, "BLOOD, BOMBS, MOB RULE BRAND APRIL 9, 1968, CITY'S DAY OF INFAMY." The headline was dead on target. Black smoke billowed in the bright sunshine, fires were being deliberately set, looting was rampant, and Wilmington, the jewel of Delaware, was being shattered by sniper gunfire. In all, on that day alone, fifty-four people were injured, many of them guardsmen called in to help. A total of 140 people were arrested. Mayor Babiarz was appreciative of the Guard's help but stunned that

Governor Terry had activated almost the entire Delaware Army and Air National Guard. The combination of rioting civilians and gun-toting soldiers with no battle experience would turn into a horrible disaster for Wilmington.

I've always enjoyed getting close to news, with some exceptions. Close calls are the stuff of legends and storytelling, but in reality, they are the worst form of terror. On the block where I stood near downtown Wilmington, sniper fire rang out from several row houses, with Delaware National Guardsmen ready to fire back if necessary. At one point, bullets were ricocheting off a nearby fire hydrant, forcing me to squeeze my frame under a car. If you've never tried to hide your body beneath a car, you have missed an oily, claustrophobic adventure. Once you've managed to squirm beneath the gas tank, your face smashed against metal, you have a decision to make: should you remain on your stomach or crawl back out, one precious inch at a time, on your battered and bleeding elbows to re-enter the narrow passage on your back, much like a mechanic looking up at the engine block but without the hydraulic lift? For a few hours I opted to stay in place, until the sniper fire stopped. My thoughts ranged from excitement to fear and finally to a realization that the story would live, but I might not. Not knowing whether the gunfire would start again, I made an exit, my body trembling as I hustled down the street to the safety of a police barricade.

That day was the ultimate trickle-down experience. A divisive governor decides to send in the troops en masse, aggravating an already tense situation. The results of his decision trickle down to the victims of his lunacy: the people rioting and the guardsmen and local police trying to stop it, all of whom become jeopardized.

There was no question: the National Guard was needed in Wilmington. But so was talk, negotiation, and community outreach. While Philadelphia remained peaceful and Camden and Trenton experienced a considerable level of violence, Wilmington was the scene of the most extreme bloodshed in the three-state area. When the smoke had cleared, a good portion of the southern part of Wilmington was routed. The state was thrown into political turmoil, and it would be years before the city of Wilmington would achieve any level of racial unity. To make matters worse, the governor kept the guard mobilized till past Christmas, a full seven weeks after he had been defeated for another term in office. Although peace had been restored fully in late spring, the guard's presence guaranteed an atmosphere of tension until the end of 1968.

Nor was that the end of the year's violence. In May, Beatles John Lennon and Paul McCartney asked me to come to New York. I interviewed them about their new ventures, and they extended an invitation to me to visit them in London.

The timing of my trip was ominous. On June 4, 1968, my plane arrived in Britain almost at the same time as Sirhan Sirhan fired bullets that would end the life of Robert F. Kennedy. WFIL TV management called with an assignment: get the British reaction to the shooting. The streets of London were plastered with the headline, "Oh My God, Not Again—RFK Shot." Over the next two days, I fed reports to TV and radio, never realizing I was beginning a thirty-day odyssey into the labyrinth of sixties revolution and violence.

Days later, another call came from Philadelphia. Pat Polillo, the news director of WFIL, asked me to fly to France, where Paris was literally burning. Student protesters had taken over the Sorbonne and other universities in protest against the policies of the government of Charles de Gaulle. Polillo wanted film reports and live radio reports by phone. Excited and anxious, I arrived at Heathrow Airport, where I paced in the lounge, readying myself for the unknown intrigue of Paris. Then, not far from me, I saw a scuffle and a group of police dragging a man away from the terminal area. Too many police, I thought. My phone call to Scotland Yard was just based on intuition, but I had to know. The press officer calmly answered my questions. "Sir," he said, "you have just witnessed the arrest of the killer of Dr. Martin Luther King, Jr." It was a heart-stopping moment. My next call was to WFIL TV. The funeral of Robert Kennedy was on the air, but management decided to break in with my phone report. The man, later identified as James Earl Ray and traveling under the alias Eric Starvo Galt, had been captured in front of my eyes. Pollilo told me to go to Paris, but to stand by to return to London for criminal proceedings against the King killer.

Paris was eerie. Amid the darkness of that Saturday night, I tasted the ominous and pungent aroma that I had inhaled once before. Tear gas was in the air, and from a roadway on the Right Bank of the Seine River, I could see large fires glowing above the heart of the Left Bank. One night later, accompanied by a United Press International (UPI) news team, I crossed the Point Neuf Bridge to the Boulevard St. Germaine, receiving a toxic introduction to the sixties politics of confrontation. De Gaulle had summoned his national riot police, including many former Foreign Legionnaires. They had three weapons of choice: concussion grenades that could tear your ears apart, tear-gas canisters, and the force of their own huge nightsticks. That was the night I learned that France could disintegrate into the kind of lawlessness that degrades the human spirit.

Thousands of students were marching near the Luxembourg Gardens. Hundreds of shielded riot forces stopped the march. But stopping the protest wasn't enough. Some of the riot police chased after students in the alleys adjacent to the main boulevards. The UPI team and I followed them, our ears ringing from the concussion missiles and our throats raw from the tear gas. What we saw was ugly—riot troops ripping the clothes off of female students, forcing them to the ground, and attempting to rape them. At one point, I hollered, "Stop that!" A riot police lieutenant responded by pulling out his concussion launcher and laying one on me. It exploded ten feet in front of me, and for two days, my hearing was virtually gone. Although I had witnessed every sort of violence imaginable in my job, it was the first time anyone had fired directly at me, in anger. We had provided a distraction that stopped the sexual assaults at that location, but unmerciful beatings continued. Thank God for America, I thought. But, as you will learn, my thanks to our democracy were somewhat premature.

The student protests proliferated in Europe, including more violent ones in Germany. Paris burned for several nights, and with elections weeks away, the government was under pressure to contain the protests and restore order. Days later, in the Bow Street Court in London, watching the arraignment and extradition proceedings for King's accused assassin, I felt that history was being lived in a brief flash of time. There I was, shuttling between France and Britain, watching a country burn and witnessing the prosecution of an apparent assassin whose act of murder had sent me to the riot-torn Wilmington two months earlier.

My travels weren't over. The station dispatched me to Berlin to cover the Autobahn blockade by the East Germans. The blockade prevented West Germans from traveling to and from Berlin. Observing the tension at Checkpoint Charlie and the other Berlin outposts, the crossing points, was an eye-opener. My cameraman, an Italian, was roughed up by some Russian soldiers who remembered that he had once sneaked across the border. It was ghastly to watch. I was untouched, a minor tribute to my citizenship.

I returned to Paris to cover the peace talks on Vietnam and to do an interview with our ambassador to France, Sargent Shriver. Shriver was the point man for the U.S. negotiating team in Paris, a Kennedy loyalist and the husband of JFK's sister, Eunice Kennedy Shriver. He would serve as George McGovern's running mate in 1972. In the ornate American embassy, the soft-spoken Shriver, rattled by the death of his brother-in-law, RFK, offered an eloquent analysis of where America was at. He spoke harshly of the war, even though he was there to defend it. He leveled his most intense criticism at what he called the "forces of extremism" that threatened to tear the country apart. His was a wise analysis.

Finally, after thirty-one days in Europe, my job as witness to history was over. My return to Philadelphia was greeted with the news that I would be covering both political conventions, the Republican gathering in Miami Beach and the Democratic convention in Chicago, where I would see Sargent Shriver's vision of the consequences of extremism come ever more alive.

The 1968 Republican convention gave me an opportunity to learn more about the party's leaders in the region. Publisher Walter Annenberg, who owned WFIL, was there. Pennsylvania governor Raymond Shafer led the delegation. There were plenty of local politicos, too, but my most interesting encounter was with the new governor of California, Ronald Reagan. Wandering through the lobby of the Eden Roc Hotel, I noticed the crowd surrounding him, gravitating toward him, and saw his face flushed with excitement. His supporters carried signs touting "Reagan for President." Absurd, I thought as Reagan waded through the crowd, a magnetic presence. Who would ever elect an actor, however polished, as president? The convention was otherwise uneventful, the only glitch being a race riot in North Miami that of course played into the hands of the law-and-order delegates nominating Richard M. Nixon. The convention ended; I moved on to Chicago.

Two months earlier, weeks before a national election, tear gas and riot troops had rampaged through the back alleys of Paris, putting down revolt. Who could ever imagine seeing American troops patrolling an American city in the midst of a national political convention? It was beyond good sense. But in 1968, the year of assassination, revolution, a bloody war in Asia, and overall chaos, common sense had vanished into the maelstrom of violent rhetoric and severe polarization.

The Delaware Valley delegates to the convention included Congressmen Bill Green and Joshua Eilberg, along with once-and-future gubernatorial candidate Milton Shapp. Shapp remarked to me, "Chicago is a great American city, a magnificent location for a nominating convention." As Shapp, Green, New Jersey governor Richard Hughes, and others arrived at the Ambassador East Hotel on the north side, however, it became apparent than sinister forces were in command. The hotel's vents were flowing with the foul wind of stink bombs, the odor so thick that you wanted to gasp for air at times. The police blamed the bombs on antiwar protesters, perhaps a good assessment, considering that thousands had converged on Chicago. Senator Joe Clark, adamantly opposed to Vietnam, was also staying at the hotel, but he was noticeably low key in his outrage over the stink-bomb incident and the other protests in the city.

Chicago was like a pack of dynamite, the fuse lit and ready to explode any second. The police department was launching its own crusade of hate and anger, its officers chasing down protesters and giving them a piece of their minds and a chunk of their nightsticks. It was especially dangerous on the streets for young news people, who were often confused with the so-called flower children, or "the agitators," as Mayor Daley called them. Daley was determined to crush the resistance, a decision that left the Democrats looking like a party out of order, under siege, and connected to the lawlessness of both the young protesters and its own police department.

When Daley walked out of the convention after blasting the protesters and his party in a speech from the podium, I experienced one of the more unusual moments of Chicago's 1968 convention. Wedged in a crush of people in the narrow aisle between Pennsylvania's delegation and some other state's, our camera team struck blood. The lens of our camera crushed into the head of a man in front of us. He fell to the ground in pain. I helped the man to his feet and watched as he wiped some drops of blood from the back of his head. The man looked familiar. He was. It was actor Paul Newman. I said, "We're really sorry." He said, "Hey, don't worry. I'm okay, young man." As it turned out, the brief encounter with the movie star was the best moment of that Wednesday night. Trouble was on the doorstep again.

Those who know me well understand that I love cops. That respect has been hammered into me after years of watching them risk life and limb. But the Chicago police, brave and courageous like all police, were marching to the drum of 1968, aware of the assassinations and fearing for the city. The result was a classic break in ranks, a lack of control, and a collapse of police procedure.

Their antagonists were even worse. Most of the protesters who came to Chicago were decent and full of conviction, but a sizable element was bent on raising hell. That they did. Everyone who witnessed the disorder of the Chicago convention has their own version of what happened. What follows is mine.

The Conrad Hilton Hotel, the headquarters hotel for the 1968 convention, was located on busy Michigan Avenue. Although the actual convention was held at the stockyards surrounding the Chicago amphitheater, the Hilton, along with nearby Grant Park, served as a central focus of protest. In mid-evening on the same Wednesday night we nicked Paul Newman, I drove to the Hilton to drop off my film for shipment. (This was before videotape and satellite, and the film had to be shipped by plane.) To complicate matters, the taxis were on strike throughout the city. Driving was not my preference, especially when I realized that the front end of the Hilton was blocked off, but I had to do it. Traffic on Michigan Avenue was moving at a crawl, forcing me to park blocks away from the hotel.

Then misfortune came my way in the form of a police barricade, forcing me to walk on the east side of Michigan Avenue, behind the barricade set up to contain several thousand protesters lined up on the park side of the avenue—the side I was on. This detour went right into the middle of the demonstrators, a cultural experience that bared all. Most of them were dressed in raggedy clothing, unshaven, unwashed, and carrying plastic bags. Some of the plastic bags were loaded with urine, blood or red paint, and human feces. This was not your ordinary American protest but a systematic attempt to create havoc.

The smell was unbearable. Moreover, the demeanor of the activists was changing by the minute. So was the attitude of the police, who were standing directly in front of the wild crowd, sometimes almost face to face. A protester shouted, "You're all violent slime pigs." "Pigs" at the time was the favorite anti-establishment nickname for anyone associated with law enforcement. I tried to get through the crowd and cross the street, but the police held me back. Suddenly, a young woman took a plastic bag and started squirting the urine at one of the officers. The officer took his nightstick and started swinging. What happened in the next few minutes was a scene viewed round the world. The Chicago police broke ranks and lunged into the crowd. The demonstrators started struggling with the police, who were unmercifully beating every person in sight who looked twenty-five or younger. The melee started spilling into Michigan Avenue. Blood was trickling down foreheads and from broken noses, teeth were flying out of mouths, and hand-to-hand combat of the most eerie kind was taking place. Within minutes, the protesters stopped fighting back, assuming the role of victims, playing out their charade on film and of course later to a national television audience.

I tried again to get across the street and was pushed to the ground by one cop, stomped on by another. Reaching into my pocket, I grabbed a press credential and held it high. Waved through by the cops and running to the front of the Hilton, I turned my head back, and my eyes captured for all time the scene of absolute chaos and insanity. The cops won, beating the protesters into submission. Chicago, of course, lost, along with the Democratic party. An aura of uncivilized behavior had developed. The commentators on TV began saying, "If they can't run a convention, how in the hell could they run a country?"

That imagery was further enhanced by the decision of President Lyndon Johnson to order the Eighty-second Airborne and a tank division into the city. The next morning, from the balcony of our motel on South Michigan Avenue, our crew members watched the troops and tanks marching into Chicago. The journey into the dark side I had begun in Europe had come home to America. I recalled the scenes of rape and carnage in Paris, the troops and riot police near the Sorbonne, and my relief that it could never happen in America. But now the young American troops, the same age as the protesters, were arriving, fully armed, part of a political mission that could only be described as massive overkill.

Hubert H. Humphrey, a good man with a love for his country, was defeated before he got out of Chicago, at least in part because his party was associated with a massive mess. Richard Nixon couldn't have asked for more.

Philadelphia's delegation flew back to Philadelphia with us, and everyone in the delegation was in a somber mood. Milton Shapp knew his party had been had. Senator Joe Clark blamed it on LBJ. Young Congressman Bill Green, a friend of the Daley family, was flabbergasted. To America, Richard M. Nixon and his law-and-order Republicans suddenly looked good.

I believe we all bear the scars of that experience. Chicago did not host another convention till the Democratic gathering in 1996. Working for KYW that time, I would pass the Chicago police and their famous checkered hats as they patrolled the boundaries of the convention site, the United Center. Sure, it was 1996, and twenty-eight years had passed. But inside me the fear was building, incessant fear that strikes at you like a dagger. Flashbacks came quickly, chilling memories of the night law disappeared and violence ruled the night of another red-letter day in 1968, the year of the ugly.

The year 1968 was not without its consequences. The murder of Martin Luther King resulted in more than just violence; it helped lay claim to the frustrations of millions of Americans forgotten by the power elite. In Philadelphia, the killing fostered a new level of routine protest—more aggressive and goal oriented. His murder and other assassinations changed the political landscape. And 1968 was a turning point in the war in Vietnam, with protests reaching a fever pitch and the American public turning against the war effort. Richard Nixon defeated Hubert Humphrey, and the road to Watergate began. The European crises eventually brought de Gaulle and other postwar leaders down, but in Czechoslovakia there was too much protest for the Russians; they invaded and ended an era of freedom.

In the Delaware Valley, the deep divisions of the war motivated almost daily protests through 1968 and beyond. The Nixon campaign's law-and-order dialogue resonated in the words of Frank Rizzo. The era of violence and its aftermath was fuel for Rizzo's rise to power. But 1968 also provided a moment of great history in Philadelphia. On September 11, four young Philadelphians showed up for the first full day of school at Girard College: Owen Gowans, age seven; eleven-year-old William Dade; Carl Riley, eight; and Theo Hicks, age nine. They shared a unique moment, becoming the first children of color to enter the school and ending a fourteen-year battle waged from the streets to the highest courts. Their entry into that school building was a turning point in the civil rights struggles of Philadelphia.

On January 20, 1969, Richard M. Nixon took the oath of office. At that moment, I was in Nuremberg, Germany, covering the military exercise Operation Reforger, an effort at the rapid deployment of American troops. After 1968, it was good to be starting anew.

For me, 1968 was not only a pivotal year in history but a personal turning point, a visit to the horrors of American society and a sneak peak at my own future. Suddenly, the impossible early dreams of becoming a real anchor newsman were beginning to look possible. Gridlocked by the tension of the times, unsure about my own ability, I marched ahead with fear and trepidation and the expectation that something exciting was waiting just around the corner.

Part Two

Success in the Seventies

Double-breasted suits, bell-bottom trousers, ties too wide, long sideburns, short skirts, and the beginning of a craze called disco—this was the fun side of the seventies. But the seventies was also the decade when the nation witnessed Watergate and all that followed. While Nixon's crisis dominated national life, in Philadelphia and across the region, another man began to dominate public life. The name was Rizzo, and the presence was bigger than life. This big man would rule, pontificate, inspire, succeed, fail, and raise hell. From 1972 to 1980 as mayor and for a decade beyond, Rizzo ruled.

The decade was a time for change on all levels. Joe Biden of Delaware became the youngest man ever elected to the U.S. Senate. Richard Nixon achieved a shameful first—resigning the presidency. In my TV studio, John Lennon became the first (and, I believe, the only) Beatle to forecast the weather. In the same studio, Gerald Ford became the first president to appear on a live local newscast. Ed Rendell, a young prosecutor who later became the city's mayor, had his inaugural run for district attorney.

At the U.S. Capitol, I watched Jimmy Carter take the oath of office. In Philadelphia, I witnessed another ceremony: Frank Rizzo, his hip fractured at a refinery fire, entered his second term. Also in the city, a group called Move made its first moves. And from 1970 to 1978, the suburbs of New Jersey, Delaware, and Pennsylvania mushroomed in population.

Last but not least, there was a big change in news format at Channel 6 (WFIL, later known as WPVI) that made instant fools of the so-called media experts. We called the new format "action news." Here and across the country, it changed the way people watched television news. Like many other achievements in America, it all began in Philadelphia.

My role in the dramatic success of *Action News* would place me on a collision course in a personal struggle—weighing ambition against my obsession with Philadelphia. For a while, ambition won that struggle. But then the magnetic field of life in Philadelphia drew me back.

But the Big Story on Action News . . .

It was April 4, 1970, and WFIL TV was about to launch a new format with a new anchor, and frankly I was so frightened I couldn't eat. The news director, Mel Kampmann, had asked me to try out a few "headline openings" for the program called *Action News*. I came up with this: "Good evening, I'm Larry Kane. In the news tonight, City Hall declares war on street gangs, and President Nixon calls for more defense spending, *but the big story on* Action News *is*. . . ."

I don't remember the big story that night, but "the big story" line would become the trademark of a broadcast format that would dominate the media market for three decades. Initially, the program was critically rejected, with newspaper columnists calling me a young, overly dramatic, machine-gun-paced newcomer. The newscast would be crushed, they said, by the reigning giants of Philadelphia television. The columnists were wrong. One year after its inception, *Action News* became number one. Herein lies the story of a success in broadcast journalism that not only changed the way Philadelphians viewed television news, but that also altered news viewing across America.

The dominance of *Action News* in the seventies was not about personalities or format alone; it was about providing what forms the essence of journalism—good, solid information. During my first four years in Philadelphia, the street was my workplace. My reporting came from all Philadelphia fronts—government, schools, transportation, law enforcement, politics, and the arts. That knowledge base certainly played a role in my ability to credibly anchor the news—which I had the chance to do before long. So I came to play, ready for action, but it was the content that counted.

In 1970, Philadelphia television news was dominated by two stations, WCAU with John Facenda and KYW TV with Vince Leonard. These stations were locked in fierce competition. WFIL TV trailed along as a distant last. WFIL management was determined to make things better, and in the fall of 1969, they launched a massive research effort. At almost the same time, they named me temporary anchor while they conducted a nationwide search for a powerful male anchor. I was happy to fill in. They had promised me a permanent position as weekend anchor once their search was completed. My first stint as anchor was a heady time for me.

As January 1970 approached, management was still looking for the anchor star. That's about when John Facenda called and invited me to dinner at San Marco's restaurant on City Line Avenue. John was a chain-smoking, hard-drinking man who had a wonderful way with people. His charm was legendary. He delivered the news for WCAU in a majestic voice and appeared to be a lifer in television, or so I thought.

Our dinner began with some small talk about things to see and do in Philadelphia. Then he went directly to the point. "Young man," he said, "our CBS station in St. Louis, KMOX, is looking for a five o'clock anchor, and they are very interested in you. It would be a wonderful opportunity, and I think you should fly out there and talk to them." Facenda then waxed poetic about my abilities and gave me some phone numbers for the St. Louis station. We had coffee and spumoni and went our separate ways.

Flattered and appreciative, I never dreamed that the great John Facenda's mission was really to get me out of town. I flew to St. Louis and was offered a five-year contract and the five o'clock anchor position. Excitement was building in me. Someone really thought enough of my work to offer me a full-time anchor job.

My signature on a letter of intent was barely dry when the phone rang. The invitation was for lunch at the General Wayne Inn in Narberth with WFIL general manager Gene McCurdy and news director Mel Kampmann. It was Valentine's Day 1970, an unforgettable Friday. I had the flu. I was hours away from proposing to Donna, and I was making initial plans to announce my resignation and move on to St. Louis. At the restaurant, unable to breathe, I sipped some chicken soup from a cup and worried about why I was there. After some small talk, they offered me the number one anchor position at Channel 6. Stunned and thinking the scene was all a mirage, I accepted without even looking at a contract. I never, ever told them about the St. Louis offer. I guess they'll know now.

Their offer had come as a big surprise. Weeks before, broadcast consultant Frank Magid had suggested that I was too young for the assignment. (I was twenty-seven at the time.) And Roger Clipp, then the departing chief executive for Triangle TV, had told me to my face months before that I was too "ethnic" and certainly not old enough to fit into Philadelphia TV. But four executives at the station fought hard to take a chance with me. They were led by Group President George Koehler; Programmer Lew Klein, a legend in local television; General Manager McCurdy; and Kampmann, the news director. Several managers in the station had even insinuated to me that Walter Annenberg, the ambassador to Great Britain, was pushing my elevation to the anchor chair. And perhaps he was. Later that year, Annenberg called me from London, seeking results in the gubernatorial election. After I told him that his arch-enemy Milton Shapp had won, Annenberg said, "Young Mr. Kane, I hear you're doing a great job. I'm glad you got the opportunity."

So the management—led by Koehler, now the chief executive—took a gamble, and between February 14 and April 5, 1970, we began a massive effort to shape our new broadcast format. The first problem was the name. I suggested Action Central. Kampmann wanted Action News. Consultant Magid thought both names were absurd. We also debated about the music. One executive suggested that our dramatic theme music was "too black," an obvious reference of disdain, considering that the Main Line white establishment had been dominating broadcasting in Philadelphia. One thing we didn't disagree about was our slogan: "Give us thirty minutes and we'll give you the world."

That promotion effort was organized by Walter Liss and Mike Davis, two creative geniuses. Liss is now a top executive at Disney; Davis runs a creative consulting firm, where he is in high demand. The two developed a series of commercials for *Action News* that became legendary in broadcasting. The first featured a short, eccentric-looking woman in a hotel elevator slapping my arm with her pocketbook and, in a matter of thirty seconds, reciting almost everything you needed to know about me. She said, as she flailed away at my arm, "Larry Kane, *Action News*, what a smile! More film! More stories! *Action News* is everywhere." By the end of our filming day, my upper arms were black and blue.

With the promotion underway, deadline day approached. *Action News* became the title, the music—a dynamic theme fit for a marching band—was ready, and the lead anchor was fidgety and awed by the opportunity. Picture my situation: I was twenty-seven, scared and insecure, and about to go up against two giants—Facenda and Leonard—in front of an audience conceived to be conservative and stuffy. We know now that that image was and is totally wrong, that in fact the viewers of the area are open to new ideas, but then it was accepted as truth that Philadelphia was a tough, unbending town. Even before we began the show, the stodgy press barons were already picking away at my youth, my credibility. Some of the columnists used words like "brash," "hot dog," "speed demon," and "cocky." They were mistaken. The right words were meek, apprehensive, and fearful. Other broadcasters were spreading the word that our faster pace would fail and that the people of Pennsylvania, New Jersey, and Delaware would never accept a "kid" anchor. Youth is revered in our society today, but in the early seventies, young people were still considered outsiders.

Away from the station, then, the mood was hostile. Inside, an air of excitement and anxiety prevailed as we lunged forward to begin *Action News*. Our format was based on three principles: high story volume, clarity at a fast pace, and—probably the most important element—regional coverage. *Action News* was not an overnight sensation, but it was close to it. We had a wonderful reporting staff led by Rich Kellman. Our first weatherman was Dr. Frances Davis, and our first sportscaster, baseball great Bill White. Lost in all the mythologizing about *Action News* is the fact that Frank Davis and Bill White were still on board when *Action News* became the number one news operation one year later. It was and still is the format, not the personalities, that drives *Action News*. Davis was replaced by John Hambleton, later a pet-shop owner, and then by disk jockey Jim O'Brien, who joined us in 1972. White left to become a Yankees broadcaster and was replaced by the handsome and exciting Joe Pellegrino, a big draw among women viewers.

Mel Kampmann was the key creative force in this success story. Kampmann was a talented, solid news director who resigned in 1974 to run a station in Fargo, North Dakota. He began the job; Ron Tindiglia finished it. Tindiglia, my best friend from 1966 to 1997, was named news director after Kampmann left. Tindiglia brought *Action News* into the modern age with live broadcasting and videotape, expansion to a 5:30 P.M. newscast, and enough inspiration to last a lifetime. More than anyone, Ron Tindiglia elevated *Action News* from a basic, fast-moving news service to a journalistic force in Philadelphia. Ron was hired by General Manager Gene McCurdy, a dynamic broadcaster who believed more than anything else that community service was a priority.

A young man named Larry Pollock became general manager in 1975, replacing McCurdy. Pollock sustained the gains and added more in a brilliant career. Pollock was the single driving force in the continuity of *Action News,* insisting on its consistency, demanding excellence, and personally supervising the promotional effort. His stewardship allowed the station to survive three crises: my departure to New York, my return to Philadelphia and to WCAU TV, and the death of weatherman Jim O'Brien. Under Pollock's leadership and with new call letters following an ownership change, WPVI didn't miss a beat. Pollock's decision to stay in Philadelphia was a critical factor in the station's success. In fact, when he assumed the presidency of all the Capital Cities-ABC-Disney stations, he made his headquarters in Philadelphia, defying the logic that New York is the heart of all media operations. Larry Pollock came here with ambition. He secured his goals, but in a poignant tribute to the joy of living in this region, he stayed here, worked here, and raised a family here. When he recently neared retirement as the ABC station's top executive, he was still in his office at 4100 City Line Avenue.

Those were the principals in the greatest success story in modern local television, a story that certifies something I've believed in for many years: there is no reward without risk in life and in television, something that scores of general managers who competed against Channel 6 learned the hard way over the past thirty years. I'm constantly amazed at the broadcasters who rely on somebody else's research, not their own gut feeling, to program a station, and at the managers who fail to grasp that, when it comes to success, the overriding factor in broadcasting is good, solid news coverage and community commitment, the kind that KYW is providing and that WPVI has sustained for so long. Admittedly, it's a challenge to find managers willing to stay in one town for years. KYW general manager Marcellus Alexander ran the CBS Baltimore station for nine years, and like Pollock in Philadelphia, the length of his tenure worked. The net result was a more successful station and a proud record of accomplishment. My point is simple: musical-chairs management is the primary reason no one has been able to chink the armor of the mighty Channel 6.

Certainly, there's more to the story of the station's rise to prominence—and there's more to how the growth of TV news and my career paralleled the history and growth of the region. Those stories, as we say in the business, are still ahead. For me, though, I will always treasure two special times in my career in Philadelphia—the advent of *Action News* and the creation of the *Bulletin* at KYW. Both programs were created and produced by people with guts and innovation, rare talents in the current television environment.

The advent of *Action News* also meant the beginning of a sea change in the way news was covered. Its accent on suburban coverage forced the other stations to follow suit, and eventually even the big newspapers started their own suburban sections. Expanding news to the suburbs was one thing; actually reaching out to the suburbs was another.

The history of the Philadelphia television industry will show that only one African American, the solid Lisa Thomas-Laury at WPVI, has achieved major star status. Others, like Edie Huggins at WCAU TV, Trudy Haines and Malcolm Poindexter at KYW, and CBS sportscaster Irv Cross were important players early on, but only Lisa caught the brass ring, thanks to hard work, endurance, popularity, and—most of all—exposure.

It wasn't until 1976 that *Action News* promoted and marketed two African-American reporters, Vernon Odom and George Strait. Odom continues as a major City Hall force. Strait joined ABC News in Washington. During the same period, WCAU TV was promoting black personalities vigorously, including Jack Jones and Edie Huggins. And at KYW, the cast was diverse from the beginning. To this day, Channel 6, the leader, has three white men manning the eleven o'clock desk. WCAU TV has key black anchors, and KYW has placed more people of color than any station in town, including my anchor desk partners, Beasley Reece and John Stehlin. Ukee Washington, one of the area's most popular personalities, is growing quickly as an anchor and stands a good chance of becoming the franchise anchor. The issue here is not one of quotas or lists but rather of reflecting properly the nature of this community. In the beginning, there was a reality at WPVI that continues today: the key to winning the ratings was gaining viewers in the white suburban communities where the bulk of the audience lives. Publicly, some broadcast executives will deny that. Privately, they accept it as doctrine.

Today, in the year 2000, WPVI is as diverse in its staff as any station in the country. Its city coverage is excellent, but it makes full use of the fact that a large share of the Philadelphia television market is in the suburbs—an estimated 30 percent in Pennsylvania, 29 percent in New Jersey, and the remainder in Delaware. That means about 70 percent of the entire market of viewers is suburban, that less than 30 percent of metropolitan-area viewers reside in the city of Philadelphia. It's no wonder, then, that *Action News* has been promoting itself with the words "We are everywhere" since the beginning of 1970.

So with that regional coverage, fast pace, and good blend of talent, WPVI had achieved speedy success. The competition started gearing up and shaking up. John Facenda was removed from the anchor chair in 1972. I still believe that was a gross mistake on the part of WCAU management. Facenda was loved; removing him guaranteed more than a decade of rating and financial losses at the station John Facenda had built. Facenda continued as a spokesman and representative for the station, but he returned to TV only to join me in live coverage of the pope's visit in 1979. It was an honor and a pleasure to work with Facenda.

Ratings success came quickly. Dealing with it was another story. To explain that story, first I have to tell a few others.

Roots and Rumblings

Ten years earlier, in June 1960, I was putting the finishing touches on my last edition of *The Lancer,* the school paper at Southwest Miami High School. After school, a bus would take me to downtown Miami for my radio shift, with the return trip home coming at one in the morning. It was a thrilling time, marked by the challenges of seeking news and broadcasting it. At the age of seventeen, who could ask for more?

My family had moved to Miami, after stays in New York and Los Angeles, in an effort to stem the growth of my mother's multiple sclerosis (MS), a disease of the central nervous system. In those days, we were told that a warmer climate might help. From sixth grade on, writing had been my hobby—writing for school papers or neighborhood weeklies. I hooked up with WQAM Radio in Miami in 1957 as a high-school football reporter, nudging my way into the news operation as a gopher, a writer, and eventually, at seventeen, a part-time newscaster. In Miami, I covered everything—murder, sports, domestic violence, politics, and tourism. By the time high school had ended, my career was almost three years old. Like any serious effort in life, it was made possible by a support network. Mine was led by a remarkable woman.

My mother, Mildred Kane, was a never-ending, glowing inspiration to my work, a realist who left me notes every night on my performance, never missing a newscast, never ceasing to be my number one critic and inspiration. She followed my career from 1957 to 1964. Never tampering with my creative juices, she nevertheless was at the time the most important influence in my life, reminding me always to consider others and to see things positively. In this business, seeing everything positively is a challenge, but her advice still lingers.

Not that I always followed it. In 1961, I broke the story of the impending Bay of Pigs invasion in Cuba. My friends in the Cuban exile community had urged me to come along for the ride to observe the invasion from coastal waters. My mother was furious, urging me not to go, almost commanding me. Still, I was prepared to go. Fortunately, logistics weren't favorable. The rest—the death or imprisonment of the brave freedom fighters—is history.

Mildred Kane was the mother of three boys, a brilliant and forward-thinking woman whose little acts of kindness are still remembered by surviving MS patients whom she helped counsel. In MS, hope, the ability to look for a better day, is a great weapon. She used her hope to move from wheelchair to walking cane, then to become the driver of a car and master of a bowling ball. My memory of her walking hand in hand with me to my bar mitzvah dinner is so clear: that was the day she had thrown the wheelchair away and used a cane. When I see the film of that night, my heart breaks, and inevitably I miss her. She was radiant and proud, thankful that the day had come to pass.

Even through her pain, she managed to remember the details of life. In my first years at WQAM Radio in Miami, at holiday time, the staff waited eagerly for the large box of French rolled chocolates with nuts that she made by hand. My young career made her proud and sometimes concerned. One day while I was on assignment at WAME Radio, the phone rang. It was my mother. "Larry," she said, "there's a sheriff's deputy here with a warrant for your arrest. He says you're passing bad checks." Astonished, I replied, "Mom, I don't even have a checking account." When I rang the sheriff's office, the confusion became apparent. The law was after a deejay at the station named Larry King. Larry was having problems in those days, years before his astronomical rise to prime-time television. My mother was relieved.

From 1960 to 1964, youth was unwelcome in radio and TV. It was a mature man's business. Women were not in evidence, minorities not even considered. Fighting the specter of prejudice against youth was difficult, but my mother's constant message was to remain consistent and to have courage. Courage is a trait she knew well. In the days when MS was even more of a mystery, she fought day by day to maintain balance and to make the most of the drops of joy she could glean in her few pain-free moments.

For some reason, my life is organized in my mind by news events. On the evening of August 9, 1964, I was in my parents' bedroom, my mother and I watching President Johnson deliver his address on the hostile action in the Gulf of Tonkin, the precursor to the war in Vietnam. She looked tired, but we talked about politics and my business. As the anchorman summed up LBJ's address, she said, "I think you'll be on TV someday." I replied, "No, Mom, I don't have the looks, and I love radio." She answered, "No, I have a feeling you'll do very well on TV." It's almost as if she wished it on me.

The next morning, she died of complications of MS. She was forty. Her entire life—the struggle, the courage, and her unbounded hope— was my real inspiration, especially when I entered the world of insecurity, anxiety, and even depression that accompanied hard work, ambition, and a desire to win. Her love and belief were more than significant: they were the keys to my becoming who I am, personally and professionally.

The other woman in my life would arrive five years after my mother's death, in the fall of 1969. The coffee shop of WFIL TV, now WPVI, was a stop I made every afternoon for a snack or a soda. It was there that I become addicted to coffee and to something else. My visits to the room became more frequent, my coffee drinking more systematic, after a chance encounter with a woman named Donna Jarrett. Donna was just twenty when I met her, a student at Temple and a part-time employee in the station's business office. She was beautiful, even magnetically attractive, but more than just a looker; she carried herself with confidence and calm.

The first time I looked into her eyes, heard her voice, got closer, and watched her walk and exchange glances with people, I had no question that I would ask her out. When I got my first look, I was interim anchor of the eleven o'clock news. Donna didn't seem impressed with who I was, although in those days *I* certainly was. With cocky confidence, I placed a call to her house. "Hello," I said, "this is Larry Kane, uh . . . the . . . uh . . . anchor at the station." She said, "Yes?" I replied, "Would you like to have dinner Saturday night?" Donna said, "I'm busy." I charged on, saying, "How about next Saturday?" She said, "I'm tied up then, too." Paralyzed by this setback, I announced that I had never dated anyone at the station, a feeble comment intended to anoint her as the lucky one. Not surprisingly, it came out the wrong way. That was the end of the conversation.

The next week, I stepped up my trips to the coffee shop, where I caught Donna occasionally glancing over. Gathering my courage a few days later, I made a second call. "Donna," I said, "I'd love to have dinner with you next week." She replied, "I can't go Saturday night." I said, "How about Sunday?" She added, "Okay, but it has to be an early night."

After my knock on the door, her mother greeted me with warmth and open arms. Her father seemed curious. Donna walked down the stairs, avoided eye contact, and came with me to the car. Once inside, I asked stupidly, "I guess you want to get married and have babies?" If Hollywood were central casting for a nerd, I would have won the part hands down. At that point, I was ready to go through the motions, have dinner, and go home. Her coolness and disinterest rattled me. "Just chalk this up as another life experience," I thought on the drive to a restaurant on the White Horse Pike in New Jersey.

Life has its surprises, though, and somewhere between the salad and the main course, our conversation got warmer. Our eyes made contact, strong contact, and I was in a trance. Her face lit up. There, in the middle of Sunday night dinner, we clicked and bonded, and my quick night out turned to thirty years and counting.

Donna and I became engaged on Valentine's Day in 1970—as you may remember, the same day that Channel 6 offered me a contract as permanent anchor. We were married on May 24. Michael was born in 1972, the night of the Watergate burglary, also a Father's Day, and just days before Tropical Storm Agnes dumped ten inches of rain in the region. Alexandra arrived in 1978, the year of Frank Rizzo's charter reform defeat. As you can see, I do indeed chart my life by news events.

What the marriage meant to my career in Philadelphia was incalculable. Donna has given and continues to give me love and strengths that have been critical in times of both triumph and trial. She is my biggest supporter, but her support carries a dimension rare in most marriages—truth. Being honest with myself has never been my strong point, and that illusion of success, delusions of grandeur, has always been a failing of mine. Donna is my reality check. There is not an ounce of falsehood in the life of Donna Jarrett-Kane, and that's why her advice has always been straightforward, without compromise and with no half-hearted rationale.

On countless nights I've returned from work with real and imagined fears, only to have her tell me that my insecurities and anxieties are on the verge of costing me my health and well being. A tough newspaper critic, a jealous coworker, a nasty competitor, untrue things written about me, and evil gremlins of my own when these challenges creep into my mind, Donna always provides an all-out defense for me, coupled with advice to put things in perspective, something I have always found difficult. I can't say that I've followed her advice every time she's offered it. But her strength and caring have been more than enough to get me through the excesses of success and the dark depths of failure.

The ebb and flow of our relationship has sustained me and—I hope—her. Many of her aspirations were suspended so she could love and mentor our children. Today, she is developing her own multimedia production company, Dynamic Images. Her success is all but assured. Whether it's during her work in our community, which has been exemplary, or through her efforts in business, people are drawn to Donna's caring, her intelligence, and her charisma. Most people who meet her find it hard to believe that this youthful and sexy beauty is the mother of two grown children. As my hair turns grayer, some people mistake her for my daughter, a compliment to her and an ego-splitting blow to me. Our children love it, and so does she.

Public recognition is nice, and so is professional success, but Donna has always counseled that success is not worth much unless you can maintain your standards and can look at yourself in the mirror and see the human being, not the image of some press release or publicity photo.

Who am I? Just a man, I'll say, who's had the support of some wonderful people, but especially two women: a mother who refused to quit living, and a dynamic and gorgeous wife who has stood with me, along with our children, in the glow and shadows of broadcasting and public life.

Friends in the Business

Those early days as anchor—nervous, anxious times—were made easier by some kind people. Some were strangers to me, though not to the people who lived in Philadelphia.

One day during my first year as anchorman, a man approached me and, to my amazement, started singing in a weird cadence, "Larrya-phonic Lar, action man, you are the greatest, my man. You are rockin', baby, rockin' the news at night." The man was short, dressed in stylish bell bottoms, his hair combed back in a Sinatra-like wave. Before I could ask his name, he pulled out a dollar bill and wrote the following on it: "Larry, wishing you success always, your friend, Jerry Blavat."

Like a businessman savoring his first sale, I've saved that dollar bill all these years. It's a bit tattered but durable, much like the friendship that followed. Blavat was a real Philadelphia star, a South Philly boy who was self-made in every sense, rising from guest shots on American Bandstand to developing his own radio and television programs. His good-luck-charm dollar bill was a real boost at a time when my success seemed elusive, if not impossible.

Blavat remains a star today, although his audience is a little grayer. Along the way, life has been good to him, but it's also been challenging. His mother's friendship with mob boss Angelo Bruno's wife prompted investigators to try and tag him with a mob label. It didn't stick. In recent years, he watched in agony as two of his best friends—Sammy Davis, Jr., and developer Sam Rappaport—died. In Philadelphia, if you weather the storm, the people of the area become the sunshine, and the people always come out for Jerry Blavat.

Inspiration is a lost art, but in the seventies there was plenty to go around. In 1970, I got calls from Vince Leonard, the wonderful anchor at KYW TV, and talk host Tom Snyder. Snyder once said about me, "He's younger, he's tougher, and nobody watches him." That was the public posture. Privately, Snyder would call me with encouraging comments about my work. So did Leonard, who not only called, but also wrote of my growth as an anchor. And Marciarose, the anchor at KYW TV and the first woman in America to anchor a big-city evening newscast, was always supportive.

Not all the anchors in the viewing area were class acts. Judd Hambrick was a young anchor, a pretty boy whom WCAU placed next to John Facenda in hopes of countering the *Action News* success. Hambrick was cocky. At a testimonial lunch for Facenda, Hambrick asked when meeting me for the first time, "Do you rent or own your home?" I answered, "We rent an apartment." Smiling broadly, Hambrick said, "That's good, because I should be finishing you off in about a year." Judd Hambrick left before the year was out, his ego shattered in the tough world of Philadelphia television. Cocky can get rocky when you play for all the marbles.

Within my first year as primary anchor, the recognition factor grew so dramatically that my daily life was affected. By the summer of 1970, there were few places I could go without being talked at, touched, or pursued. This sudden fame left me missing my privacy and haunted by a bizarre form of public claustrophobia, a terrible reluctance to go places because I feared that all eyes were on me. Some people live for public recognition; mine has always been a burden.

Much to Donna's chagrin, I started avoiding large crowds. Going to a movie was harrowing, trips to the drugstore annoying. During personal appearances, people touched and hugged me like I was a member of the family. By the mid-nineties I was treated like the dean of news, with more recognition and a quieter respect, but in the beginning, the adulation and commotion was above and beyond.

Kane, You Are a Pussy

Along with the fame came ominous moments caused by threatening letters and phone calls. One in particular gave me an inside look at the vagaries of the Philadelphia justice system. Philadelphia justice is a mosaic of influence and power. On a summer morning in 1972, I learned how that mosaic can change according to who you are from a municipal court judge named Lewis Mongelluzo.

A few weeks before, a young man had phoned and written to me, threatening to cut me up and spread my body parts on various monuments through Philadelphia. That was the first time I had received such threats, and they scared me. I reported his phone calls, they were traced, and he was arrested. A preliminary hearing was scheduled for the 18th Police District in West Philadelphia.

I had agreed with the prosecutor that the best course of action would be psychiatric treatment under a first offender's program. But, to my surprise, I was called to the bench by Judge Mongelluzo. He asked me to come behind the bench, where he introduced me to his wife, his clerk. And then he said, "What do you want me to do to the kid? I think we should send him up for a year or two to teach him a lesson." I said, "Your honor, that would not be right, and—" He interrupted. "Larry Kane, let's get this guy's ass in jail. That's what everybody wants, because we don't want anybody messin' with you." I replied, "Please, your honor, get him some help." He said, "Okay, but the guys in City Hall are gonna be pissed."

The young man was ordered to have psychiatric treatment. I was happy but curious to know what had happened. Later in the day, I called Mayor Frank Rizzo and asked him if he had heard of the case. He said, "What are you talking about, that weirdo freako who wanted to kill you? Kane, if I were the judge, I would have sent him up and thrown away the key. Kane, you are a pussy."

While I have received threats since then, no other mayor has described me that way. But then again, as you will learn, no other mayor was like Frank Rizzo.

News Wars

The fast rise of *Action News* put incredible pressure on us to keep the train on track. With the press still harping on our fast style of packing dozens of reports into a half-hour newscast, News Director Kampmann embarked on an effort to expand our reach. His effort came in the form of two prime-time documentaries. One was "Public Bridges—Private Riches," an exposé of the public officials who were getting rich from the PATCO high-speed line and the construction of the Betsy Ross and Commodore Barry Bridges. Twenty-seven years later, these two bridges are still not receiving heavy traffic and, in retrospect, seem unnecessary. The second documentary was called "Decision of a Life-time," which followed the *Roe v. Wade* decision and provided a close-up look at the abortion crisis. The program featured a live abortion performed on a Catholic woman at a Center City clinic. Despite protests from both the Catholic church and abortion advocates, the broadcast aired in prime time, and members of the public made their own judg-ments about abortion clinics. Suddenly, *Action News* was in the serious news business, and that was good.

With success guaranteed at WPVI TV, the competition started gearing up. In the course of just over a year, WCAU took John Facenda off the air, dumped Judd Hambrick, and tried something new—a youth movement. They hired Mike Tuck, a handsome young man, and Jack Jones, a protégé of Facenda's, dressed them in turtleneck sweaters, and tried for a casual style. It didn't work. In desperation, they hired Barney Morris, a weak anchor from San Diego, who fell flat on his face. WCAU brought back Tuck and Jones and continued pairing anchors through the seventies.

The real competition came from KYW TV, where a community-minded, activist general manager named Alan J. Bell rose to the moment. Bell was determined to get the audience, but unlike the man-agement at WCAU TV, Bell stuck with his anchor, steady Vince Leonard, and buttressed him with Mort Crim, a velvet-voiced veteran, and a new-comer, Jessica Savitch. Savitch was attractive, charismatic, and obvi-ously talented. She seemed to caress the camera with her eyes. A girl next door with a sexy edge, she became the talk of the town. She also had a secret weapon, a man by the name of Dave Neal. Dave Neal's story is the untold saga of Philadelphia TV history.

Neal, who was born Dave Gomberg, was a KYW news executive who personally crafted the image of Jessica Savitch, launching her on assignments that quickly established an image of credibility. One mem-orable story, for example, was a personal look at how women coped with rape, a subject that was taboo on local television. Neal also created franchises (specialty assignments) for one of Philadelphia's great reporters, Dick Sheeran, whom he named the Energy Warden during the 1973 energy crisis. Sheeran was the people's watchdog for cheaper energy. Neal's impact on the lives of reporters would spread to his work at Channels 6 and 10, but always, in her life and after her death by drowning, Dave Neal's biggest legacy was the crafting of Jessica Savitch. Whether it was deciding on her makeup, choosing her personal appearances, or educating her about the city, Dave Neal was there, helping to drive her to the top.

Neal also had a brilliant eye for inventive coverage. In 1975, *Action News* was the last station to get live cameras for on-the-scene coverage, which was ironic, because through magnificent promotion most viewers thought WPVI was *the* live station. By this time, having been dumped by KYW, Neal had joined WPVI as assignment manager. Our live camera, the only one we owned, was debuted on a six o'clock broadcast. The camera crew managed to shoot three live reports that night with the lone camera. The newscast opened with a report on a murder: the background was an abandoned home off north Broad Street. Minutes later, Neal had the crew turn the camera around to point down Broad, and our City Hall bureau chief fronted a political report, with City Hall itself, majestic in the distance, as the backdrop. At the end of the broadcast, the camera turned east for a live report on a jobs fair. The background this time was Temple University. Dave Neal had struck again—one camera, one location, three stories. Neal was creative and crafty, but his shining achievement was helping Jessica Savitch.

Savitch needed the help. She was the most ambitious broadcaster I had ever met and wasn't afraid to show it. Her reporting skills were suspect, however, along with her instincts for understanding life. While he was still at KYW, Neal had arranged several meetings between Savitch and me where we talked business, one in the Famous Fourth Street Deli at Fourth and Bainbridge. Jessica was curious. "Are you going to leave Philadelphia?" she asked. I replied, "Possibly, but it would have to be really good." She said, "Well, if you leave, I have to leave, because I need to get on a fast track. It's my destiny to be the network anchor. I was born to be that." Fascinated, I said, "How about other things, like family and fun?" Looking bewildered, she asked, "Are you kidding? Being a network anchor is my life."

Jessica stayed in Philadelphia for five years and then catapulted to NBC News, where she reported on Capitol Hill and was the first woman to anchor the NBC weekend news. But there was no Dave Neal in Washington. Her life of driven ambition was empty of the kind of marketing that Dave provided. Capitol Hill was a tough assignment. She went through two marriages, a spousal suicide, and setbacks. She died in the New Hope Canal when her boyfriend's car slipped into the water.

That was in 1983. In 1991, our son, Michael, was attending Ithaca College. There, in a modern corridor, I passed by a plaque naming a training facility "The Jessica Savitch Studio." Her estate had rewarded Ithaca, her alma mater, grandly. I thought of her—eager, excited, pursuing the dream—and I hoped that the students who were educated in that studio would never feel the pain of raw ambition that she felt. When I counsel students who aspire to the heights of television, I always tell them, Try to grab the brass ring, but in the process, find a life apart from television, the kind of life that can sustain you when the strain of achieving wears you down.

When Savitch left Philadelphia, her co-anchor Mort Crim was not far behind. KYW TV succumbed to desperate measures, hiring a series of anchors who would ruin the station's credibility. The station created a new format, the Direct Connection, a fast-moving, sensual newscast with special effects. Flash replaced good hard-news coverage. So as the eighties approached, *Action News* continued to flourish, through both the steam of its own creativity and the mistakes of its competition.

What Were They Thinking?

Freezing rain is nightmarish weather—my personal worst. In the winter of 1973, I proved it. My car skidded as I was turning into the driveway late at night, winding up on the lawn of my house, stuck in ice. And there it sat. This was embarrassing enough at night, but when daylight came, the shame of my bad driving was displayed in the bright sunlight, my green Camaro stuck in the ice, with nowhere to go.

After trying to extract the car myself, I called the local service station. They said they would send a tow truck, and I went back in the house to take a shower. A few minutes later, the chimes sounded. Hair wet, body dripping, I ran to the front door and saw that the tow truck had arrived. When I stepped out to talk to the driver, a man with a microphone emerged from behind a bush. I recognized him as Matt Quinn, a reporter for KYW TV. He said, "Mr. Kane, can you give us the real story on what happened to your car?" Shocked, freezing in my bathrobe, I said, "Why, you must be the reporter from Channel 29!" This was my way of having some fun with Mr. Quinn. He replied, "Sources report that you drove the car onto your lawn." I said, "You have reliable sources."

When Quinn left my ice-covered lawn, I thought his presence had all been part of a gag by the KYW newsroom. When I returned to the WPVI newsroom at 11:30, hysterical staffers told me that I had appeared on KYW. Apparently, my ice-bound car had been the final story on the Channel 3 news, complete with the brief interview. They had their laugh. I was astonished. Why would they give me exposure on *their* station? Then my phone rang. The voice said, "Larry, this is Vince Leonard. How's your driving?" I asked, "Vince, why did they use me in your newscast?" He said, "Beats me. Maybe they were trying to make fun, but frankly, Larry, I hate to see you get that exposure right here. Maybe they lost their minds." Maybe, but the following weeks would reveal a destructive trend at KYW.

For a few months, KYW TV edged us out in the early news. Then the station's promotion department made two errors. They hung a huge banner over the KYW building at Fifth and Market Streets announcing, "We're Number One!" Then, in the biggest fumble of all, they produced a commercial in which Jessica Savitch thumbs through names in the phone book in the course of telling people that KYW is number one again. In the last scene, her finger reaches the name "Kane," as in Larry. She says, "Yes, Mr. Kane, we are indeed number one." The spot backfired. Viewers felt it was petty. In Philadelphia, being tough is good, but being unfair is unforgivable.

Public Appearances, Public Spectacles

Part of the job of an anchorman is being an integral part of your community. In the first few years, I made four or five community appearances a week, leaving me with vivid memories of the interiors of synagogues, churches, schools, day-care centers, American Legion halls, shopping centers, and bowling alleys. I cut ribbons, made speeches, signed autographs, gladhanded, and ate enough chicken dinners to last a lifetime. I felt like a political candidate, except that my constituents were voting with their dials.

Most of the excursions were on behalf of groups and services that needed help. Television is a powerful medium, and if my presence could comfort someone in need or nurture a young person, the effort was gratifying. Future reporters and anchors need to understand that they have a responsibility to use the power of television to enrich people's lives. Most anchors and reporters in Philadelphia television have given back little to the viewers who support them. Channel 6 portrays itself as a station of community service, and it does a fine job, but its lead anchor is rarely seen in public, and only Lisa Thomas-Laury, the great 5:00 P.M. anchor, is truly involved in the community. Orien Reid, who recently retired from WCAU TV, and Pat Ciarrocci and Ukee Washington, my colleagues at KYW, set the standard for community involvement. My own involvement with helping the fight against MS and my speaking and fund-raising schedule have been taxing but very gratifying. Show me an anchor who participates in the community, and I will show you a success—a success measured not in ratings, but in the ability to do good deeds for others. My advice: if you want to be a star, start by giving to the needy rather than being needy yourself.

It's difficult remembering each stop, each appearance, but in over three decades of very public appearances, a few stick out in my mind, and for good reason. One of those appearances became a treacherous road through the minefields of public debate.

Pottsville is a beautiful little town in Pennsylvania coal country. Donna and I traveled there in late 1971 to meet and address a consortium of service clubs, including the American Legion, Rotary, and Kiwanis clubs. Driving into Pottsville, I realized that I was fulfilling an ambition. The town was the home of one of my favorite novelists, John O'Hara, who wrote about the haves and the have-nots of small and big towns with clarity and insight. O'Hara also began as a journalist, and that counted to me. My hope was for a short visit to the O'Hara library, but we were running late, and as it turned out, maybe we should have stayed home.

During the trip from Philadelphia to Pottsville, Donna and I exchanged points and counterpoints in our great debate. The question: should I give my Agnew attack speech? Would they run me out of town? There's a wonderful newsroom aphorism that covers questions of propriety—When in doubt, don't. But I contended that the First Amendment guarantees free speech, and if I couldn't offer my point of view, as far as I was concerned, our Constitution wasn't worth a spit. So in my youthful, macho mania and my sincere conviction as a free American, I ignored Donna's advice and decided give Pottsville the unabridged version of the Agnew speech.

Here I am with one of my best friends, the typewriter, in the newsroom in 1976. (Photo courtesy of Donna Jarrett-Kane)

Me and my parents, Jack and Mildred, in 1943. (Photo from the author's collection)

In 1956, settled in Florida, my mother continues her battle against MS, surrounded by her family. From left to right are me; my father; my middle brother, Bruce; and my younger brother, Monte. (Photo from the author's collection)

Here I am with Donna and the children, Michael and Alexandra, at Lorimer Park in Montgomery County in 1981. (Photo courtesy of Kathleen Friedman)

My good buddy Jerry Blavat, an early supporter and a real star in Philadelphia. (Photo courtesy of Jerry Blavat, Geator Gold Radio Network)

In 1982, the year of the Mayor Green fiasco, I serve as commencement speaker at Cabrini College. (Photo courtesy of Cabrini College)

New Jersey governor Tom Kean honors me for my efforts to promote adoption.
(Photo courtesy of the Honorable Thomas H. Kean)

Orien Reid, consumer reporter for WCAU TV, joins me at the 1987 MS Walk.
(Photo courtesy of the National Multiple Sclerosis Society, Greater Delaware
Valley Chapter)

Here I am narrating the Pageant of Flags at one of the eleven July 4th ceremonies I participated in at the request of the city of Philadelphia. (Photo courtesy of the City of Philadelphia, Office of the City Representative)

Moments before Philadelphia's July 4, 1977, Independence Hall ceremony, Frank Sinatra and Mayor Frank Rizzo chat while I wait nearby. (Photo courtesy of the City of Philadelphia, Office of the City Representative)

Donna Kane meets Donna the lion. The lion, donated by Frank Palumbo to the Philadelphia Zoo in my honor in 1976, peers from her cage in front of Palumbo's restaurant. (Photo courtesy of the Zoological Society of Philadelphia)

At the Devon horse show in 1973, I meet up with the legendary Howard Cosell. (Photo courtesy of Donna Jarrett-Kane)

ABC anchor Harry Reasoner and I pose during a promotional tour in 1974. (Photo courtesy of WPVI-TV)

In a television first, President Gerald Ford joins me for a live appearance on WPVI Action News, *days before the 1976 election. This was the first live appearance by a president on a local news program. (Photo courtesy of the Gerald Ford Presidential Library)*

Here I am, hosting and moderating a forum involving the entire 60 Minutes team before a Philadelphia Chamber of Commerce luncheon in 1996. From left to right are Morley Safer, me, Charles Pizzi (president of the Chamber of Commerce), Mike Wallace, Ed Bradley, Andy Rooney, and Leslie Stahl. (Photo courtesy of Liz Wuillermin)

Co-anchor Alan Frio and I during an MS Walk event at Boathouse Row in April 1988 (Photo courtesy of the National Multiple Sclerosis Society, Greater Delaware Valley Chapter)

First, some scene setting. Vice President Spiro Agnew, a man who could have written the textbook for Demagoguery 101, had spent a good two years defaming and diminishing the credibility of the news media. Although Agnew was a vacuous political attack dog, his message was resonating across the land, and people were reacting in a wave of resentment against all forms of news media. Even my own father suggested that my business was burning up the American dream with negative messages.

So, undaunted, courageous, and rather stupid, my nerve up and my guard down, I walked into the Legion Hall to a thundering standing ovation. The event included a family-style dinner, reach-out-and-help-yourself style, with some local beer thrown in. The food was marvelous and the company friendly, and the citizens of Pottsville were cheery and pleased that I had showed up.

My address covered a summary of Pennsylvania politics, White House intrigue, Kent State, the war in Vietnam, and press freedoms, with an accent on the freedoms part. I gave a strong defense of the First Amendment, accentuating the dangers of people like Agnew trying to shape what we see, hear, and read. "Good news is good, bad news is bad," I said, "but when people do not have information, they cannot act, they cannot judge, and the lessons of a repressed media are written in blood on the pages of history, in Cuba, Russia, China, and in the greatest example of press censorship, Hitler's Germany." The speech concluded with a savage attack on Agnew, who was using his bully pulpit to coerce the media.

There is a special communication with the woman you love. It starts with a curve of the lip and ends with those brown eyes staring into space. It says, without a word, "You're in trouble." If looks could say "I told you so," then Donna's face told the whole story.

There was no applause when I finished the speech. I asked for questions. There were no questions. Silence. More silence. Finally I said, "The people who come to this Legion Hall fought in wars to preserve my right and your right to talk freely. Does anyone have a problem with that?"

Still no questions. Thirty seconds passed by, but it could have been thirty years. Tick tock, the clock is ticking, and there is nowhere to go. Finally, realizing my predicament, a woman in the back rose up and asked about my views on abortion. I said, "Considering the recent reaction to my outspoken remarks, I'll take a pass on that question, if you know what I mean." More silence, then a roar of laughter and applause. Thank God for that woman and the opportunity she gave me.

The questions started coming; the debate was at times hostile, although sharply focused and worthwhile. When it was over, I thanked the Pottsville viewers for inviting me and affording me the opportunity to understand the extent of public anger toward the news media. "We both learned a little tonight," I added. Their send-off was warm and cordial.

As I sat down in the driver's seat of the car, Donna looked over, grinned, and said, "See, I'm always right about those things." I replied, "Yes, you are, but I'd do it again." She responded, "I know, and you did a great job tonight."

That appearance was memorable for its truth and tension. Others brought me a higher knowledge of the geography, peculiarities, and nature of the people in the tristate region. I would never take back those hundreds of speeches, because I learned quickly that you can't survive as a big-city anchor by sitting on your rear and looking in the mirror. But survival also means taking risks, like high-profile assignments and even marching in parades adorned with plumes and feathers.

Pomp, Pageantry, Embarrassment

If you want to learn about a community, examine its customs—its celebrations and peculiar routines. In Philadelphia, two events stand out, July 4th and New Year's Day. No other city in America celebrates those holidays in the same way. But then again, no other city has the Liberty Bell and the Mummers.

History is always a lesson, and in Philadelphia, you don't need a history book. You can walk the history, feel the cobblestones beneath you, and try to imagine the unpaved streets, filled with dirt and horses, on the day when America was born. Philadelphians love July 4th with a special fervor. Block parties in South Philadelphia and the Northeast run from morning till night. The people who live in a neighborhood called Strawberry Mansion move to the wide-open grass of Fairmount Park, enjoying the river view and watching thousands of barbecue fires. July 4th in the park is the aroma of hot dogs and potato salad and the ceremonial carrying of folding chairs. Philadelphia is a city of folding chairs and awnings. The chairs provide instant relaxation for the weary, and the awnings, a major attraction on row homes, give protection from the summer sun. On July 4th, the flags flying in the neighborhoods beam the pride, and the people at Independence Mall revel in the fact that, on the birthday of the Republic, this is definitely the place to be.

The centerpiece of this Philadelphia legacy is the July 4th celebration at the steps of Independence Hall. July 4th has been officially celebrated many ways in Philadelphia. In recent years, led by City Representative Kathleen Sullivan, it caps off a week-long celebration of arts, music, and street festivals. And for the last thirty-four years, Philadelphia's July 4th has never passed by without a famous person being honored or recognized. John F. Kennedy, Nelson Mandela, Lech Walesa, Jimmy Carter, and others have traveled through the corridors of Independence Hall on July 4th.

From 1969 to 1979, I was called on to emcee the city's official ceremony and read the Declaration of Independence. During those July 4th mornings, I met Bob Hope, Jack Palance, Jimmy Carter, E. G. Marshall, Gerald Ford, and others. The event always offered pomp and ceremony and some interesting scenarios. FBI director L. Patrick Gray was there, months before his corruption indictment. But for me, of all those days, one ceremony stands out—July 4th, 1977, the day Frank Sinatra was honored.

The 1977 event drew a huge crowd that extended from Independence Hall past the quadrangle on Market Street, two long city blocks, and it drew as much security as the visit by President Gerald Ford had a year earlier for the bicentennial. Police surrounded the mall, and sharpshooters were positioned on nearby buildings. At 9:30 A.M. the reception began inside the hall, where Frank Rizzo was pacing so fast he was almost at an aerobic run. "Mr. Mayor," I asked, "what's wrong?" "I'll tell you what's wrong," Rizzo roared. "What's wrong is that Sinatra is goddamn late. I don't care who he is—you don't stand me up in my hometown." Seconds later, we heard the whirr of a helicopter overhead, and someone ran in with the news that the chopper was landing on a helipad near the Old Original Bookbinder's restaurant. There, crack members of the Philadelphia highway patrol were waiting on their motorcycles, at the ready, prepared to accompany Sinatra's car to the rear of Independence Hall. The ceremony was to begin at 10:00 A.M. It was already 9:50, and Frank Rizzo was heating up.

Sirens started blaring, and Rizzo's demeanor improved considerably, his face breaking out in that special Rizzo grin. Sirens meant the motorcade was on its way. Rizzo walked to the back door, where he greeted Frank Sinatra and his security force. Sinatra, a slight man, embraced Rizzo, and the two shared a few private moments before exiting to the stage. As Sinatra appeared in the doorway and climbed the steps, a roar arose from the crowd that was deep-throated and strong. The bobby soxers and their husbands or partners were all grown up but still ready to scream.

The ceremony proceeded with a parade of flags, more music, perfunctory speeches, and my reading of the Declaration of Independence. When I finished, Sinatra leaned over and said, in a line out of a Hollywood movie, "Hey, kid, you were great. Way to go, kid!"

The crowd went haywire when Sinatra received his medal and offered a brief speech about the joys of living in America. I watched the spectators, the Philadelphia eyes welling up with tears, as the biggest superstar of the postwar generation talked about growing up in New Jersey, getting a few breaks, emerging into stardom, and thanking God and America for it. Later, the newspapers would chastise Rizzo for giving Sinatra a medal of freedom. The newspapers were wrong. Sinatra personified the dream of Philadelphia life—hard work, belief in spirituality, and respect for tradition.

Tradition is important in Philadelphia, sometimes to an extreme degree. That's why my brief career as a Philadelphia Mummer was so fascinating. The Mummers are a most unusual act—funny, musical, grand, and stylish, a mystery to the rest of America, a treasure to the people of our tristate region, and an assemblage of performers not without controversy. The Mummer's Parade begins early on the morning of January 1st and consists of four parts. Each part is made up of groups of performers from neighborhood Mummer organizations who work all year round for that New Year's march up Broad Street—or, due to a recent change, on Market Street. First come the Comics. They are just that—comedic marchers satirizing current themes. Second come the Fancies, parading in the costumes they have created, full of glorious colors, sequins, and feathers. The String Bands follow. These are the people who made banjos glamorous again. The final part is the Fancy Brigades, a bit more of the Fancy routine, this time with music and more choreography.

The Mummers organizations are political to a fault, protecting turf, fighting the city for money, and, in a long history of bigotry, excluding people from the parade because of race, gender, ethnic origin, and sexual orientation. Few blacks and women are represented, although women have been marching in greater numbers recently. The Mummers have also been greedy, forcing the bidding so high for their TV rights that in 1994 the big three stations in Philadelphia pulled out of the bidding. That left the Mummers with a hot product and no takers. Fred Calandra, the late leader of the String Bands, would always say, "Lar, they're goin' to screw it up because of money." Calandra was right. After his death, opportunists knocked on the doors of the TV stations and got no answer.

Nonetheless, the Mummers provide a spectacular show, drawing hundreds of thousands of people. During the six years I anchored the parade (1981–1986), I made solid, lasting friends whose only prejudice was against their competition and whose pride was being a part of Philadelphia. One of those friends was Frank Conforti, who we called "The Voice of the Mummers." Conforti is a South Philly guy, an expert on all things Mummer. It was during the 1983 parade that he dared me to march next time around. What can I say? Donna wasn't with me, and I lapsed into lunacy. So on January 1, 1983, I pledged to march in the next Mummer's Parade. The 1984 parade seemed a long time away.

The Klein Fancy Club adopted me, preparing a fancy costume of blue and white sequins along with a body suit and a very tall hat. I had sparkles of glitter from head to toe. The first "rehearsal" at Klein headquarters convinced everyone that I did not belong in the Mummer's Parade. A special concession was made. Small wheels were put on my two-hundred-pound getup, and we decided that my fateful march would start at Broad and Washington, shortening the journey considerably. The Klein Club would be separated from me by a hundred yards because of concerns that my high profile and lack of talent might impact on their chances of winning.

The morning of January 1, 1984, was crisp and clear. During the broadcast from 7:00 to 11:00 A.M., nervousness began sweeping through my body, aggravated by my knowledge that Donna and the kids would be watching my mad march on television at a reception at the Bellevue Hotel. Shortly after eleven, I drove to Broad and Washington, changed hastily into the sequined and feathered costume, and took my place in the line of the march. I was ready for a new role—I would be the man who pulled my weight by pulling my small float.

The costume was heavy. As I moved toward South Street, faint stirrings in my bladder sent a surge of panic through my body. But I pressed forward, scattering feathers and sequins as I went. When the Bellevue came in sight, I got a grip on myself and tried to change my thought process, focusing on visions of a far-off mountain range and a bright blue sea. The big turn was coming up that would put me in the sight of the judges, left at City Hall, up Fifteenth Street, and another left at the reviewing stand. In a state of despair and disappointment, I approached City Hall, where a cavernous cheer erupted, the sound echoing through the concrete canyon. Those great Philadelphians were cheering me on the way to the finish. They knew the foolishness of my trek, but in the lore of my Philadelphia, one thing is certain: if you become a part of the roots of the city, a piece of the pride, the love always returns with fervor and glee.

When I approached the WCAU broadcast booth, adrenalin flowing, happy that the ordeal was almost over, the inner extrovert emerged. Unrehearsed, I began a Mummer's dance, twirling around in my dress of glitz, waving my weighted-down arms at the crowd, and dipping my head in that Mummer's strut. The crowd had sustained me. Afterward there was celebration and talk of my adventure, but also a vow: I would never do it again.

The costume was put in storage at the Mummer's Museum, where it is occasionally displayed. The Mummers continue their New Year's magic. The TV audiences are a bit smaller, but the Mummers remain as Muzak for the soul on New Year's Days. Some people retain faint memories of my walk of fame, or shame, in 1984, but these memories are overshadowed by the continuing performances of the great men and women who are real Mummers, the pride of Philadelphia and South Jersey. God bless them.

Ode to Palumbo's

Somewhere in this world is a lion named Donna. Her last known whereabouts were the Philadelphia Zoo, but she could be anywhere. In March 1976, Donna was not at her zoo home but pacing in a narrow cage, roaring at those who passed in front of a nightclub and restaurant known as Palumbo's at Ninth and Catharine Streets in South Philadelphia. Donna, named for my Donna, had been donated to the Philadelphia Zoo by Frank Palumbo, owner of Palumbo's and supporter of politicians, ordinary folk, and animals.

The occasion was a service club fund-raiser and testimonial in my honor, packed with elected officials and jammed into three separate rooms at the multilevel Palumbo's. The rooms were busy with the power people, including the mayor, most members of City Council, judges, and an assortment of Philadelphians, mostly from south of City Hall. The speeches were brief, the company was wonderful, and the event gave me another chance to see Frank Palumbo, a man who had encouraged me from the beginning to endure the growing pains of living in Philadelphia. From my earliest days in Philadelphia, Palumbo would offer me words of encouragement. When I covered stories at the nightclub, he would emerge from his office and tell me that people liked my work. For a twenty-something learning the big city, these were important words.

Palumbo's nightclub, and later his Nostalgia restaurant, served two purposes: it was the scene of thousands of parties, bar mitzvahs, confirmations, and weddings, and it served as a political nerve center in Philadelphia. The menu was usually the same—ravioli or spaghetti, salad, veal, and wonderful bread, usually topped off by spumoni. The diners were seated close together, watching the entertainers on a small nightclub stage. Greats of the time like Jimmy Durante and Mel Torme made Palumbo's a regular stop. With its smells, food, red carpeting, and various rooms, Palumbo's conveyed the fabric of life in South Philadelphia. From Mummer's events to political fund-raisers, I attended gatherings there and began to know the secret stairways and different banquet rooms as though they were my own home.

Frank Palumbo was a most unlikely restaurant and nightclub operator. Painfully shy and unusually quiet, Palumbo would hide away during major banquets and affairs in his side office, occasionally emerging briefly to speak with his guests. He left most of the social amenities to the love of his life, Kippee. Kippee Palumbo became one of Philadelphia's first ladies, a beautiful woman who was a Hollywood and TV actress in the fifties and, like her husband, a philanthropic legend.

Getting to know Frank Palumbo was a mission impossible, but an unusual interview brought me closer. In 1975, Palumbo was disturbed about an *Inquirer Magazine* article suggesting that his intense privacy and philanthropic zeal were perhaps a cloak for some sort of secret life.

The article never confirmed any link to the underworld or any world other than the daily grind of running a club and restaurant, but there were enough insinuations that Palumbo decided to act.

Through his good friend, *Daily News* columnist Larry Fields, Frank Palumbo agreed to a television interview with me, the first he had ever done. The interview was remarkable, but my work had nothing to do with it. Palumbo opened up about his parents' use of the Palumbo's building to house and feed poor Italian immigrants earlier in the century. Then, to my surprise, he tackled his image head on. I asked, "Do you have some connection to irregularities, or bad elements?" The usually shy Palumbo, smiling, said, "Larry, I have no contacts with the mob, if that's what anyone is suggesting. None whatsoever. My books are open, my records are clear, and I try to do what I can for the city." His eyes seemed to well up with tears when he said, "I may not show up much on the floor of the club, but my presence is felt. My wife and children know who I am and what I am. I'm just sorry that people may have gotten a bad impression from the article." There was more about family, politics, and his love of animals.

The interview ran as an exclusive and was well received. I've often wondered why Palumbo sat for the interview. Nothing in the article implicated him in anything. He refused to be interviewed for the *Inquirer* piece but was wide open with me. Perhaps a wound was reopened, a remembrance of other eras, other insinuations. There is a truth in Philadelphia life. When an Italian-American businessman is successful, a stereotype erupts in people's minds that tells them he is surely associated with the forces of evil. That stereotype continues today, a constant reminder of our American inclination toward subtle and not-so-subtle prejudice based on ignorance.

The real story of Frank Palumbo has never been told. For a period of almost thirty years, Palumbo was a powerful force in elected politics. Years later, in his tiny office, counting the money from the day's receipts, Palumbo explained his role to me. He was like a fight promoter, he said, a man who enjoyed finding a talent and making sure he was the horse for the course. Among his finds, people he nurtured to election, were Frank Rizzo; Tom Foglietta, a congressman and ambassador to Italy; various members of City Council; a host of judges; and many employees in the court system. Some of the servers in Palumbo's at night were Philadelphia court employees by day. Palumbo also helped raise funds for candidates and, for a man not elected, wielded amazing patronage power. It was good business. There wasn't a major political force in Philadelphia who did not hold a fund-raiser at his place.

Palumbo's burned down in the nineties, a little more than ten years after Frank's death in 1983. Once again, the phantoms of misinformation tried to leak the news that the fire had been set. The fire marshall said not so. There was no insurance on Palumbo's. When it burned, the physical structure was reduced to ashes, but the memories live of pasta, vegetables, tables for ten, the music of the orchestra, and the figure of diminutive Frank Palumbo quietly, very quietly, checking the room out, making sure everybody was happy, and doing what he did best—Palumbo's.

Kippee Palumbo hasn't let the fire put out the flame. Active in the community, vibrant as a grandmother, the widow of Frank Palumbo is seen frequently at community events. Donna and I are amazed at her vigor and strength. But get her talking and you'll quickly discover how much she misses that big building on Catharine Street and the man who built it.

John Lennon's Lost Weekend in Philadelphia

What did John Lennon have to do with Frank Rizzo and Pennsylvania governor Milton Shapp? Nothing, of course, you say. But in May 1975, they had an odd connection.

When I arrived in Philadelphia, so did a small legend, my history of travels with the Beatles. As a radio news director in the summers of 1964 to 1966, I traveled with them to twenty-eight cities in North America and Canada, reporting to a network of fifty stations. We got to know each other well, and after the tumult of the tours came to an end, we stayed in touch.

John Lennon was in a bad place in the mid-seventies. The Beatles had broken up, and he was facing deportation because of a marijuana conviction. The campaign against Lennon was hostile and heavy-handed. He needed help, and Philadelphians gave him some cover.

John was living with his wife, Yoko Ono, at the Dakota Apartments on Central Park West in New York. He was, according to reports, despondent over a career that was going nowhere after the Beatles' breakup and the campaign by the Immigration and Naturalization Service to get him out of the United States.

Almost at the same time as Lennon was fighting in the courts, WFIL Radio was planning a "helping hand weekend," a marathon fund-raising event to benefit a number of needy community organizations. The management at WFIL, which was located in the same building as WPVI, suggested that Lennon might want to come to Philadelphia to host the fund-raiser. I got a note off to John with two main points: part of the marathon would benefit MS, which had killed my mother, and, considering his deportation battle, his involvement in a major charity event could prompt some letters of support from public officials like Rizzo and Shapp. Lennon sent word that he would be there, and we hastily made travel arrangements.

I met him at 30th Street Station. John, who was losing his hair, emerged from the Metroliner alone, looking for me. He ran to me and we embraced, and he said, "Larry, thanks a million for getting me out of the house." I replied, "Thanks for coming, and let's take a tour of the town!"

We drove to Independence Mall, where I gave John the quick tour, reminding him that the Liberty Bell was the symbol of our revolution against his native Britain. There and at other locations, there was a turn-about: Lennon got a kick out of watching people recognize me, and he said, "Laddie, you've done well."

The radio marathon got underway at 5:00 P.M., and in the radio studio I got my inspiration. Jim O'Brien, the weatherman, was off that Friday night. Whispering to John, I said, "How would you like to do the weather?" He grinned that devilish Lennon grin, the one that told the world he was up to something, and he said, "Groovy, baby. Let's do it, boss." Lennon was really into the radio show, and his on-air introduction sparked a switchboard jam the likes of which hasn't been seen in years. There he was, international superstar John Lennon, away from Yoko, doing some real good and having a ball. But the ball was yet to come.

As the six o'clock newscast approached, producers prepared Lennon for the weather forecast, coaching him on highs and lows and cold fronts and the jet stream. He didn't seem to care but just sat on a chair in the corner of the studio, watching the newscast, his face in that daffy, weird Lennon look. There, in the hot studio, I came to realize that the man who set the world on fire with his music and his madness was thrilled to be back in a spotlight again. When the time came, Lennon was introduced, and he started taking the magnetic weather strips, those with numbers and the names of cities, and tossing them indiscriminately at the weather board. "Well, there's a high here," he would say, flipping Denver onto the East Coast and rain clouds onto the Mojave Desert, "and a low there, and people everywhere are singing where is the blues . . . ha ha ha." Then he summed up the forecast by saying, "So the outlook is sunny, but the weather is funny, and you should find a yellow submarine." Lennon was a hit, but no one got the genuine weather forecast on Channel 6 that night.

Having finished his stint as weatherman, he retreated to his suite at the Marriott for some R and R. Then he returned to our radio station, where he hosted the rock and roll program till mid-evening, when he again returned to his suite. The sales department at WFIL Radio had promised to make John comfortable, but comfortable was apparently a code word for something else altogether. I don't know what happened in that suite, but every time he returned to the station, he would whisper to me, "Larry, what a ball. Every one of them was gorgeous. Great weekend."

Despite the intrigue in the hotel, Lennon spent many marathon hours on the air until Sunday night, when we wrapped it up. He worked hard and made the deejays feel good about broadcasting with him, offering tidbits about his personal life and memories of Beatles experiences. He also talked about me, fondly and with great humor, reminding everyone that his famous manager Brian Epstein had had the hots for me on tour. Brian died in 1967, so he wasn't around to answer the allegations, which were true. I asked John, "Were you jealous?" He answered, "Was there something to be jealous about?"

John returned to New York, and over the next five years we talked several times on the phone. He had fond memories of that weekend in Philadelphia and appreciated the letters on his behalf. Eventually he won his fight to stay in America, a place where he could walk the streets in freedom and have little or no fear. As he did in Philadelphia, John traveled without security, enjoying the sights and sounds of New York. That desire for freedom from fear led to his encounter with a deranged fan, Mark David Chapman, who ended John Lennon's life with bullets in December 1980.

On the night of his death, when I read the copy on the air, I was saddened and disgusted but felt fortunate to have known the man who defied convention and used his celebrity to lecture humans on their frailties of hatred and war. The memory of John Lennon always stays with me, especially when I hear the dominance of his voice on Beatles songs and when I recall that magic weekend when John Lennon lost himself in Philadelphia.

Flyers Win: Station Scores!

Philadelphia is a major-league sports town, with fans who demand nothing less than excellence. The old Philadelphia Athletics and the Philadelphia Phillies, especially the Whiz Kids of 1950, made this one of the great baseball towns of America. Chuck Bednarik and the 1960 Eagles would launch a golden era of professional football in this region. The Sixers, in 1967, led by Wilt Chamberlain, brought home championship wins.

And then there was hockey. When the Flyers won their first Stanley Cup in 1974, they set a new standard for sports franchises in the community. The team was comprised of some rugged young Canadians led by a toothless wonder named Bobby Clarke. Clarke, a diabetic, had so much energy and poise that he single-handedly put hockey on the city's map. The 1974 victory was a delirious diversion, a lustful orgy of Philadelphia pride. A million people came out to celebrate on Independence Mall, some of whom had never seen a hockey game but were thrilled with the sense of Philadelphia victory.

A year later, the Flyers made the Stanley Cup finals again, facing off against the Buffalo Sabres. Who would know that the Flyers' series would conflict with primary election day 1975, giving WPVI TV the chance for a victory that, in broadcasting terms, was an absolute shutout. That was also the first and only time I broadcast on two stations in the same night.

WPVI news director Ron Tindiglia joined me in plotting a broadcasting coup that, to my knowledge, has never been duplicated. The fifth game of the Cup finals, set in Buffalo, was on the same night as the primary election for mayor. There was no question that the majority of viewers would tune into the game on WTAF TV, Channel 29 (now WTXF TV). That meant that hockey viewers interested in Frank Rizzo's second primary for mayor would have a difficult time getting the information on Channel 29. Tindiglia's plan was simple—offer our services for special reports during breaks in the game. I called Flyers chairman

Ed Snider and some friends in management at WTAF TV. The idea was greeted with elation, and secretly our station began planning the logistics of the operation.

On election night, the Flyers took the lead against the Sabres. After the first period, the studio crew assembled, and the cue came from the control room at Channel 29. I said, "Good evening, I'm Larry Kane with an *Action News* update for Flyers fans on Frank Rizzo's try for a second term." Three times more on that election night, we broadcast returns during the game. It was a doubleheader. We got two for the price of one, and with the Flyers' ratings high, the majority of area viewers saw WPVI election returns on the air of WTAF.

The day after, management from the other stations protested loudly to the Flyers' organization, but the damage was done. In the spirit of American enterprise, Ron Tindiglia and the *Action News* team had scored a victory days before the Flyers won their second Stanley Cup in game six against Buffalo.

That victory brought a parade on Broad Street, from City Hall down to the sports complex. That meant a schedule of wall-to-wall coverage, with one curious interruption. Not far from Broad and Washington Streets, the motorcade that included players and coaches stopped. Philadelphia police were mysteriously shuttling Flyers goalie Bernie Parent from the flatbed truck to a row house. "What's happening?" I asked. No one had a clue. While we vamped to fill the time, it occurred to me that maybe, just maybe . . . uhm . . . but no . . . not here! My instincts were correct. One of Philadelphia's most popular sports heroes, human being that he is, had raised his hand and asked to go to the bathroom. The publicized pit stop was but a short diversion from a spectacular Philadelphia day.

The Flyers' success also served as a boost to the spirit of Philadelphians, perhaps sparking an era of recovery from the raging inferiority complex that had plagued the region. The Phillies won the World Series in 1980, the Eagles made the Super Bowl in 1981, and the Sixers won the NBA championship in 1983. What an era. In less than ten years, all the sports franchises had made or won championships. But there was a problem. The Flyers—their president, Ed Snider, and the players—had set the standard for all Philadelphia sports teams so high that, over the decades, it's been impossible to reach again. In Philadelphia, unlike other cities, there is no parade, no celebration, not even much appreciation for second place.

The Great Debate

Fourteen months after the inauguration of *Action News,* controversy faced me down, but I had company. Political debates are always tricky. Scheduling them is painful, and dealing with the intrigue and squabbling is always unpleasant. In 1986, I agreed to moderate the gubernatorial debate between Bob Casey and Bill Scranton. Casey drove Scranton mad. Shortly after the debate began, he started sniffling, and he continued to sniffle throughout the debate. Scranton's complexion turned beet red. Distracted by Casey's stuffed-nose act, he did not perform well. Did Casey have a cold? I don't know. Whatever it was, it worked.

I remembered that day in 1996, when Congressman Jon Fox and challenger Joe Hoeffel, the county commissioner, held a series of debates sponsored by the Montgomery County League of Women Voters. They were bitter affairs and sometimes stretched the limits of common sense. In a Harleysville debate, irritated over a Fox campaign flier suggesting that he was soft on sex offenders who preyed on children, Hoeffel peered over at Fox and said, "Jon, you know very well about my record. You distorted it. I would never hurt children. I have two children, Jon, something you will never get to know about." It was a nasty jab, considering that Fox and his wife, Judy, had no children. Did Hoeffel know something about their capacity to have children? A hush fell over the crowd, even among Hoeffel's supporters. Hoeffel lost, but the mostly affable and intelligent county commissioner eventually defeated Fox and became the congressman from Montgomery County. Knowing Hoeffel well, I'm sure he regretted the Harleysville debate.

My most vivid debate memory, however, comes from 1971. The challenge was almost insurmountable—to put together a debate between two political legends, moderated by three competitive anchors, without politics coloring our effort.

Tension surrounded the early morning breakfast in a private room at the Marriott Hotel on City Avenue. It was the first time that the venerable John Facenda, legendary anchor at WCAU TV; Vince Leonard, the main man at KYW TV; and I had ever met together alone. Our assignment was difficult: to put together a televised debate that would satisfy mayoral candidates Frank Rizzo and Thacher Longstreth.

Facenda drank his coffee and chain smoked. Under fire at the time because of sinking ratings, he had little to say to me. Leonard joined me for some eggs. We exchanged pleasantries and then got down to business, the business being the orchestration of two debates that would serve the electorate well and keep our immaculate reputations intact for the ages—no easy task in the hot political climate of 1971.

The 1971 mayoral campaign was a nasty, contentious affair, sparked by a primary election bitterly fought in the streets and on the air. In those days, political campaigns were covered with expertise and excitement, unlike the lip service that some stations give to politics now. The job of the anchor trio was to have an exciting format with vigorous questions. We decided on a format in which each of us would anchor one third of the broadcast and which would allow the candidates to ask each other questions. Leonard seemed content, but Facenda had one concern. As an Italian American, Facenda insisted, it was important that he ask questions about Rizzo's reported meeting with Angelo Bruno, the underworld chief, in which Rizzo was said to have warned him sternly about committing illegal activities. Facenda said he did not want it to appear that he was ducking the issue. We disagreed but bowed to his request.

The first debate, to our relief, went smoothly. The second was held in the WCAU studios. It was my first time there, and I felt like an alien walking into a new environment. Before the debate, Thacher Longstreth's main adviser, Cliff Brenner, insisted that his man get the final question during the segment where candidates queried each other. Al Gaudiosi, the Pulitzer Prize-winning reporter who managed the Rizzo campaign, had no objection. I wondered why. When time for the final question came around, Longstreth looked at Rizzo and said, "Frank, this has been such a good debate. I challenge you now to another one to give the people a chance to hear us one more time. How about it, Frank?" Rizzo, smiling, looked at him, and countered, "Thacher, why should I give you another debate? Thacher, it would be stupid. Why should I do it, Thatch, when no one really knows who you are anyway!"

Longstreth got the last question. Rizzo got the last word, which he usually did. Gaudiosi knew very well that when it came to the final punch line, the punctuation of an argument, nobody did it better than Frank Rizzo.

Broadcast Moments

There are moments in television that the viewer never sees—which is too bad, really, because they are sometimes the most exciting ones.

The blue police cars that arrived at 4100 City Avenue, the location of WPVI TV, in July 1972 looked like an army assembled for major combat. There were about ten regular cars, five wagons used to transport prisoners, and unmarked police cars containing several members of the stakeout squad, which includes sharpshooters. It was an impressive array, and I was the reason for it.

When you broadcast the news for many years, it is rare to get a rush of nervousness and adrenalin, unless you make a horrible mistake. Fear of going on the air is rare for me, but on that Tuesday I had to go off the air and back on again, and before returning I experienced an adrenalin surge that felt more like an electrical shock.

We were about halfway through the eleven o'clock news and I was reading a story about youth violence when someone walked behind me. Suddenly I heard the words, "Mr. Kane, we demand justice." I thought to myself, "He's going to kill me." Images of Arthur Bremer shooting George Wallace a month earlier raced through my mind. The man then grabbed my coat, we struggled briefly, and the director in the control room faded to black and to a commercial. Then the real fun began.

Jim O'Brien, our weatherman, went into hand-to-hand combat with the protest leader. Sportscaster Joe Pellegrino ran after the three other invaders and pinned one of them against the wall. When the news returned to the airwaves, O'Brien was near the point of severely beating my visitor. Along with the highs and lows, blood appeared on the weather wall, near the state of Illinois. The viewing audience never saw the violence, but it was a heavyweight struggle.

After what seemed like hours, the program ended and police officers came in to arrest the protesters, who called themselves the Gay Raiders. Their purpose was to draw attention to gay rights, and they certainly did. I refused to press charges, knowing that incarceration would glorify their error in judgment.

The *Daily News,* the *Inquirer,* and the *Bulletin* ran the story on page one. It isn't often that people break into a newscast in progress, but that wasn't the last time. This gay commando squad interrupted Walter Cronkite's newscast and later managed to infiltrate the *Tonight Show* with Johnny Carson. Its leader was a crafty young man named Mark Segal, a rebel with a cause. Mark scared the hell out of me before going on to greater heights with his network "appearances."

Today, Mark Segal is a mainstream capitalist, publisher of the enormously successful *Philadelphia Gay News.* His colleagues in the gay community have made their mark in business, journalism, and politics.

There is still homophobia in Philadelphia, but minds have been liberated, and hopefully there will be no need for further incursions like the one in 1972. Ironically, the Philadelphia region has shown itself more tolerant of sexual divides than of racial divisions, and the city itself is one of the most comfortable environments for gays in America. You can give Mark Segal a little credit. After all, he became a delegate to the Democratic National Convention and is now so mainstream that he dines at the Palm, the "be seen" restaurant of Philadelphia's power elite. Mark and I had lunch there a few years ago. I couldn't believe I was breaking bread with the man who had sent my insides exploding so many years ago.

At a party honoring Mark's work with the newspaper, I made a videotape salute in which I said, "Mark, you took Cronkite, you got Carson, but Mark, I will be always be remembered as your first. And you always remember your first, don't you, Mark?" The audience roared with laughter.

A year after the Segal affair, we experienced more shock in the studio at WPVI TV, and this time it came about at the most unlikely moment, at a turning point in the political career of Arlen Specter. In 1973, Specter was up for re-election. That brilliant political strategist Elliot Curson had a creative slogan: "Arlen Specter—He's Younger, Tougher, and Nobody Owns Him." In truth, he was younger and tougher than the other candidates, but somebody did own him: the man who staged one of the greatest upsets in Philadelphia political history.

F. Emmett Fitzpatrick was a firebrand defense attorney with a sharp wit and an even sharper temper. As the Democratic candidate, he was given little chance by the pollsters of defeating Specter, the popular Republican incumbent. When he squeezed by Specter in an election marked by light turnout, the most surprised person was probably F. Emmett Fitzpatrick.

During the eleven o'clock news on election night, my special guest was common pleas court judge-elect Lisa Richette, a Fitzpatrick ally and sworn enemy of Mayor Frank Rizzo. Richette was also an upset victor, having beaten the Rizzo machine, and she was all smiles as she sat down next to me on the news set. The first thing I noticed were her eyes, dark and deep-set and staring at the innermost crease of my trousers, where the inner thighs connect to the area below the zipper. "Can it be," I thought, "is it possible that the judge is signaling some special interest? Or perhaps she's just looking at the pattern of my bell-bottom trousers." As the interview continued, I began to be self-conscious over the focus of her attention. What was she looking at, and why? During the commercial break, the new judge started laughing so hard she almost fell off the seat, and I said, "So what's up?" She replied, "Uh . . . oh . . . Lar . . . your fly is wide open." I zipped up my fly and turned a deep shade of red, as in embarrassed-beyond-belief red.

Though it's hard to believe, the night got worse. Emmett Fitzpatrick had staked his reputation on his aggressive approach toward crime and punishment—and reporters. When he arrived at the studios for a late-night interview, he looked at me with the stare of an angry man and said, "Your buddy Specter got the shit kicked out of him. No more exclusives for you. From here on out, there's a new team in the DA's office. Got it, Larry Kane?" Why people prefer to call me by my first and last name is always a mystery to me. I guess they view me as "a" Larry Kane, as opposed to Larry Kane. Would you go up to Bill Clinton and say, "Hello, Bill Clinton. How's Bill Clinton today? Pleasure meeting you, Bill Clinton"?

Fitzpatrick continued to verbally challenge "Larry Kane." He said, "Larry Kane, things are changing as of tonight." I said, "Congratulations." I wanted to scream some four-letter words. I wanted to say, "Emmett Fitzpatrick, go make love to yourself and the horse you rode in on, and you are a male genital." Instead, I meekly said, "Congratulations, Emmett." Emmett Fitzpatrick was really a pretty decent guy, but with me, anyway, he acted like a loser instead of an upset winner. Years later, I began to appreciate the man for his lawyerly talents and an unknown fact: he quietly raised money for many causes in Philadelphia. The real Emmett Fitzpatrick was never seen by the voters, and so, four years later, he was defeated in a race for a second term by a young attorney named Edward G. Rendell.

Weather Star Meets President

Texan Jim O'Brien was a big success at WPVI. People loved his fast-talking style and his real-talk references to the weather. O'Brien was a hard-working and driven broadcaster who sought excellence in everything he did. The mouth that roared was a surprise star in Philadelphia. By original profession, he was a deejay, but he could have been anything he wanted to be: he was driven to win and sometimes driven to excess. When he perished in a skydiving accident in 1983, I was overcome with emotion at the reality that a man who had lived so hard could die so fast.

By 1976, after about four years at the station, O'Brien was clearly a winner for WPVI TV. With his success, came the price of celebrity—irritability, supreme ego, and an unbridled temper. That temper was clearly in evidence a few days before the presidential election of 1976, which pitted Jimmy Carter against Gerald Ford.

President Ford was visiting Philadelphia for a campaign stop and the taping of a campaign commercial. In the pursuit of news, if you don't try for a story, you generally don't get it. So with a lot of skepticism, I called Drew Lewis, a powerful Pennsylvania Republican, and asked him to clear an interview with Gerald Ford. Lewis said he would try. He tried and tried hard, because in mid-afternoon I received a call from the Ford campaign telling me to expect the president to show up during our six o'clock news. Wow, I thought, this is bigger than big—the president of the United States, live in our studios, during a newscast.

I advised our producers, who told Jim O'Brien to be flexible by giving up some of his weather minutes. Jim rushed up to my desk and said, "Listen, Mr. Big Nose for News, ain't no way I'm gonna give up my time for any damn president, any political sonafabitch. You got it, buddy?" His face was turning red, his demeanor was angry, and he walked out of the newsroom yelling to me, "Besides, he ain't coming. No way." Then he added, "I'm goin' home, buddy." Because O'Brien was such an integral player in our success, I was concerned about his feelings—but not too concerned. After all, an exclusive with the president was worth a P and M session from O'Brien, the P standing for pissing and the M for moaning.

Six o'clock came, and O'Brien was nowhere to be found. The studio was occupied by Secret Service agents and Philadelphia police. The president was scheduled for about 6:23, and O'Brien would be on before him with the weather, if he returned to the studio. During a commercial break, the door of the studio flew open, and the president of the United States walked in with his entourage. A few seconds later Jim O'Brien strolled in, ran up to the president, shook his hand, and said, "Sir, this is a special honor to have you here with us. I'm honored to be here in your presence. Welcome to Philadelphia, sir." He went on and on, offering accolades and pouring his gratitude out to Mr. Ford. He did everything but kiss the president on the lips. As I prepared for the interview, O'Brien was told to cut down his weather forecast by sixty seconds. He obliged with great fervor, saying, "Of course, anything for the president." I always knew that Jim O'Brien was a Republican.

My interview with Ford lasted five minutes, and to my knowledge it was the first-ever live interview with an incumbent president on a local news broadcast. Of course, it didn't do him much good. Four days later, with his pardon of Richard Nixon hanging around his neck as an albatross, Gerald Ford was defeated by Jimmy Carter.

No one ever defeated Jim O'Brien, except, on occasion, Jim O'Brien. O'Brien was fierce and unbending in his passion for excellence, and that ironclad will of his would forge great moments and unusual actions. In Jim O'Brien's world, there was the man you saw on television, joking and making even the most miserable weather seem attractive. But when the studio lights went off, O'Brien could be a terror.

Let me start from the beginning—the discovery. In the fall of 1970, the station's news director, Mel Kampmann, and I were invited to a seminar for area high-school students in a studio at Channel 6. One of the guest speakers was a deejay from WFIL Radio. The man's message was one of self-help, a conviction that you, more than anyone, were responsible for your trip through life. The speaker was handsome, his jet black hair accentuated by Elvis-style sideburns. He spoke like an evangelist, his words flowing quickly, as he used his Texas dialect to make a point. He said, "Don't you tell me that you can't, tell me that you *can*. Don't give me one darn reason that you can't achieve. And let me tell ya, buddy, cream, also known as hard work, rises to the top. And waste, also known as laziness, floats to the bottom. You get it, man?"

The kids were mesmerized by this fast-talking, charismatic Texan. And so were we. Mel leaned over to me and said, "Who is this guy? We should talk to him." But in a typical case of analysis paralysis, management hesitated on trying out Jim O'Brien. So O'Brien took some part-time weather work at WCAU TV. It's a little-known fact that O'Brien had a short stint there and that, amazingly, the people at WCAU didn't understand his promise. So we eventually installed O'Brien as the permanent *Action News* weatherman, and there, with his quips, ad libs, and sense of clarity, the man from Waco grew to become one of the biggest stars in Philadelphia television history.

O'Brien wrote the book on hard work, beginning with his 6:00 A.M. radio show and working through the 11:00 P.M. news. The hours eventually took their toll. After one particularly shaky newscast, O'Brien roared into the newsroom and confronted Producer Rick Friedman. He complained that his time for the weather forecast had been cut down, and he yelled, "Listen, you sonofabitch, don't ever fuck with me again. Got it, asshole?" His face turning red, he grabbed Friedman under his arms and slammed him into the world map. Then he left the building, and so did the producer, shaken and in fear.

The next day, O'Brien apologized to Friedman with a softness and sensitivity that could turn his mania into magic. But I was not happy and gave him a fill of expletives. I ended by saying, "Jim, who gave you the license to be a bully?" O'Brien never answered. For his part, Friedman, who loved Jim's work ethic and talent, was unfazed. There would be many other moments, outbursts of rage and anger. But in the most important moment of his workday, when the red light on the camera glistened in the studio, Jim O'Brien, as a weatherman and later as anchor, was a man enriched with talent and armed with charisma.

O'Brien and I had a wonderful relationship, marred only by a few bouts of anger. I would never be as close to him as his buddy, then-sportscaster Steve Levy, but our on-air chemistry was spectacular. The broadcast relationship was cherished, and when things erupted in the psyche of the man, I was happy to periodically intervene to protect him from his greatest enemy—himself.

Banana Republic

Late in 1986, bananas kept arriving in small boxes, even envelopes, in the daily mail at WCAU TV. By the time they reached the newsroom, the bananas were crushed or overripe, and the smell was horrible. The strange banana packages were addressed to me, with accompanying letters inside. The letters were laced with caustic invectives and a high degree of sarcasm; one in particular described me as the back end of a donkey. The stage had been set for this banana protest the week before, on a special broadcast of David Copperfield's magic show on CBS.

It was a Friday night, and Copperfield's program was on from eight o'clock to nine. Copperfield is a super hit with children. His format often includes magic tricks that last the entire hour, and on the night that will live in infamy, the trick was to find a banana. Where was it? How would he get it back?

Concurrently, a municipal union strike was in the final stage of negotiations. We received word at 8:49 that there was a settlement, at which point the magic show's producer, Paul Gluck, made a fateful decision. Gluck, a long and faithful friend and a native of Philadelphia, rushed me to the studio to break into prime-time programming. We were first with the facts, but last in the hearts of children, who missed the punch line to the magic act. The phones started ringing and did so continuously through the eleven o'clock news.

Today, Paul Gluck, an Emmy-award-winning, two-time Philadelphia news director, is an executive at WHYY TV and remains a close friend. Gluck is one of the premier broadcast journalists of this era, recognized nationally as an innovator and a creative force, a man in high demand. He's also a man with a great sense of humor. We talk often about the night that the banana never returned, laughing hard, our uncontrolled jocularity masking the truth: on that fateful night, we slipped on the banana trick.

Dying Can Be a Fun Experience

Newsroom humor often descends into the galaxy of the macabre, the gallows-like comedy that most normal people find useless and tasteless. What causes this weird behavior? There is really no excuse for it, but there is an explanation. News people deal with so much death and destruction—their minds fed a diet of devastation—that a torrent of terrible news can take its toll. The mind provides a perfect defense mechanism: jaded humor that is the purest form of escapism. Usually, we just practice it on each other, but sometimes it makes its way onto the air. That's when it gets dangerous.

Another peculiarity of television news is that some personalities are prone to cracking up on the air, losing decorum, providing laughter where it doesn't belong. In that regard, there was and is no better crackup artist than Alan Frio. Alan, a South Philadelphia native, worked with me as co-anchor of the eleven o'clock news at WCAU TV from 1984 to 1989, a marvelous five-year period of journalistic excellence, decent ratings, and lots of laughter. Frio remains one of the most durable anchors in the nation. Alan and I became good friends, thereby setting the stage for a relaxed broadcast environment, so mellow that sometimes the guard was not just down—it dropped out of sight.

The night that Desi Arnaz, the former husband and mentor of Lucille Ball, died was a red-letter day in Alan's sub-career of laughing. The news of Desi's death was expected; he had been ill for some time. The story was placed near the end of the first news segment of our eleven o'clock newscast. There was no time to preview the video. I read the story, and my last words were, "Desi Arnaz, dead at the age of sixty-seven." At that moment, the video displayed a logo of the Lucy show, and the sound came up with the program's theme, ending with the ruffle and flourish of a band, almost like a celebration of Desi's departure. At that moment, producer Paul Gluck, of banana fame, whispered into Alan's earphone, "Luceee, I'm dead!" As I was reading the end of the story, Alan started laughing like a hyena, his eyes welling with tears of laughter, his head falling to the desk, where he wrapped his hands around his ears. Alan Frio was incapacitated by mirth. When the commercial break began, I laughed so hard my stomach hurt, but Alan was beyond laughter: he had jumped off the set and run to the rear of the studio, where he remained in hiding until the end of the program. The broadcast continued with me solo, my mind constantly wandering back to the image of Frio hiding behind the wall, clasping his hands around his mouth to muzzle the sound of his laughter.

To this day, we laugh about the night Alan had to excuse himself from the newscast. After the episode, I said to Alan, "When Lucy dies, I don't want to be anywhere near you. God help us when Lucy dies."

We received word of Lucille Ball's death on Alan Frio's final day at WCAU TV. Frio was leaving in 1989 to host a syndicated program for Paramount. Fortunately, Alan was paired with someone else that day. Being a man of good intentions, I avoided seeing him all afternoon. No eye contact. No Lucy talk. Alan's final show went flawlessly, but watching carefully as he read the story of Lucy's death, I could see a slight grin emerge on his mouth. As the words came out, the grin got wider— his face turning red, his eyes bulging out. He never cracked up, but he was dangerously close.

The Top Angry Phone Calls

Memory is fascinating. You can easily recall the good, but remembering the bad and the ugly can be challenging, daunting, even impossible. Still, certain moments never fade away, remaining as mental mementos of episodes that left you low and livid and sometimes disappointed with yourself. I'll share the log of the angriest and most troubling complaint calls I've received over three and a half decades, calls that rattled my senses, shattered my ego, and often made me see things in a different light.

Charles Bowser was an independent candidate for mayor in 1975, finishing second to Frank Rizzo and humiliating the Republican party in the process. Bowser is a successful lawyer and a behind-the-scenes power whose public tranquility belies a fiercely intense man with a burning desire for righteousness. When Bill Green decided not to seek a second term in the fall of 1982, reports were circulating that Bowser was interested. Two quality sources told me that Bowser was considering a run. I tried to reach Bowser, but he was away. The story was reported as a part of my political notebook. The phone rang a few hours later.

The voice on the other end was high pitched, a nervous voice twitching with agitated excitement. Bowser said, "Larry, this is Charlie Bowser on vacation in New England. Who the hell do you think you are? What kind of crap is that?" His voice got even higher as he said, "You know that's not right, but you're starting trouble, aren't you?" I interrupted, "But Charlie, the sources for this are people close to you." Then, compounding the problem, I added, "Besides, you know you're going to run." It was a comment I should have avoided. There was a pause on the line. Suddenly, Bowser said, "I've had it with you!" and hung up. The conversation jarred me. Bowser did not run for mayor in 1983, but he was one of the most powerful influences in the administration of W. Wilson Goode, eventually serving on the mayor's commission investigating the Move confrontation, an event that I'll relive for you later.

Frank Rizzo's wrath was scathing when he felt he was wronged. During the 1987 mayor's race, Rizzo was indignant about a poll that WCAU TV commissioned showing him far behind incumbent Wilson Goode. The phone rang at 11:30 P.M., as soon as I was off the air, and Rizzo gave me a dressing down. The call lasted ten minutes. Rizzo described me in such lurid detail that even I was beginning to wonder if that was me he was talking about. After the tirade, I said, "Mayor, can I say something?" He said, "No," and hung up, but not before uttering two more words. The second word was "you." The next morning, Frank Rizzo called and, in that engaging way of his, softened the blow by explaining his anger. The truth is that Rizzo, in his individual dealings with people, was a soft touch.

John Facenda, the "voice," provided a most disturbing conversation. After rejecting the St. Louis CBS job that John had so neatly arranged, I called to let him know the job was not for me. I was staying. John said, "All right, then, that's that." A few minutes later, Facenda called me back. His voice had a tinge of anger. John said, "Why would anybody turn a job like that down, knowing full well that chances of success here are slim to none? Why, tell me?" My reply was simple: "I like Philadelphia. This is where I want to be." There was silence, small talk, and the conversation ended. The lump in my throat seemed bigger than the pit in my stomach. After all, this was John Facenda I was speaking to, a legend, an icon, a revered Philadelphian.

A viewer's call in the mid-eighties will stand out always as a testament to the perils of being wrong and sloppy. The late John Anderson was a popular Philadelphia city councilman. On a long-ago night, a murder suspect named John Anderson was in the news. That evening, as I read the John Anderson murder suspect story, the graphics box behind me showed a picture of Councilman John Anderson. From a technical point of view, since I couldn't see behind me, I had no way to know. At program's end, there was hilarious newsroom laughter but no laughing from this end. My call to John Anderson's answering service was clear and apologetic. The call I received from a viewer minutes later was nasty, unpleasant, and justified. The woman said, "You are a puny excuse for a newsman, disgraceful, full of yourself. You belong in the gutter, the sewers, for stinking up John Anderson's image. I'll never watch you again." I don't know who she was, but who could blame her?

These calls were bad, but my very worst night of phone calls will always be remembered at KYW TV as Lipinski night. During the Winter Olympics of 1998, drama and suspense was building as young Tara Lipinksi competed for the figure-skating gold medal. Because of the time difference, many viewers preferred to stay in the dark about the outcome, hoping to enjoy the drama of the prime-time broadcast.

During the taping of our nightly "teases," the promotional announcements designed to lure viewers in, I read the words, "A night of gold for Tara, the report at eleven." I assumed the "tease" would be broadcast after her victory. Assumptions in broadcast news can send you to the garbage heap of mistakes and misery. When the "tease" was broadcast *before* the event, the phones started ringing. People were mad, disgusted, threatening to never watch us again, and in the worst-case scenario, placing the blame on the anchorman, who of course happened to be me. The initial onslaught of calls began on Friday night, but calls continued through the weekend. The calls to my voice mail were so passionately profane that they could make a grown man cry. I almost did.

Every time the Winter Olympics rolls around, I will remember Lipinksi night for its sheer telephone terror. Let this be a lesson to all future broadcasters: when you screw up, you can run, but you can't hide from the wrath of the viewers.

Isn't television fun?

New York, New York: Goodbye, Hello Again

As a broadcast journalist, living in one city and working in another is like being married to two people—absolute culture shock. It is that premise—that you must live where you work—that was the undoing of my brief fling in New York City.

When I left New York in 1978 to return to Philadelphia and begin work at WCAU TV, the ratings at WABC, where I had been the solo anchor of the eleven o'clock news, were the highest in New York history. But my welcome was not as hot as the ratings. The New York press vilified me for working in New York and daring to live in the suburbs of Philadelphia. My desire to remain in the area was based on the fact that I like it here, pure and simple. So I hired Joe Primavera, a former Philadelphia police officer, to drive me to New York every day. For a while, it worked, but the truth is that you have to live in a community to report on it. My life had become flashes of New Jersey turnpike exits, late-night drives, and continued doubts about leaving the Philadelphia market.

There were also the sharp knives, slithering at my backside, at WABC TV in New York. Roger Grimsby, the veteran anchor, was disturbed by my presence and played mind games very well. One day, during a ferocious snowstorm, I called live, on the air, to report on conditions on the Jersey turnpike. After the report, Grimsby said, "Thanks, Larry, and by the way, how's the limo?" Months later, he called me "limo Larry" in print. Grimsby was a cruel man. He was also troubled. On several nights, as we made our trip home, we noticed him sprawled between garbage cans outside of his hangout, Chips Bar on Columbus Avenue. We dragged him into the car and dropped him off at his home. His drinking, often a source of newsroom humor, was ugly and demeaning. He never acknowledged our little rescue efforts. He did, however, find the time to alert a magazine to exactly where my car was parked so they could photograph the Pennsylvania license plate. On the other hand, Roger's co-anchor, Bill Beutel, was a perfect gentleman. I still wonder how he was able to work alongside Grimsby for so many years.

Why did I leave Philadelphia TV in the first place? A combination of peer pressure and ambition had fueled my desire to move on—that and, of course, the opportunity to anchor at the network level. The decision was a professional victory but a personal mistake. In life, hindsight is always masterful, while projecting the immediate future is almost impossible. I've learned the hard way that your own truth is more important than someone else's truth—that it's best to trust your own instincts. My desire for upward mobility was overwhelmed by my wish to live here.

Why did I return? I knew very well that coming home again would be no easy task, but, win or lose, I wanted to stay here. That was that. Despite the provincialism of the New York press and the constant attacks on my commuting habits, the job was going well, so much so that Ken MacQueen, the manager of WABC, had offered to buy us a townhouse in New York so I could commute and still have a place to stay. Ken said, "I don't care if you live in Virginia. The viewers couldn't give a damn, either. Just stay here." The company even enlisted ABC sports icon Howard Cosell and news anchor Harry Reasoner, who had been so helpful to me when I first came to New York, to lobby me to stay. Both were persuasive, but the Philadelphia factor was overwhelming.

When I declined, the next decision was where to go in Philadelphia. WPVI expressed no interest in having me back. WCAU and KYW both worked fiercely to hire me. I made sure that both offered the same money so my decision would be made on the basis of where the right place was, not on who had offered the most. The manager of KYW, Alan Bell, was impressive. Bell was one of America's most progressive managers. But in the end, WCAU was the place. It offered more stability in the event of setbacks.

Of course, if I had simply stayed and nurtured my success at WPVI, all of this would have been unnecessary. Today, I would be the dean of anchors, graying as I am, at *Action News,* instead of at KYW *Eyewitness News.* Jim Gardner would be in another major market plying his craft. Instead, I am residing at KYW TV and enjoying it thoroughly. Life's strategic errors can be played two ways: you can wallow in your tears or take the opportunity to make things better. Having done both, I assure you that the latter is a better choice. I have no regrets about going to New York, returning to Philadelphia, or eventually joining KYW. One thing has remained constant: I never stopped living in the Philadelphia area. Our children grew up and thrived in the same neighborhood. That stability, and mostly Donna's parenting, made the difference.

So I left New York behind, and along with it probably a network anchor career. Philadelphia is where I wanted to be. Since 1978, I have never looked back.

Part Three

Crisis and Change

F riends will often say, "What a great life you have in Philadelphia." It's certainly true that the highs have been through the stratosphere. It's also true that the lows have been beneath the depth chart. In that regard, two events stand out: an embarrassing legal battle with a mayor and an intolerable struggle with the boss of a TV station. Fortunately, the business of news offers respite in difficult times, and the next phase of my career and the life of the Philadelphia region provided enough big news for an entire generation. The twelve-year period changed Philadelphia forever and my direction altogether.

The events were impactive. A city neighborhood was bombed, history was made at the ballot box, elected officials rose in power, and some officials went to jail. Along the way, John Heinz and Frank Rizzo died, the latter's death causing me to look back at one amazing man and his life vigorously lived. New Jersey proved that a single vote is very important. The pope's local connections, along with the Chernobyl nuclear calamity, took me overseas. The hostage crisis in the Middle East and Iran brought me face to face with local victims. An earthquake in Italy showed me the face of tragedy but also, once again, Philadelphia's generosity.

For me, personal safety became an issue, especially when a grenade exploded a few feet away in Israel. Moderating televised debates became a second job. And more than ever, my judgment and that of my profession were challenged, especially on the day that doom was lurking ninety-seven miles west.

Too Hot to Handle: Meltdown in Middletown

The middle of the afternoon is a strange time in a newsroom. People are hurrying to and fro, foreheads creased by the frustrations of the day. Worry is the face of a newsroom, especially worry about the hole of news that has to be filled. Worry is the middle name of most news producers, who are by nature a special breed, trained to prepare for alarm but to hide their anxieties lest the rest of the newsroomers drown in the quicksand of panic attacks.

The record will show that the afternoon of March 28, 1979, was, all things considered, a quiet news day. I was drinking coffee at my desk when I heard the sounds I've only heard once before, on another quiet afternoon, that of November 22, 1963. Before computers, the clickety-clack wire machines would ring bells when bulletins were coming down. When President Kennedy was shot, the Associated Press and United Press machines rang out ten bells. A ten-beller was very big. The fear that entered my body the day of the JFK murder is something that never goes away, and that's why, when ten bells rang on March 28, 1979, I started to scream in the newsroom of WCAU TV, "It's a big one! I know it! I've only heard a ten-beller once before, and that's when JFK died." Our news director, Eric Ober, another ten-bell veteran, ran out of his office, breathing heavily, racing to the wire machines. We both looked in horror at the words, "Federal officials report there has been an accident at Three Mile Island nuclear power plant in Middletown, near Harrisburg." The first report mentioned the possibility of radiation leakage and suggested that such an accident could spell disaster for millions of people from Pennsylvania to New England.

My first thought was to get the story on the air, but then, how do you tell people about something they've never heard of before, a nuclear accident in their own backyard? Would people panic and start driving eastward in a mass exodus, or would they remain calm? Thoughts raced through my head, including pictures of Donna and the kids. Did I belong at home at such a moment, and would they be safe if there was indeed a nuclear catastrophe?

The newsroom camera was readied. Ober and I huddled with Andrew Fisher, the assistant news director. Both started giving orders like generals. Camera crews were on the move west toward the scene. Live cameras were headed to the train stations to gauge the reaction of commuters. Within ninety seconds of the original ten bells, WCAU TV broke into the soap opera *Guiding Light,* and there I was, bringing the news of the accident. Calm is very important in a situation like that, so I talked in a relaxed tone, devoid of the anxiety that was hounding me, hoping that my words would motivate reason, not provoke panic.

Within seconds of our cut-in (the professional term for breaking into a program), the phone lines were flooded with two types of calls—people seeking more information, and viewers fuming that we had interrupted their soap opera. It has always boggled my mind when viewers call during the middle of coverage of assassinations, funerals, or public emergencies to complain about missing their programs. Perhaps, on the afternoon of Three Mile Island, the viewers didn't realize that in a worst-case scenario they would soon have no programs—and perhaps no lives.

Despite the calls, our coverage continued through the afternoon. As news filtered in, we began to realize that the apparatus of government had failed miserably, that the flow of information was coming in so fast and in so unruly a manner that there was a real possibility of civil unrest. The Feds were a mess: no one was a point person for information. We were getting reports ranging from small radiation leaks to a massive breakdown in the core reactor. No one could confirm anything. No one could answer our questions.

There is nothing worse than working in a vacuum of information. This is not just a whine of journalists. When people don't get information, they make bad decisions and get hurt. The lack of information in the early hours of the Three Mile Island (TMI) emergency was a violation of the basic standards of good government, and it wasn't until Dick Thornburgh rode to the rescue that people finally calmed down. When he realized that the federal regulators were fumbling the situation, the Pennsylvania governor took charge and established his own command post, providing regular updates to the media and his constituents. Within hours, the facts were clear: TMI had undergone a serious accident, but it would not place at risk the millions of people in the mid-

Atlantic region. Thornburgh's take-charge attitude not only defused the situation but added luster to a young but vigorous political career.

The news that severe danger was not imminent brought relief not just to the community but to the newsroom. Producers, reporters, and writers who use dark comedy to deal with tragedy were not joking when they talked and wrote about TMI. A strange thing happens to journalists when they have the potential to be in the crosshairs of danger. The joking stops. Reality steps in. Suddenly, you're not just writing the story; you could become the story.

Seeing Green, as in Bill

There is one period in my Philadelphia life that will stand out for its impact on me and its effect on Philadelphia history. Let me point out that this episode provides evidence that, once they are committed to you, Philadelphians are respectful, sympathetic, and loyal.

On the rainy Saturday morning of March 27, 1982, I sat on the couch in our den, staring into space, tears flowing down my face, my body paralyzed by stress and fear. Donna was sleeping after a long night of anguished conversation. I placed a call to my best friend, Ron Tindiglia, and when he answered, I said, "Ron, the 747 is in a sharp descent, the landing gear is stuck, and there is no foam on the runway." He asked, "What happened?" Barely audible, I tried to explain the events of my worst professional crisis.

Bill Green had always been a mystery to me. As a young Philadelphia congressman, he seemed to have a great political future. Over the years, we had gotten to know each other at news events, especially at the stormy Democratic National Convention in 1968 in Chicago. Green was affable but somewhat distant, a man on a roll, but a man who seemed unsure of himself. Nevertheless, he was easy to cover and always cooperative.

In 1971, he ran against Frank Rizzo in the Democratic primary for mayor. Rizzo handily defeated both him and Hardy Williams, a popular state senator and the first African American to run for mayor. But Green's dream to be mayor was answered in 1979 when he was elected and began a low-profile mayoralty with limited objectives and marked by strained relations with a scandal-tainted City Council. By 1982, he was an apparent shoo-in for re-election, clearly on his way to a second term. But then an event happened that may very well have changed the course of his career and of Philadelphia city government.

Early in March 1982, WCAU TV began an exhaustive investigation of reports that Green had taken a kickback to award a contract for sludge removal, a report fostered by freelance journalist Frank Geary, a former *Bulletin* staffer. It was hard for me to believe that Bill Green would commit a crime. After all, he wasn't a risk taker. But by March 23, the station purported to have all the facts and was ready to run.

Sensing the severity of the story, I demanded to know the primary sources for this report, but my request was turned down by the station's general manager, Jay Feldman. The news director, Tom Dolan, invited me to listen by speaker phone to confirmations of the story with seven secondary sources, including some Philadelphia political heavyweights. They all confirmed, without detail, that Green was the target of a federal investigation. The U.S. attorney, Peter Vaira, refused to talk to us, lending credibility to the reports. So the stage was set for a catastrophe.

On March 25, beginning at five o'clock, WCAU TV, with me at the helm, began reporting the Green story. In a sharp retort, on live TV, the mayor blasted the station from City Hall in such extremely emotional terms that it surprised even his top aides. The war of words was on, and I was uncomfortable.

By midday on March 26, with the newspapers now involved in an unabashed orgy of criticism toward the station for airing the report, Vaira finally issued his denials, and we discovered there was no basis in fact to the story. We had blundered. On Friday night, I went upstairs to the general manager's office. I said, "Jay, I'd like to write an apology." He answered, with a look of disdain and disgust, "Write whatever you want." In the coming days, Feldman would then retreat into short-term obscurity, letting me take most of the hits for a botched-up job.

When I delivered my apology at eleven o'clock on Friday night, I discovered that some of my friends were really not. The apology was heartfelt and emotional. Yet from my peers, there was hardly a show of support. Sportscaster Al Meltzer put his arm around me and said, "Don't worry." Meltzer was kind, but few followed suit. Herb Clarke, the weatherman, didn't say a word. My co-anchor Deborah Knapp sat in silence.

Newsrooms can be unkind places. Over the years at WCAU TV, I had tried to exert leadership and to assist people in their hours of need.

After the Green broadcast and the apology, there was "dead air," as we call it in the business, from people I thought were friends or acquaintances—Terry Ruggles, anchor Knapp, and others. Of the reporting staff, only Bill Baldini (named in the eventual lawsuit just because he was present at Green's denial news conference) and Harvey Clark were supportive. On the broadcast set, Knapp and Herb Clarke maintained their silence. In the newsroom, my friend, consumer reporter Orien Reid, openly embraced me and my dilemma.

Anchor Knapp's attitude was especially disturbing, since I had offered tremendous assistance to her husband, Henry Bonilla, by helping him get television production work. During some turbulent times in her life, my wife and I were always there for her. She and Henry invited us to their wedding on the banks of a river in San Antonio. Deborah eventually left WCAU TV, blaming me for her exit. About that, my conscience is clear. As far as Henry Bonilla goes, the story gets better. He is now the Republican congressman from the San Antonio area. Deborah is a popular anchor there. They are a Texas power couple.

So with some deep hurts, I was persona non grata in my own newsroom, and the silence lasted for weeks. Although I hadn't crafted the story, I shared the blame for not challenging the information enough and for allowing them to use me as the front man for a precarious report.

By Saturday morning, I was a wreck, and the calls started coming in. Frank Rizzo was the most prominent caller. Rizzo sounded stricken with grief at the station's bad fortune, and he insisted that we had been set up for disaster. The former mayor reprimanded me: "Why the hell didn't you call me? I woulda told you it was bullshit, but maybe you were on to something." Rizzo had no prior knowledge of the developing story but wished he had. Rizzo was wired for information, but on this one, he didn't have a clue. Bill Green had told mutual friends that he was convinced Rizzo was behind the story, but Bill Green was dead wrong.

Another caller was Bishop Louis DeSimone, auxiliary bishop of the Roman Catholic archdiocese of Philadelphia, a friend and the man who earlier had accompanied me on the tortuous trip to earthquake-ravaged Italy. He said, "Larry, the people like you and respect you. Just do your job. This shall pass. Your contributions far overshadow this problem." Weeks later, Bishop DeSimone and Archbishop John Cardinal Krol would call Mayor Bill Green and urge him not to file a lawsuit. Green was gracious but declined their intervention.

Green refused to accept apologies and filed a five million dollar damage suit entitled *Green v. Kane et al.* The suit was originally handled by Judge Stanley Greenberg, an odd choice for such a high-profile case. Greenberg had been convicted in 1970 in a check-kiting scheme and had been banished from hearing cases. But in the world of Philadelphia law, lawyers take care of their own. Greenberg was supported by the leaders of the law community. He sought and received a presidential pardon from Richard Nixon in 1973. In 1975, he was elected to a ten-year term, and in 1982 he received *Green v. Kane et al.*

The Judge's appointment led insiders in the Green administration to start calling me to warn me that something smelled. Greenberg's appointment disturbed me as well. It wasn't because of his criminal record, cleared by the pardon, but because he had ties to Green's family and the law establishment. In the summer of 1982, my calls from insiders increased, and the message was simple: the mayor wants a big settlement.

As the legal proceedings got underway, the written press went on the attack. Columnists and reporters were using me as a battering ram for media excesses. The *Inquirer* dealt the harshest blow, referring to me in an editorial as the station "announcer." An "announcer" is a term used for a broadcaster who has no connection to legitimate journalism, a person who announces station breaks and commercials. There is no greater insult to a good broadcast journalist. Years later, Gene Roberts, the Pulitzer Prize-winning boss of the paper, apologized to me for that reference and for the paper's failure to oppose a frivolous lawsuit, especially one filed after a full-scale apology, an apology made to four hundred thousand viewers.

The columnists who attacked me included Jill Porter, a *Daily News* writer, who was especially vicious and who didn't even know me. At the time, her boyfriend was a member of the management team at rival KYW TV. Jill still writes for the *Daily News* and her boyfriend, Fred Hamilton, became her husband and a successful executive at the Franklin Institute. Porter's nastiness was matched by many other print journalists, but some reporters also stood up to defend me, including the legendary Tom Fox and Pete Dexter, who later became a Hollywood screenwriter. Complicating matters, Don Fair, a press aide to Mayor Green, was the husband of Cheryl Fair, a top executive at rival WPVI TV. Fair helped to craft Green's angry response.

On the Monday morning following my apology, I awakened at my usual time, 9:00 A.M. I had not gotten a good sleep; in the hours of darkness I could hear the sound of my heartbeat. Real fear had found its place in my body, locked inside and with no way out. I carried out my morning ritual—a mile swim, a light breakfast, and a check-in call to the station. In all my years of broadcasting, I had never called in sick, but that day I considered it. My mind was racing. To Donna, I said, "How would it look if I stayed home?" Donna was deeply concerned about my mental well-being. But we both understood the consequences of taking the day off. So I started gearing up.

The morning hours seemed like a lifetime, although phone calls helped me pace the time. My best friend, Ron, checked in, along with a former WCAU news director, Bill Lawlor. Rizzo called again to see how I was coping.

Driving to work, I kept thinking that people were looking at me, which was not true but a reflection of paranoia, nervousness, and the lump in my throat that wouldn't go away. Once again, daydreaming, I tried to interpret my fear. I had no concern about security: I could always make a living. The embarrassment was hard to absorb, along with the cruelty in the print media, but all of that was ultimately bearable. What mattered the most to me professionally was my credibility. Would my ability to gather information be obstructed, and would the flow of news stop? As I walked into the newsroom, these fears were twisting and turning in my mind. All eyes were on me as I sat down at the desk, sorted through the mail, and started going over the news of the day, avoiding eye contact. In a slow trickle, writers and technicians circled around and cautiously offered greetings. There were pats on the back and words of encouragement—but still no visible support came from the anchors and reporters.

Their silence in the coming weeks would be deafening and cruel. I saw evidence of my personal disaster everywhere, real and imagined. A week after the Green episode, our family traveled to Disney World for a scheduled vacation. On the aircraft headed down to Orlando, they played the movie *Absence of Malice,* a drama about a newspaper that committed libel. I didn't watch.

In the weeks after March 25, facing humiliation and enormous personal pressure, I experienced two incredible things. To my astonishment, General Manager Feldman failed to come to my support, letting me take the fall for the entire episode. He purported to be my friend, and even invited me to be in his wedding party later that year, but the man who pushed the story to broadcast without pause was clearly elated that the name of the lawsuit was *Green v. Kane et al.* and not *Green v. Feldman.*

Then a phone call came that changed my entire perspective on the calamity and gave me courage. The president of CBS TV Stations and owner of WCAU phoned to see how I was doing. Neil Derrough asked if I was continuing my hard-hitting political report, "Larry Kane's Political Notebook," which I had been putting together for the past four years and presenting on the eleven o'clock news. It was an inside view of the latest goings-on at City Hall and at all levels of government. I replied, "Neil, I think we should suspend it for a while." But he snapped back, "Are you kidding? I want you to continue reporting the news as if nothing happened. That's your job. If the report happens to be negative about Bill Green, then tough shit. Nothing is going to stop us from reporting news." Derrough was a courageous manager whose First Amendment instincts always came to the forefront. Managers in the nineties could learn a lot from his idealism and his courage. Derrough's call, Donna's support, and the daily reality checks from my buddy Ron Tindiglia took me through a difficult time.

And there was another factor that helped me pull through: the calm and courtesy of the viewers. I got some nasty letters, but mostly I received a quiet, solid support, a show of trust and faith in my work that showed in the ratings. In fact, the ratings of the station stayed solid and even increased for months after the episode. The Green affair was on the top of my mind, but it faded quickly in the minds of viewers, an indication of loyalty and perhaps respect.

Neil Derrough's support and the forgiving public attitude inspired me to get back on the political track. By the summer of 1982, I was once again breaking political stories. I was proud to be the first journalist to report that William J. Green would not be seeking re-election, a story provided by high-level sources close to the mayor's office. Green was apparently irritated that I was the one who broke the story.

The lawsuit became a factor in the story of Philadelphia politics. To this day, supporters of W. Wilson Goode are convinced that he might never have had the chance to run for mayor in 1983 if Bill Green had avoided the lawsuit. Green's hunger for the lawsuit convinced Goode's fund-raisers that he should start hinting about a run. Charles Bowser, the former deputy mayor of Philadelphia, was also a possible contender. With Goode breathing down his back, Bowser in the wings, and the prospect of getting some cash through other means, Green opted not to run.

Our attorney was John Harkins, a Philadelphia legal power, a great thinker, and an absolute realist. Harkins had surmised early in the game that Green would not seek a second term. An apology for false charges would seem to be enough, he reasoned, so it was evident that Green wanted money. By October 20, 1982, we had reached a settlement, the specifics of which I'm banned by court decree from discussing. Harkins had predicted the settlement amount and even suggested the time frame, but he was angry that the judge, Stanley Greenberg, had not been pulled off the case.

The settlement came one day short of my fortieth birthday. Donna threw a surprise party for me, and life seemed sweeter. I'd walked in from the darkness, and the Green episode was behind me—except for a surprise invitation from the mayor.

A day before Green left office, he called and asked me to drop by City Hall. When I entered the mayor's office, which was packed with cartons of his personal mementos, he asked me to sit down and have a cup of coffee. Green said, "I got you, didn't I? You gave me one night of hell, I gave you six months of grief. Got ya." I replied, "So what's your point?" He didn't answer. Then I asked a question. "I've always wondered, Bill. If you knew you were innocent, why did you go ballistic when it happened? You could have buried me by accepting the apology and moving on. You could have been a mensch, but instead you chose to sue. So you got your bucks, and you're running with the cash and leaving office. You know that some of the secondary sources in the story were allies of yours. With allies like that, who needs enemies? All you keep obsessing about is Frank Rizzo, but he had nothing to do with it. I guess it was money, wasn't it?"

Green sat stone-faced and said, "There's a reason I asked you here today. I want to make sure there are no hard feelings, because I may run for the Senate, and I'd like you to be fair." With a bit of anger I replied, "You don't understand the media at all. My job is to be fair, to you and everyone else. You're the man with the problem. But I will assure you that my objective will always be fair reporting."

We shook hands and I left. Bill Green never ran for the Senate, though he did have one chance at getting in. When Senator John Heinz died in a plane crash in 1991, Green was the first choice for appointment to the seat. Governor Bob Casey wanted to anoint Green, but Green had a powerful enemy in Philadelphia. State Senator Vince Fumo, whose power was critical to Casey's political agenda, put the nix on Green.

Fumo's intervention guaranteed Green would not get the job, and instead Harris Wofford was appointed senator.

A year later, I spoke at a fund-raiser for the Allied Jewish Appeal. Waiting for a cab at the Franklin Plaza Hotel, I was approached by Howard Gittis, chairman of the law firm that Green hired in the case, Wolf Block Schorr and Solis-Cohen. Gittis offered me a ride to the station, giving me an opportunity to quiz him about the case. "Howard," I said, "during your deposition of me, you questioned me for five minutes and sent me home. Why?" He answered, "I told Greenie [Green's nickname] you don't want to fuck with the man with the gun, and Larry's going to be around long after you. Besides, you didn't know much." Devilishly, I answered, "How do you know?" He replied, "Because I knew you were telling the truth."

Gittis, a former Philadelphia Bar Association chancellor, is now Ron Perelman's number one. Perelman is the colorful chairman of Revlon and McAndrews and Forbes. Bill Green is a lobbyist for that company. Peter Vaira, the U.S. attorney at the time of the episode, took a job a few months later with Wolf Block, the law firm associated with Green. Of the secondary sources the station relied on for the Green allegations, some are still public officials, three others have lucrative businesses in Philadelphia, and one is dead.

The Green affair may have ended a mayoralty, resulted in a purge at the CBS law department that gave the green light for the story, and in strange ways jump-started my career. I had walked through fire and come out whole. Nevertheless, for the benefit of reporters, editors, and anchors involved in investigative reporting, let me once again repeat that old newsroom aphorism: When in doubt, don't.

The Move Confrontation: A "Live Event"

The technical advances that coincided with my life in Philadelphia were breathtaking and impactive, and these developments were especially visible on one memorable May night. But before we get to that debacle, let me start at the beginning.

An odd feeling. I was standing on a rooftop, looking over the Mediterranean, scanning the pastel-and-white buildings of Israel's largest city, Tel Aviv. It was shortly after one in the morning—6:00 P.M.

Philadelphia time. I was sweating bullets—nervous, excited, ready for an experience. Through my earpiece, I heard the words, "Stand by Larry, ten seconds." The countdown continued. When it was over, six thousand miles from home, I began talking into a camera, reporting reaction to the Camp David Accords, my face and voice almost instantly relayed to thousands at home. This was my first broadcast via satellite, a small cylinder rotating the earth, beaming me across the continents and seas.

Technology changed the world of communications and the way news was covered. Technology also saved me from a traffic disaster.

During my freshman year on the City Hall beat, I discovered a way to drive from the northwest corner of City Hall to the Channel 6 studios on City Line Avenue in less than six minutes and thirty seconds. Don't try it. But if you're ever stuck heading west, take the Sweetbriar cutoff from West River Drive, pass Memorial Hall, take a right on Belmont, and you'll reach City Line Avenue in less than seven minutes. You must be willing to exceed the speed limit, however, which is not recommended.

The reason for my rush-hour rushes was 16-millimeter film. To make our deadline, film had to be processed and developed at least thirty or forty minutes before airtime. That is why my 1966 Chevy Bel Air, pock-marked with dents from various sixties protests, with my pedal to the metal, was moving so quickly in the late afternoons.

In 1968, on assignment in Paris, I had to travel to the airport to ship the film, which would arrive at the station twenty-four hours later. In 1974, videotape arrived, ending film's run, but I still had to rush it to the TV station. Videotape changed that in 1975, since it could be sent electronically by microwave dishes attached to the news trucks. That high-speed drive from City Hall was no longer necessary.

Then, of course, satellite arrived. In a span of thirteen years, television news moved from the slow film process to instant videotape and dramatic satellite technology. Offering more than just convenience, these developments changed the way you got your news and posed a serious challenge to journalists. With the advent of live television, gone was the age of the reporter who could sit for hours, writing and editing a story. Live transmission meant that veteran reporters who couldn't think on their feet were soon unemployed. It was also a challenge to reporters who had no mastery of spoken words and no intimate knowledge of the stories they were covering. Suddenly, television reporters had to be quick on their feet and totally informed. To be perfectly frank, not all reporters in that era were ready for live TV.

The immediacy of live TV was also dangerous to politicians, who didn't have time to spin their answers to tough questions. Mayor Frank Rizzo and District Attorney (and future senator) Arlen Specter could dance with the best of reporters, but politicians lacking savvy crumbled under pressure. During his second term as Philadelphia's mayor in the late eighties, Wilson Goode tried avoiding live interviews, while his successor Ed Rendell sought them with delight. Politicians learned quickly: you simply cannot claim to be misquoted when you're saying it yourself in a live interview.

The era of instant coverage brought another problem—other people. There is nothing more incongruous than watching a reporter at the scene of an accident, crime, or disaster trying to convey accurate information while surrounded by arm-waving people screaming into the microphone, proving that, even in times of crisis, people are always looking for their fifteen seconds of fame. But live is what live coverage is, and I guess people are what they are, too.

With all that as background, let's return to the night of May 13, 1985. Drenched in sweat, my mouth dry and back aching from sitting in the same position for eleven hours, I looked over at the clock on my office wall. It was 1:15 A.M. When I emerged from the studio chair, hope suddenly erupted within me that the evening's events had been one of those nightmares that are so real you can smell them, touch them, see them in color. But this was no bad dream. Hundreds of thousands of people would have preferred a dream to the ugly events that had just occurred on the 6200 block of Osage Avenue in West Philadelphia during the day and night of May 13, 1985. May 13 has gone down in regional history as a day of infamy, a day on which the famous became infamous literally overnight.

The week had begun peacefully. Sunday, May 12, was Mother's Day, and while I was giving my annual Mother's Day speech at my synagogue, Old York Road Temple Beth Am in Abington, the beeper in my right pocket alerted me that a story was unfolding. That Sunday was a crucial day in what has become known as the Move confrontation. Members of Move, a back-to-nature group living in a group house in West Philadelphia, had been harassing their neighbors with threats, profanity, and loudspeakers blaring in the night. The group had previously engaged in a shootout with Philadelphia police in 1978, resulting in the death of a popular police officer, James Ramp.

The people of Osage Avenue wanted Move quieted or gone. Little did they know that their effort to seek the city's help would drive hundreds of Osage residents out of their homes, while other human beings would leave the block as bodies unearthed from a rubble of wood, metal, and brick.

Throughout that Sunday, I learned when I called the station, tension had been building. For weeks, the Osage Avenue residents had called the city for help, saying they were fed up with horrible odors, profanities shouted on loudspeakers, and the general disruption of their lives. A crowd was gathered in front of the Move house, and public officials were trying to negotiate with Move members. There were tough words from Mayor Wilson Goode; his managing director, Leo Brooks; and Gregore Sambor, the police commissioner. By evening, the street was an armed camp. Hundreds of helmeted police were in place. As dawn arrived on Monday morning, the shooting started.

More than any other event in recent Philadelphia history, the Move confrontation and its consequences were partially shaped by television coverage. Wilson Goode even testified after the fact that the TV screen in his office had been cloudy. He said he couldn't see that the fire started by the bomb was burning the house down and that the firefighters were standing idly by while the fire burned. Yet for those with clear screens, the live coverage exposed the failed calculations, actions, and inactions that led to the deaths of eleven people and the destruction of a two-block area of West Philadelphia. Without the live cameras, who would have seen that the fire department had followed orders to let the fire burn?

Decisions by broadcast journalists about how to cover the unfolding confrontations played a significant role in how the city's leadership was judged and how the neighborhood was compensated. Those decisions came from two different motives: what was right for the community and what was wise for the station. Not all of Philadelphia's TV stations had the public's interest at heart during those fateful hours. In times of emergency, broadcasters must take special steps.

The shooting erupted in the early morning hours of May 13. We found out months later that it had been a one-way barrage and that the Move members had had very few arms, perhaps just one pistol. WCAU's live coverage began in the morning and continued until the firing stopped at midday. Observers saw no indication of what was going on inside the Move house. The pause in the shooting, ordered by police commanders, gave Mayor Goode an opportunity to restate publicly that the city would use whatever means necessary to take control of the house.

This was a time for serious questions. Harvey Clark, a reporter for WCAU TV who had made close contact with Move members, was probing, challenging everyone he spoke with. He moved through the streets surrounding Osage Avenue, gauging the situation. Clark was talking with two groups, Move sympathizers and city officials. From the Move sources, he reported to viewers that occupants of the house were ready to build a barricade to keep police at bay. From officials, he tried to get answers to basic questions. Just how many children were inside the building? What was the plan, if there was one? Or was this a catch-as-you-can, ad-lib affair? His questions to city officials were mostly greeted with blank stares and "official-speak," that artful dodging of issues that people in power have such a talent for. In the newsroom, we eagerly awaited Clark's calls, along with a call from our secret agent. Pete Kane, an award-winning cameraman, was staked out in a building across from the Move house, his camera ready with a view of the building, his telephone and two-way radio available for total communication. Kane had the picture in his viewfinder. Later, his work would be pivotal for both the station and the mayor.

Leadership should be judged by its ability to take on risk in difficult situations. Too much of my business is filled with "cover your behind" managers who are more interested in protecting their hides than in doing the right thing. But luckily, that day, Jay Newman was in charge at WCAU. Jay was the news director, guided by the general manager, Steve Cohen. Both were adamant: the station would see the story through. Clark had told us that an all-out assault was planned. Newman and Cohen set in motion a series of events that would ensure the story was covered well: an additional truck to submit live pictures was dispatched, along with two outstanding journalists, reporters Charles Thomas and Dennis Woltering. Newsroom producers were briefed on protocol during civil disorder. Newman, an energetic and thorough manager, sought approval from Cohen to go nonstop, if necessary, with one caveat: the CBS News with Dan Rather would have to air at 6:30 P.M. Pre-empting the CBS Evening News would have been treason in the company.

My day was long. I started broadcasting at 8:45 A.M. while the fire was being fought and returned to the air several times during the afternoon with updates. During the afternoon break, I looked outside at the lush growth of leaves and petals that make May such a beautiful month in Philadelphia. Nature was blooming, I thought, while human beings were exposing their ugliest side. Azaleas were showing crimson while seeds were being planted for a nasty time ahead. My thoughts turned to the children inside that house. Anger filled me—anger over the inability to break the impasse, anger that thousands of rounds of ammunition had been fired at the Move house, with still no indication of what was going on inside. Were the Move members all dead? Or was their silence a part of some sinister plot? Months later, as I have noted, we would discover that Move had possession of perhaps one pistol, but on that Monday afternoon we in the media, and much of the public, imagined a small army ready to blow the neighborhood to smithereens.

During the afternoon break at the station, I called every key source on my phone list. Information was limited. The Goode administration's next steps were uncertain, although most insiders expected some military-style action to force the occupants out. That, I thought, would be frightening.

The inner tension I was feeling had become unbearable. Sensing a traumatic conclusion, my instincts told me to relax a bit to rebuild my energy for the crisis to come. I read some magazines, had some coffee, and nervously swallowed a turkey sandwich—a wise move, considering where I would end up in the coming hours. In the newsroom, people were tense and testy, facing the fright of the unknown, facing questions: Would Move screw up? Would the city screw up? Would we screw up while reporting a tense, explosive situation?

We returned to air at 4:00 P.M. with reports circulating that a final assault would be staged by the police. Throughout the next hour, we provided a summary of the day's events at the Move house. At 5:00 P.M., the broadcast continued with live reports focusing on the current situation and how Osage residents evacuated on Sunday were coping. Not well, mind you, considering that their homes were in the line of fire of thousands of police. Harvey Clark reported that police action was expected any moment. The most interesting report came from cameraman Pete Kane, who was set up in the house across the street. Pete said, "Seems like police are pulling back, area in front of the house a dead zone, police lines are expanding in the rear, something's up."

Something *was* up. Members of the Philadelphia bomb squad had spent decades disarming explosives, preventing them from killing and maiming people. That bomb squad had never dropped a bomb in anger until May 13, 1985.

The sun was shining brilliantly over the 6200 block of Osage Avenue. Suddenly, Clark reported, a helicopter appeared. Another news helicopter? No, a Pennsylvania state police helicopter. None of us in the studio were immediately interested: it could have been routine surveillance. The chopper came lunging toward the Move house, where it dropped a sack on a small rooftop bunker constructed in the northwest corner of the house. The sack was loaded with C-5 plastic explosives. The bunker exploded in flames, and a fire began. For the first time in American history, a municipal governing authority had dropped a bomb on one of its neighborhoods.

Minutes later, we broadcast the video of the bombing captured by our camera crew on the street. That was sensational enough. But because of the total-coverage scenario envisioned by Jay Newman, our reporters and cameras were ready to report something more remarkable. Now, more than ever, the presence of live cameras would come to bear on Philadelphia history.

I have covered so many row-house fires in our region that my sense of impending danger is high and accurate. Pete Kane's camera showed a fire spreading in the Move house, smoke billowing from the front windows and the roof, a hint of flames beginning to emerge. Across the street, two solitary fire trucks sat idle. It was risky, but I said on air, "I can't be sure, but it seems that the fire is spreading rapidly. It appears that the fire department has decided to let the fire burn. Perhaps the city is trying to smoke Move out, but row-house fires spread quickly. This could torch the entire neighborhood. I wonder what's going on." At that moment, Jay Newman's voice was in my earpiece, the instrument used for communication to the anchor. Newman said, "Lar, I want you to make your own decisions on where to go and who to talk to. Just carry it, man. Okay?"

The next two hours were a round robin of reports from Clark, Kane, Woltering, and Charles Thomas. Eventually we had to pull Pete Kane from his secret hiding place. He was black and he was young, and we didn't want him shot. A case of mistaken identity would be unbearable. For added security, Newman called the police commissioner's office, advising them that Kane was in the house and would be exiting shortly. As six o'clock arrived, the live picture we broadcast showed smoke billowing out of an adjacent home. I said, "This fire is definitely spreading. Will the fire department fight it? What about the kids inside—any indication that they are evacuating?" Harvey Clark reported from around the corner. "Larry, [the situation] confounds me. Smoke is rising from Osage Avenue, and there doesn't appear to be any effort to battle it." My thoughts turned to the inferno that was now the Move house. I wondered if the mayor had ever heard that old newsroom adage (here I go again), "When in doubt, don't."

Then a decision was made that rocked the foundations of CBS. Steve Cohen, the general manager and also a brilliant journalist, decided not to run the *CBS Evening News* with Dan Rather. It was heresy, pure treason in the CBS world, but Cohen was determined to stay with the story nonstop, even if it meant pre-empting the most prestigious daily broadcast on CBS. So we continued our reports. The people at CBS News were livid until they realized the scope of the story and the tragedy.

As light was fading, gunfire was reported in the alley behind the Move house. Two Move occupants raced out of the house—Ramona Africa and young Birdie Africa, both seriously burned. Ramona claimed later that the police had fired at her and others, preventing their escape from the burning house. But the story of the moment was the fire, because the flames were spreading in both directions from the Move compound. Clark, his face burning in the searing heat, was careful not to incite any further violence in the city in his on-air reports. Off camera, he was incredulous. "How could a city bomb its own people?" he asked.

Too late, the fire department started sending all available units to Osage. By this time, a full city block was burning. The late start, coupled with the bombing, would prove to be a colossal mistake in judgment that would hurt Philadelphia's image around the world.

In the WCAU studio, the pressure was on. Move was a radical group that was detested in Philadelphia, but there would be attempts to link the bombing to racial tension, and that could cause more violence. More than ever, my job—and that of our team in the field—was to put things in perspective. Our reports had to be clear, our tone business-like. This was no time for inciting more fear, in that neighborhood or in any other. The ratings would show later that WCAU TV had a large audience that day and night. I had assumed that we *would* be watched in record numbers because the other stations had thrown in the towel.

On the night of May 13, 1985, WPVI TV, my alma mater, had a movie scheduled, part two of *Murder in Miami.* The station management decided to stick with the movie in prime time. KYW, my future station, gave the Move situation more extensive coverage but didn't even lead its eleven o'clock newscast with the story. By good instinct and default, we owned the story and the audience. For the first time in fifteen years, the armor of Channel 6 was shattered, and the station was embarrassed. KYW TV was slow on the story, although its coverage, when it was on, was fair and thorough.

The responsibility and ethical behavior displayed that night by WCAU TV played a major role in keeping the city calm, a tribute to risk-taking management and to the reporters, who were bound by their obligations to the wellness of the community as a whole. There was no grandstanding, there were no glaring and sensational headlines—just the facts and the pictures. We were on the air until 1:15 A.M. There were no commercials, no prime-time shows—just news and information. When I walked out of the newsroom, bathed in sweat, imprisoned by fear, I was comforted by a realization that, in the face of an ugly night, we had done the right things.

The next morning, exhausted from the night before, I was awakened from a deep sleep by a phone call from CBS TV Stations chief Neil Derrough, the same man who had so courageously defended me in the Green affair. Derrough said, "Congratulations. You were number one last night. What a victory." His praise should have delighted me. But my pride in my and my colleagues' accomplishments was dampened by the truth: my city, my community had been disgraced, bombed by its own leaders. It had truly been a day of infamy.

The Move episode was followed by three separate investigations. A special commission spread the blame to elements of the executive branch, but no criminal charges were made. Mayor Wilson Goode was declared politically dead, but he rose from the ashes to narrowly defeat Republican candidate Frank Rizzo in 1987. Move lingered as a story as efforts to rebuild the neighborhood got underway. It still lingers in my mind today.

Of all the memories of the Move confrontation that remain scorched in my mind, one image stands out: an image of watching the building burn. As I watched, I wondered how anybody could possibly get out and what it was like in there. Ramona Africa, who spent seven years in a state prison for related charges, would never tell how it came down. But one night I was shown the excruciating pain the compound's occupants must have felt in that oven of death.

In 1993, the InterAct Theater Company staged an original play called *6221*, a drama of the confrontation from start to finish. Opening night at the University of Pennsylvania's Annenberg Center served as a reunion for many who had lived through the disaster. Members of the bomb squad showed up, some talking about their years of psychiatric treatment. People from the neighborhood came. Ramona Africa was there to join in a forum that I would moderate when the curtain fell.

Ramona, always fiercely intense and the last public voice of Move, was happy to see me again. Over the years, she had seemed to trust me more than she trusted other reporters. We talked, then watched the premiere.

The play was superb, especially its scenery and its script. The performances were gripping—maybe too gripping. During the intermission, Ramona expressed her gratification at seeing the re-enactment. She said, "It's real, really real." Turns out it was too real. The final act recounted the fire and depicted the screaming, burning Move members trying to get out of the inferno sparked by the city's bomb. Suddenly, Ramona left the playhouse. When the play was over, I found her weeping in a lobby alcove. "I couldn't take it," she said. "It was so real." Trembling, she added, "No one understood that they never got a chance to get out, so they burned alive." That's all she said, but additional words were needless. Ramona Africa's face told the gruesome story.

She was not the only living victim of Move; there was also Wilson Goode. In the final days of 1984, Wilson Goode's first year in office, I had anchored and helped produce a special called "Wilson Goode—The Man, The Mayor," a story of a spectacular first year in office. The mayor beamed as he talked about restoring confidence in government and, most of all, restoring hope in Philadelphia's future by defusing racial tension. The first black mayor had been warmly received, and on our interview date, the normally stoic Goode was smiling so broadly that I wanted to say, "Wait, freeze it. This may never happen again." The fact is that, after 1984, W. Wilson Goode had little to smile about.

Goode's political descent began the day of the Move confrontation, the day that changed the public view of his administration forever. The tragedy of Wilson Goode is that, even in the trying days after Move, he never let anyone inside his world.

Personally, Goode was intense and private, although at moments he let his guard down. An exciting moment for Goode, he once told me, was arriving home, eating potato chips, and drinking Pepsi. On the job,

Goode was a natural-born policy wonk. He ruled his office and government with military precision. His treatment of the media was no different. If an interview was scheduled for 3:00 P.M., it was going to start at three. If you came late, Goode gave you that ice-cold stare of his that could ruin a sunny day. Yes, Goode was misunderstood, but the fault for that falls on the doorstep of Wilson Goode. Beyond that ironclad facade stood a sensitive and caring man who would quietly provide little acts of kindness to his constituents. Few people were turned away from the mayor's door. After Frank Rizzo's death, for instance, he instructed his police department and bureau heads to do whatever was necessary to make the burden of the Rizzo family a bit lighter.

On the streets, Wilson Goode was treated like a star. He was easily recognizable, and even after Move he was greeted warmly by citizens. His administration brought a big-city skyline to Philadelphia, finished the Center City tunnel that connects all the regional rail lines, upgraded the transit system, and established regional mayor's offices so that people in various neighborhoods had better access to him. Perhaps his most important decision was selecting former Secret Service agent Kevin Tucker as police commissioner. Tucker, a rare outsider in the department, was nevertheless respected and helped restore public confidence in the police department after the Move bombing.

Wilson Goode also provided a living civics lesson for future mayors in the arena of press relations. A mayor is served by a press secretary, and that person can cause irreparable harm or positive benefits to a mayor's public image. Goode's press secretary was Karen Warrington, who was notorious for browbeating reporters in heated telephone calls. That is, of course, part of the job. Warrington is a talented woman who cares about the state of Philadelphia, but her dealings with the media were excruciating. If a report was negative toward Goode, she would at times infer that race was the reason. It is the role of a press secretary to take flak for her client, but combat never works.

I've wondered what role Mayor Goode played in those phone calls and complaints. It's hard to believe that Warrington, a savvy journalist, would act without his approval. Today, Karen Warrington continues to serve brilliantly in the public sector. Most of us who dealt with her in those years empathized and understood her role. If Wilson Goode was directing her, his own administration was the victim. In stark contrast, Ed Rendell, who privately holds deep grievances against the media, rarely sent his press chief, Kevin Feeley, on the attack. There's a lesson here for all current and aspiring politicians: never browbeat the press. It doesn't work and usually backfires. If you have a grievance, air it, drop it, and go to the next item on your agenda.

Here and there I run into Wilson Goode, and I smile, privately thinking about how hard he tried and how hard he fell. We often reflect on the morning after his first win in 1983. His family was gathered around the breakfast table at the old Center City Sheraton. Pride was in the air: you could see it in their eyes. Wilson Goode, the man whose poker face and stern style would scare subordinates, was beaming, hugging his children and embracing his wife, Velma, conscious that he had broken the political glass ceiling. My first reaction was deep pride for the man and the dream fulfilled. It is a disheartening memory, so disappointing to think that the dream was realized, but the job was unfulfilled. When the end of his mayoralty came, Goode retreated to what he knows best—spending eighteen-hour days, commuting to and from Washington, as the regional education chief for the U.S. government.

To many Philadelphians, Wilson Goode will always be an enigma. But he's really not a puzzle. Goode is a thoughtful man who had a very bad day once and lives to regret it. When he says to me, "Larry, a night doesn't go by when I don't think about that day and those kids," I believe him. When the history books are written, W. Wilson Goode (the W stands for Willie) may actually get better treatment than what he's received in the short term. He doesn't have the political skill of Ed Rendell or the brute power of Jim Tate, nor does he have the powerful charisma of Frank L. Rizzo, but like Rizzo, he has a heart of gold. Those of us who covered him are quite confident of that.

Every year, my mind circles May 13 on my mental calendar. And whenever I see Ramona Africa or talk to Wilson Goode, I flash back to that long night—the decisions at City Hall that wrecked a neighborhood, the choices at a television station, the broadcasting of a precarious live event that kept a city whole during a dark and dangerous night in its history.

As God Is My Witness . . .

Philadelphia is often called the Quaker City, a tribute to the early Quakers who pioneered the spirit of friendship and giving hundreds of years ago. In the modern era, the city's power establishment was primarily Protestant, even though over two million Roman Catholics live in the three states. The city's Jewish community is now the fourth largest in America. Religion is at the core of this city and at the core of American life, so it's no surprise that religious beliefs and events often generate big news.

The afternoon sky was deep blue, the sun fading in the west, and the leader of the Roman Catholic world was praying atop a temporary platform, surrounded by thousands of flowers and more than a half-million people. Pope John Paul II's visit to Philadelphia in October 1979 was a brilliant, shining, and spiritual moment in Philadelphia history. John Paul's Philadelphia visit was a show of gratitude to Archbishop John Cardinal Krol, a man I would cross paths with many times in Philadelphia and whose life would intersect mine at the most unusual moments.

Over a period of years, at news events, award presentations, and personal appearances, I became familiar with the influential Philadelphia Catholic archdiocese and its news-making force, Cardinal Krol. Cardinal Krol was a giant among the world's Catholic leadership, his standing enhanced by the quiet role he played in marshaling the cardinals to support the election of his friend Cardinal Karol Wojtyla as Pope John Paul II. In Philadelphia, Krol ruled the five-county archdiocese with a strong hand, streamlining the educational system, pruning the budgets, and fostering his private agenda, a strengthening of ethnic pride, with an accent on all things Polish. When the pope came to Philadelphia on that spiritual pilgrimage in 1979, it was a cherished moment for Cardinal Krol, a reaffirmation of his faith and commitment, with mass being celebrated within a block of the cardinal's highrise office. His unique relationship with John Paul underscored the reasons that I would travel to Italy on four occasions, to Poland twice, and to Alaska in the winter of 1981.

John Krol always seemed to like me, even when I fired tough questions at him about the rigidity of the church on such items as feminism, abortion, and gay rights. After news conferences he would often walk me into his office to talk about politics and the times. He was fascinated with my thoughts about how events in the Middle East related to my Judaism. Quite often he would lecture me on the evils of society. Unlike many religious leaders, he was pro-life across the board, opposing abortion and the death penalty at the same time. The cardinal's staff feared him, because his grim stare could bore a hole through your heart. I always had the impression that he was concerned about letting his guard down, though sometimes he did, as we will see later.

In December 1980, three devastating events unfolded. John Lennon was shot to death in New York, powerful Philadelphia union boss John McCullough was shot and killed at his home in Somerton in the Greater Northeast, and, thousands of miles away, the people of southern Italy were rocked by a disaster of enormous consequences. The Lennon death was difficult for me to bear. It was only five years earlier that John had come to Philadelphia for the radio marathon. McCullough's death was a sign that mob warfare would open up again in Philadelphia; on the night of the killing, I walked into McCullough's living room and shuddered at what was left of his body. The night was made even more difficult by the fact that I was leaving for Italy to cover the Italian earthquake for WCAU TV the next morning.

At first, the earthquake seemed of minor interest to Philadelphians. But within days, the Italian-American community, sensing the despair in Italy, responded with a major fund-raising effort, and I was off to southern Italy with Father Louis DeSimone of St. Monica's parish in South Philadelphia. Cardinal Krol had asked me to go and work directly with Catholic Relief Services, his fund-raising arm, and the station had readily agreed.

The situation west and south of Naples was grim—three thousand dead, a hundred and fifty thousand homeless, and the earthquake sending its waves of savagery into the beautiful hills of Avellino province. We walked through small towns, slowly passing makeshift morgues, seeing people whose lives were devastated. In the town of St. Angelo De Lombardi, I cried when I saw the destruction and the surviving families huddled by makeshift fires. This Italian journey resulted in an unprecedented campaign of aid, with Philadelphia rebuilding entire communities and especially aiding the town of Montella, which to this day honors the city of Philadelphia with monuments and plaques.

With that story as a backdrop, my relationship with Cardinal Krol deepened. On February 28, 1981, less than two months later, Cardinal Krol and Ed Piszek, the owner of Mrs. Paul's Foods, extended even further the Polish connection they strove to build in Philadelphia. As a show of gratitude for WCAU's Italian mission, the cardinal invited me on the most unusual of papal missions. We flew in Piszek's Lear jet from Philadelphia to Anchorage, Alaska, where the pope was making a six-hour layover on a flight to Rome from Japan. The cardinal insisted that there be a Philadelphia delegation to greet the pope during his short stop on American soil. Krol flew separately, but our little rocket ship of a jet had a passenger list that included Jim Murray, general manager of the Eagles, and Stan Musial, the Hall of Fame baseball player who was one of my boyhood heroes. Musial and Piszek were prominent Polish Americans. Murray, with the generosity of Eagles owner Leonard Tose, had helped send thousands of dollars to Catholic Relief Services after the Italian quake. Piszek was a giant in the Polish-American community and was known in Eastern Europe for his decades of philanthropy. The missions of John Krol were joining together in the air space over America.

The flight to Anchorage gave me a chance to meet Stan the Man and to discover that he was a quiet, strong man and a good listener. Musial asked me about our children, and I mentioned that our son, Michael, was in Little League. He nodded, and that was that. Piszek took charge on the trip, providing us infinite scraps of information about John Paul. I came to believe what I had heard, that Ed Piszek was one of the few people on this earth who could call and visit the pope on short notice.

The jet landed in a flurry of snow, and we headed to the hotel for a good night's rest before what would turn out to be an emotional day. John Paul arrived in late morning and was greeted by a small airport delegation, including John Cardinal Krol. Krol quickly steered him to the press area, where I shook the pope's hand and our cameraman got some wonderful video. I will always remember the sight of Jim Murray offering his late father's rosary to the pope and the tears streaming down Murray's face as the pope blessed it. Murray, who had named his baby boy John Paul, was overcome with emotion.

The pope's mass was warmly received by the starstruck Alaskans. He boarded his jet a few hours later, waving goodbye and holding for the world to see a Philadelphia Eagles jersey bearing the name Jaworski. Once again, the Polish connection had been made.

On our final night in Anchorage, we had a farewell dinner. Musial walked in with a crumpled brown paper bag and said, "Larry, I did my best. It's the only one I could find. I hope it's okay." I had no idea what he was talking about. I opened the bag and picked up a baseball. It wasn't an official major-league ball, but on it was a dedication: "To Michael, from Stan Musial." Based on my one brief comment, he had walked the streets of Anchorage looking for a baseball for our son and had purchased one at Woolworth's. His taking time for that one kind act is something I will always remember.

The Catholic connection between Philadelphia and Italy continued in December 1981, when I returned to Italy with Louis DeSimone, who had recently been named an auxiliary bishop. Some of his parishioners suggested that his media exposure during the Italian earthquake the previous year had catapulted him into stardom, but in fact he was elevated by Cardinal Krol because of his years of service. Thus he became the first Italian-American bishop of Philadelphia, and his second mission to Italy was a follow-up on the Philadelphia relief effort.

DeSimone was one of Krol's men, placing him on a list that now includes Catholic leaders across America, including the late John Cardinal O'Connor in New York. Krol was dedicated to his flock, especially to those priests he nurtured. Krol was a powerful force, and I got an intimate look at his power during the final trip on the Philadelphia earthquake mission in July 1982. The cardinal had been asked to visit the town of Montella, which had been badly scarred by the 1980 quake. As mentioned above, Montella was a target of Philadelphia's fundraising. Modular homes and a new community center had been constructed, and gratitude was flowing.

Donna joined me on a grueling, hot afternoon as I covered Krol's journey. He was greeted in the community like a war hero. At times he looked like a pied piper, with crowds following him everywhere. Krol was tough and rarely smiled, but he was a man of dignified presence who carried himself with confidence and conviction, a man whose stern face and serious aura could melt down in moments when he embraced a child or took the hand of a faltering older woman. Back home in Philadelphia, Krol was feared by his subordinates because of his demand for excellence and obedience. He didn't have to dress you down with words: his eyes could penetrate your being with one glance. But there was a side of John Cardinal Krol that few people would ever see, and the next night in Rome we would see it up close.

In a show of gratitude, members of the Philadelphia delegation had been invited to a dinner party at the spacious penthouse home of Amintore Fanfani. Fanfani had served three times as prime minister of Italy and was a major force in the nation's political structure. The dinner was held on a magnificent terrace on one of Rome's seven hills, overlooking the Vatican. Seats at the tables had been assigned by Cardinal Krol. The cardinal's table included Donna and some other guests.

I was placed with four Italians, who, I would quickly learn, spoke no English. Not a word. As the dinner progressed, Krol would glance over at me with that sly smile as if to say, "How are you coping, Larry?" Donna seemed comfortable, and Krol, who had a love of beauty, seemed content to be with Donna, Mrs. Fanfani, and some other guests. The cardinal's face was glowing red from the hot sun of our visit to the earthquake zone, enhanced, no doubt, by some of Fanfani's tasty wine. When the guests retreated to the inside sitting room, the cardinal, wine in hand, headed for the piano, where he gave us a concert of love songs. His voice was good, his fingers were soft on the ivories, and his smile was the widest I had ever seen. His rendition of "And the Band Played On" would have made James Cagney proud. It was hard to believe that the leader of two million Catholics had rhythm and could let his guard down so easily. This was a rarely seen side of Philadelphia's cardinal. For a public man, it was a private moment to savor.

John Cardinal Krol's career was marked by celebrations in 1985 of his twenty-fifth anniversary as archbishop. This milestone prompted me to travel once again to Rome, this time to try to get some comment from the pope on Krol's career. Through the power of our cardinal and the invaluable assistance of Philadelphia's own John Foley, now an archbishop stationed at the Vatican, my job was made much easier. I sat in seat number one at the papal audience; Imelda Marcos, first lady of the Philippines, was in seat number two. When the pope walked by, he accommodated me with some thoughts on his friend John, the cardinal of Philadelphia. My hand was clasped in his, a physical way of urging him to linger longer. I wasn't returning to Philadelphia after just thirty seconds of John Paul: I needed more. My grip got a little tighter, and as it did, the pontiff talked some more about John Krol, the cameraman on the side of us. Glancing over, the Swiss guard nearest to me started wincing; a plainclothes officer reached for his pistol holster. Quickly I let go, realizing that I had tempted danger by grasping too hard with the leader of the Catholic church. When the papal audience was over, the leader of the guards lectured me with deep courtesy on the perils of pushing too hard. He received a gracious thank you from me, with my full appreciation of how close I had come to a personally created fiasco. Still, the handclasp had paid off. My host, Archbishop Foley, was pleased: there was enough videotape for a full papal tribute to Cardinal Krol on the air. Krol was thrilled, and as the years went by, during many interviews, he expressed his gratitude.

The cardinal repeatedly recommended that I make a trip to Poland to witness the dying days of the Communist empire. So, in 1986 and again in 1989, I visited Poland. The first visit was an aid mission arranged by Krol and Philadelphia philanthropist Ed Piszek after the Chernobyl nuclear disaster, the second a chance to interview Lech Walesa, the labor leader and democracy crusader, and to watch personally the collapse of Communism. On both trips, doors were opened and opportunities offered because of the man in charge back in Philadelphia.

John Cardinal Krol was controversial at times. His defense of the Palestinian cause in Israel damaged his relationship with my fellow members of the Jewish community. His pro-life crusade, respected by thousands, was disdained by many others. The black community felt that there were too many Catholic churches and schools closing in black neighborhoods. And his prayers and support at Republican national conventions placed him squarely in a conservative corner. But any of his controversies were far outshone by Catholic Charities, which brought aid and comfort to thousands of people in need, mostly in eastern Pennsylvania and, at random, to those overseas who had never heard his name. To this reporter, he was always kind and thoughtful, as when he invited me to dinner at his official residence on Cardinal Drive just off City Line Avenue and blushed, clearly embarrassed, when he realized that he had chosen pork as the main course for the meal.

Catholicism, of course, is not the only potent religious force in Philadelphia, nor was Cardinal Krol the only religious mover and shaker. Leon Sullivan is a man who changed Philadelphia more than almost anyone in his generation. Sullivan was the pastor of North Philadelphia's Zion Baptist Church when he created the first welfare reform program in America, calling it Opportunities Industrialization Centers, or OIC. The idea was clear—train people without jobs to perform well in the workplace. From a small headquarters in Philadelphia, OIC spread worldwide in the late sixties and became a model for the recently legislated welfare-to-work programs today.

Sullivan was a towering figure (he measured six feet, six inches tall) and a great orator. And there was something else about him that created true bonds with people. His eyes were penetrating; when he looked at you, you felt you were the only person in the room. Communicating for Leon Sullivan was personal. His voice was powerful, his emotions rang true to his message of opportunity, and he brought up a whole generation of activist politicians in Philadelphia. Philadelphia's current mayor, John Street, says that, more than anyone, Sullivan's powerful message of learning and working and achieving independence affected Street's own meteoric rise to power. Street was a food vendor who worked his way through college and law school to become president of the City Council and then mayor.

My first encounter with Sullivan was on June 29, 1967, when President Lyndon Johnson paid a visit to Philadelphia. Johnson's motorcade traveled through North Philadelphia. I was in the press entourage, and I thought something was wrong when the line of cars stopped in its tracks. The president stunned the Secret Service by stopping the motorcade and making a surprise visit to the OIC at Nineteenth and Oxford Streets, calling the program "the nation's most effective antipoverty project." LBJ's visit included a private chat with Leon Sullivan. Johnson was one of four presidents who supported OIC with federal monies. The day of the visit was the day of my first conversation with Reverend Sullivan. I asked him about racial tension in America, and he said, "Young man, the answer to easing racial tension is one magnificent four-letter word, jobs."

As the years went by, Sullivan had another calling. Fighting hard to end apartheid in South Africa, he was the author of the Sullivan Principles, which outlined the basis on which American businesses could work with South Africa without violating the rights of the repressed majority in that country. Sullivan was appointed to the General Motors board, and he used his clout to erase bigotry at General Motors and other large companies.

In recent years, Leon Sullivan founded the African–African-American summit, designed to bring American interests closer to those in sub-Saharan Africa. The 1998 summit, held in Accra, Ghana, was attended by over five thousand delegates, including nine heads of state.

It seems that whenever I see Leon Sullivan, he's always pressing hard to find money, resources, and talent to help people who live in desperation and despair. If Congress really wants to reform our welfare system, it should summon Philadelphia's Leon Sullivan, also known affectionately as the Lion of Africa.

My time in Philadelphia encompasses some militant conflagrations over civil rights and basic human decency. Sullivan's rhetoric was as biting as that of many of the leaders of the early civil rights struggle, but his arms were stretched out to bring people together rather than splitting them apart. Inclusion of people and ideas was the Sullivan approach. His pioneering activism, rooted in spirituality and blazing with respect for individuals, set an example that ministers followed gladly for four decades of Philadelphia life.

Ethnic pride coupled with religious fervor makes a powerful and compelling mix, especially in a nation divided sometimes by demagogues and the intolerant. As a Jew, the odds were against me in the beginning, especially since there were no Jewish anchors in Philadelphia in 1969. That changed, and with it, we all discovered the real nature of Philadelphians and their counterparts in South Jersey and Delaware. Despite a community polarized by racial and ethnic tension, Philadelphians appreciate and respect a job well done. Professional sports have provided a buffer against individual hatred, and so has broadcasting. The acceptance of my work, regardless of my faith, was a part of the changing face of Philadelphia life. This was a lesson that some broadcasters, wary of diversity, learned much too late.

Once WFIL TV became successful, an ugly, insidious movement surfaced at the station caused by the fear that my Judaism would somehow be exposed, an irony considering that most everyone in the area knew I was Jewish anyway. So, with good intentions on the outside and fear in their hearts, some executives urged me to work during the Jewish High Holy Days. I rejected that suggestion, explaining to management that working on Jewish holidays is tantamount to treason in the Jewish faith and a betrayal of my own beliefs. Then a secondary problem developed. Should I support Jewish community causes to help those in need? Some said no. I said absolutely: if I could do work for Catholic Relief Services, why should my faith prohibit me from helping the Jewish community or, for that matter, any religious organization?

So despite other people's fears that my identity as a Jew would hurt my career, I set in motion a series of events that would end once and for all the not-so-subtle prejudice in our newsroom. The decision was simple: I would, as I desired, become an advocate of Jewish causes, with the same enthusiasm and energy I brought to all my other pursuits. I would be accepted for who I was or, if the answer was rejection, I would walk away. It never came to that. People here cared little about my religion and more about my credibility. They contradicted the hypocrisy of some broadcasters who believed that "the people" can't handle reality.

There was, however, a time when my spirituality collided head on with my news assignment. On my first trip to Israel, I arrived at the intersection of my personal beliefs and political reality.

I had been dispatched to Israel to cover people's reactions as the Camp David Accords were signed on March 26, 1979. The purpose of the coverage was to gauge the reaction of Philadelphia-area Jews living in Israel. The story was of high interest to the large Jewish population in the three states of our viewing area, and it gave me the opportunity to view the Israel I had grown up with in Hebrew school, the miracle of a nation whose existence is the pride of just about every Jew.

Our journey took us to Yamit, a settlement just below Gaza on what was then Israel's border with Egypt. Yamit was to be bulldozed and given to Egypt, along with the rest of the Sinai desert. The residents were irate, and as we pulled into the community, the smell of burning tires filled the air. Streets were blocked by small demonstrations. It was not pretty. Israel was fiercely divided at the time over the peace process, much as it is today.

Since the five-day assignment was going smoothly, we decided to take a break, settling on a small restaurant in Arab East Jerusalem, a place adjacent to the Rockefeller Gardens. There we entertained a young Philadelphian and his wife. He was a commando, she was pregnant, and both assisted us with our coverage.

The restaurant was called the Dolphin. Small and intimate, the eatery provided respite from hours of work. We talked about our families, our lives, and the food, which was first class. I was on the crème caramel when I heard a "ping," then a second "ping," and then the opening of a door. On sheer adrenalin I yelled out, "Hit the floor!" We did. If we hadn't, we surely would have died. Within a matter of seconds, two hand grenades exploded on the sidewalk and inside the restaurant, shattering glass and sending slivers of metal and nails into the room. Blood trickled down my forehead, but it was from a minor cut. Others were also bleeding from superficial wounds that looked worse than they were. The cameraman, Tom Watson, in an Olympian feat, had high jumped across the room and was hiding behind the bar. The producer, Andrew Fisher, was in a fetal position behind two chairs.

The next few seconds were terrifying. Who did it? Would they be coming in next to finish us off? A floor creaked. I saw two boots—khaki boots—and a man with an Uzi machine gun. He slowly walked in, surveying the diners crouching behind chairs and tables. The man was from the Israeli army, and when it was safe to stand up, we saw a frightening scene. A car outside had been mangled by the blast, and the damage inside was intense. Chairs had been torn to shreds; glass was everywhere. Fisher stood up, astonished, and said, "They won't believe this back home." Today Fisher is a major figure in broadcasting, a top executive at Cox Communications, and we often talk about our close call in Jerusalem. The story behind the violence was simple. The restaurant was co-owned by an Arab and a Jew, a partnership that irritated some of the locals, who had decided to send a message. In a nation of five million people, I was unlucky enough to be sitting in the middle of the only terrorist act committed during the signing of the Camp David agreements. Once again, I had learned that, as a reporter, it's much better to report a story than to be a part of it. And I never got to finish dessert, and I must confess I've never ordered crème caramel again.

Israel has provided vivid memories, to be sure, but none as dramatic as those from a trip to southern Lebanon in 1988. The location was an Israeli Army strongpoint, a hill overlooking a group of villages. Buses pulled up and delivered hundreds of Israeli schoolchildren. For two hours they talked to the soldiers, inspected their weapons, and enjoyed lunch. When they left, I said to my host, General Yorum Yair, "What a great experience, the chance to visit the outpost. The children seemed to get a lot out of it." Yair, a war hero known as Ya Ya in Israel, replied, "This is not for them. It's for the soldiers. I want them to look into their eyes and remember them every time they are dozing off on the surveillance cameras late at night. I want them to remember the faces and think of the consequences if they are not alert, how some terrorist could fire a rocket at their homes and kill them. No, Larry, this wasn't for the kids. This was for the soldiers." Suddenly, my boyhood vision of the brave Israel came to life.

In all, I have made five trips to Israel, including trips to cover the nation's fortieth and fiftieth anniversaries. On the surface, the job of telling the story of the nation's growth and controversies has been exhilarating. Inside, the presence of Israel tugs at my very being, churning up visions of prejudice and pride. Israel is seductive, its cities vibrant with the juices of Judaism and the miracles of modern life. I've always been filled with pride at the accomplishments, the making of the state and the defending of the territory. Disappointment comes along with that pride, though—a feeling of hurt that, along the way, politics has made Israel into a controversial nation. But for what it is and what it represents, Jewish people need to be eternally grateful, because we truly are a minority, and we are among the targeted, even in our nation's school systems.

The locker room at West Miami Junior High was an odd place to be sitting on a bench, crying. I had just come in from the soccer field, where a gym teacher had come up to me, ripped the chain with the Star of David off my neck, and said, "Son, no religious symbols around here, ya hear!" Of course, other students were wearing religious symbols, just not Jewish ones.

Years later, in the civilized adult world of Philadelphia, an executive took me to lunch at the Union League, at the time the most exclusive club in Philadelphia. Eyes turned as I entered the room. Jews rarely went to the Union League in 1969. (Today, Jewish members are welcomed with open arms at the League.) Then, I discovered, the invitation to lunch had been extended for one reason: the kitchen and custodial staff wanted to meet me. Those employees were warm and gracious, but the entire event was one big slap.

They hurt deeply, these moments of prejudicial conduct, and that kind of emotion sticks around for years. When Americans bristle at the anger of minorities, they can't feel the pain of the accumulated indignities suffered over a person's lifetime. They are hard to pull from the outer lining of your character. They make you wonder about your identity. They give you two choices: hide your real being, or stand up for who you are. It is here, in the quest for identity, that Israel comes into play.

Israel stands alone as an emotional refuge for Jews who fear the worst and sometimes find it in the acts of others. Israel remains the most unusual country in the world because of its commitment to serve as the last resort, or first choice, for people living in tyranny.

In April 1989, I covered the most ambitious journey ever devised for a Jewish community. It was called Mission 1000, and as a part of that mission, two planeloads of people flew from our region determined to make a statement—that in the middle of the turmoil on the West Bank, Jews were united in support of the homeland, even those who disagreed with the policies of the government, those who cherished their American freedom to speak out. The trip was sponsored by the Jewish Federation of Philadelphia, led by the late Bob Forman, one of the great community leaders of his time and chief executive of the federation.

The Jewish Federation is the umbrella agency for most Jewish organizations, serving in a similar role to Catholic Charities. Over the years, the organization has been the beneficiary of marvelous leadership and some obstructionist politics. In 1981, I spoke at a testimonial dinner for longtime *Jewish Exponent* journalist Leon Brown. The theme of my address was the subtle anti-Semitism proliferating in our region. My comments were pointed because my concern was deep. The next morning, a leader of the federation called me, wondering if I had gone too far and if the accent on anti-Semitism might escalate the problem. Politely, I told him that his concern was tantamount to a surrender to the forces of evil. Today, Jews—including the federation's leaders—talk freely about the legacy of the Holocaust and the anti-Semitism around us, but there was a time when many leaders preferred to sweep it under the rug.

When I began this journey through the world of broadcasting, I was the first Jewish anchor in Philadelphia. Now there are six. It disturbs me that some of these anchors are still reluctant to support Jewish causes outwardly and actively for fear that their identity would alienate their audience or that support of Judaism could be construed to cloud their credibility on certain stories. My profile has always been high, as has that of Jill Chernikoff, the anchor at WTXF; Dave Frankel at KYW; and Steve Levy at WCAU TV. Others in the business shy away from Jewish community involvement, a sign, perhaps, that after all these years we are still paranoid about who we are.

1991–1992: Death on the Doorstep

If 1968, the year of assassination and revolution, was a turning point for America, then the years 1991 and 1992 marked moments of trauma and dramatic change in Philadelphia and the region. For me, it was a time when the challenge to my career took me to the brink, and new opportunity suddenly unfolded. The region has never been the same. Neither have I.

Frank Rizzo died on July 16, 1991. Donna and I were having lunch out when the beeper went off. As we hurried home, my mind was filled with apprehension. I found out that Rizzo had suffered a heart attack when I called the station. My hands were shaking as I began the drive to WCAU TV, and those tremors were accompanied by mental flashbacks of my times with Frank Rizzo. I thought about the sheer courage of the man and about how far he would have gone if the steel of his public image had been tempered by his real emotions. Rizzo was a softie. Always was. He attended more wakes and funerals than any public offi-

I meet the space age in my first satellite broadcast, from Tel Aviv to Philadelphia, in the spring of 1979. (Photo courtesy of Donna Jarrett-Kane)

I moderate a panel discussion after a performance of 6221, a play about Move. With me, from left to right, are Ramona Africa, playwright Tom Gibbons, police officer James Berghaier, and producer and director Seth Rozin. (Photo courtesy of Ramona Africa)

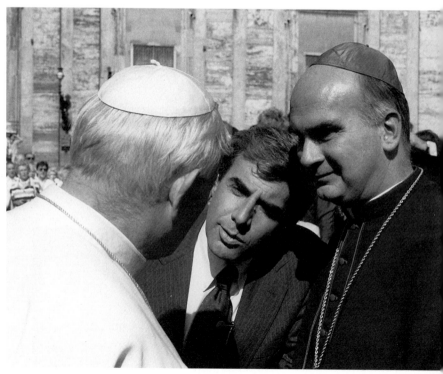

In seat number one at the papal mass on October 13, 1985, I interview Pope John Paul II while Philadelphia-born Archbishop John Foley stands by. (Photo courtesy of Arturo Mari, L'Osservatore Romano)

Shimon Peres, once and future prime minister of Israel, in a casual moment following an interview with me in Jerusalem (Photo courtesy of the Jewish Exponent, *where it first appeared)*

I begin my coverage from Israel on the Mission 1000 project as Philadelphians gather on the tarmac in Tel Aviv in April 1989. (Photo courtesy of the Jewish Exponent, *where it first appeared)*

Philadelphia mayor Frank L. Rizzo and me, following a City Hall press conference. (Photo courtesy of the Philadelphia Inquirer)

Diane Allen, a New Jersey state senator and a veteran anchor who co-anchored with me at WCAU TV. (Photo courtesy of Diane Allen)

In 1996, with future mayor John Street looking on, City Council honors me on my thirtieth anniversary in Philadelphia broadcasting. From left to right are KYW manager Jerry Eaton, future City Council president Anna Verna, me, Councilwoman Joan Krajewski, KYW news director Paul Gluck, and KYW director of communications Joanne Calabria. (Photo courtesy of the City of Philadelphia Records Department)

Here I am on the set of the nation's first prime-time, local news magazine, The Bulletin with Larry Kane, *premiering in July 1993. (Photo courtesy of Liz Wuillermin)*

We take the Bulletin *show on the road for a tinseltown interview with Will Smith. (Photo courtesy of Donna Jarrett-Kane)*

On the set of Will Smith's Fresh Prince *show in Hollywood, I interview Philadelphia music superstars Boyz II Men. (Photo courtesy of Donna Jarrett-Kane)*

Delaware governor Tom Carper, still stunned by the disappearance of his secretary, Anne Marie Fahey, joins me for a live interview at the 1996 Democratic National Convention in Chicago. (Photo courtesy of Margaret M. Cronan)

cial. He told me once, "They work for the city. I gotta be there." Rizzo breathed Philadelphia into his being. Sure, he loved his cronies, but he devoured people on the street with affection, too. In the end, I knew it was he who wanted to be loved.

As I raced to the station, hoping he would survive his heart attack, I thought of his wife (who would tell me over coffee a few weeks later what a magnificent husband he was and, much to my amazement, that she had been his most trusted adviser on everything from law enforcement to the city budget). Then tears welled into my eyes as I thought about knowing him, covering him. I prayed for one more conversation. Even one more angry confrontation would be better than having Frank Rizzo fall silent. I wanted just one more time to hear him chide me for not spit-shining my shoes or tell me, "Kane, you look like shit. Get a haircut." My thoughts turned to his battles, to how he seemed to relish controversy, how he was proud of his beliefs, fearful of enemies, and hidden in the depths of his mind. I thought of his private sulking after failure, of his inability to accept that some people just didn't like his views. But he knew, deep down in his heart, that most people liked him so much that the politics of personality overwhelmed the politics of ideology. Rizzo once said to me, "You guys need me. I'm food for your hunger. Without me, there ain't news in this town." As I drove south on the Roosevelt Boulevard Expressway, my eyes darted to the left and the skyline, to the great mass of row homes in North Philadelphia, and finally to the rich, lush green of Fairmount Park. No one saw Philadelphia like Frank Rizzo did. He bathed in it in his mind, lived its spirit, challenged all of us with his hope, and tested our limits with his bravado. There would never be another like him.

When I arrived on the news set to join the live coverage, I realized even more fully that someone who had been a part of my life for twenty-four years might soon be gone. The fine NBC News correspondent Andrea Mitchell, who fought tooth and nail with Rizzo during her tenure here, would feel a special loss later, she said, as though a powerful force had left the earth. Mitchell was Rizzo's prime media antagonist in the mayoral years, a great reporter with an instinct for the jugular. They chewed each other up and spit each other out, sustaining a war of words that never really ended. She cried when the end came. That afternoon, the end was very close.

The minutes were ticking away when suddenly someone ran in with a piece of paper. The words on the paper had been written in Magic

Marker. They said, "Larry, Rizzo is dead." I pulled myself together and, voice quavering, said, "I have just received word that Frank L. Rizzo, two-term mayor of Philadelphia, has died." I paused, then began a five-minute monologue on his life. The words just flowed, but my voice cracked because I was about to cry. It was the strangest feeling, I thought, as though a member of my family had passed. An era had ended, one that had been a piece of my life for a quarter of a century. And I couldn't forget something he had said during our final interview. "Larry Kane," Rizzo said, "Larry Kane, I made you what you are." He grinned, and so did I. He added, "You couldn't have made it without me." He was wrong about that, but the years would have been boring and staid without the presence of Frank Rizzo. Through his actions and in his conversations, he taught me more about Philadelphia than anyone else did.

After two hours of broadcasting the death of Frank Rizzo, I left the studio, opened the door to the men's room, and cried my eyes out. The rest of the night was no different. The battle to keep myself together during our coverage had almost been a losing one, because it was so tricky and demanding to erase the images from my mind—Rizzo laughing so hard the room shook; Rizzo slapping my back on election night so that I almost fell off the chair; Rizzo, scornful and angry, lecturing me on fairness; Rizzo at riot-torn Bok High School in South Philadelphia protecting black students under assault; Rizzo walking into a room, eyes darting, people mesmerized by the walk and the talk; and Rizzo taking me out on a police patrol to comb the city at night, looking for troublemakers.

His funeral was one of the largest in American municipal history. I covered it from start to finish. As the funeral cortege traveled up Broad Street, the camera shots of the people will always stay with me—the faces of respect and the tears trickling down the cheeks of Philadelphians of all backgrounds, proving once again that people here always respect the real thing. No public official was ever more real than Frank Rizzo. His life, his story, was the most important in my years in Philadelphia.

The seventies was the Rizzo decade, and the nineties brought his end. His is a story of opportunities gained and lost. But in the end his was a story of a real Philadelphian who reflected the dreams of others who couldn't make it out of their neighborhoods. My encounters with Frank Rizzo in the sixties helped shape my views of Philadelphia life and sharpened my learning curve. From the school-board riot in 1967, I gleaned an awareness of the power of his presence, of his potential for controversy, and of his power to do good. Another episode transformed my relationship with Rizzo and, for better or worse, brought me closer to the man and his controversies.

Roxanne Jones was leader of the Welfare Rights Organization, an organization of activists determined to seek a higher quality of public assistance. Roxanne, like many standard-bearers for reform, later took the elective route and became a state senator. Senator Jones died in the mid-nineties, but if she were here, she could tell a story of the siege at the state office building at Broad and Spring Garden Streets that would epitomize the art form of protest at the tail end of the sixties.

Welfare recipients did the unthinkable, taking over control of the big building without violence. They "held" the building for a few days in early 1969, making their point, before negotiations ended the siege. Covering the story was tedious. (Many news stories require long periods of standing, waiting, looking for a clue, eating, drinking coffee, contemplating the future, and hoping for an end.) But the outcome of the building takeover was surprising. Ironically, it became the catalyst for closer contact between me and Police Commissioner Frank L. Rizzo.

The protesters had settled in at a group of offices and were effectively blocking the main entrance. Their organization was flawless. Every few hours a representative would speak to the press in calm tones, explaining the reason for the takeover. Peace was at hand, but Pennsylvania state troopers ringed the building anyway. The biggest challenge for the protesters was securing enough food to subsist, as the troopers blocked the entrance of any foods besides baby formula. All other foods, even milk, were taboo.

In a few days, the welfare rights organizers ran out of story lines, and quiet settled in at the corner of Broad and Spring Garden Streets. That was before the woman with the milk container showed up. She was young and nervous. In her right hand was a gallon container of milk. She walked up to an erect state trooper, who looked to me like a local version of the Queen's palace guard.

A figure in a long black coat who was watching this mini-sideshow waved me over to a car parked on the west side of Broad Street. There, in the front passenger seat, sat the king of cops. Rizzo knew my name and where I worked, but little else. He said, "Mr. Kane, that woman with the milk is going to stare down that state trooper and then give you guys a picture that will make the eleven o'clock news. That's why she's there. You got it, kid?" "Are you sure of that?" I asked. Rizzo said, "Gimme a break. She's here to raise hell. Make a picture. Guaranteed it'll make page one. It's a setup, dummy. I'll bet you lunch that she makes the trooper into a milkman or takes a slug at him." "You got it," I said, "but make it an expensive lunch." He replied, "It's a bet."

The building was state property, so Rizzo, though eager to be called in to help, was just a spectator on the curb with his cadre of lawmen. I strolled back to the entrance. The woman was now seated on the pavement, her legs crossed, her arms still holding the plastic milk container as though it was gold headed to Fort Knox. A half hour later, as news crews and newspaper photographers gathered, the woman stood up and walked slowly toward the state trooper. She said, "Coming through." He said nothing, just stood with his chin up and his eyes staring into space as his tall frame blocked the entrance. Tom Fox, the late and great *Daily News* and *Inquirer* reporter, looked over and said, "She's going to spill the milk all over him, every single drop." I said, "No way." Fox, like Rizzo, had an instinct, a talent for seeing ahead. Rizzo emerged from his car to get a closer look at the show and sauntered up to me. "Get your cameraman ready," he uttered, almost whispering. Moments later the woman said again, "Coming through." The trooper stood firm. The milk carrier took the lid off the container. In one smooth motion, she hurled milk on the front of the trooper's uniform. Then, in a coup de grace, she lifted the container and poured the milk over his head and shoulders. Madame Milk was quickly arrested without incident. The trooper never moved, soaking up the milk in his trousers and shirt, the white stuff creeping down his trooper hat.

The photo made page one in all three city papers, and the scene provided, as the producers would say, "great pictures" for the evening news. Moments after the incident, I ran to a pay phone to call in the story. The radio operation had also asked for a taped report, posing a small dilemma. I was supposed to record the report on the spot, and I needed a stop watch to time it, or at least a watch with a second hand. Glancing into the sidewalk beside me, I saw a young man approaching. I said, "Could I borrow your wristwatch for a minute or two?" He agreed, eager to help, interested in what I was doing. After the report was phoned in, he said, "Hey, what do you think of that guy Rizzo?" I replied, "Why?" He responded, "Just was curious, you know." I said, "He's very interesting and seems to have a real aura of leadership about him. Seems like the real thing." He said, "Believe me, he is." Then he added, "By the way, people call me Frannie, but my real name is Frank

Rizzo, Jr." Today, Frank Rizzo, Jr., is a popular city councilman at large, a Republican who is highly respected by his colleagues. Often we reminisce about the night of the milk attack and his testing me with that question.

Since I had lost the bet over spilled milk, I called Frank Rizzo's office to pay up. Lunch was at the old Ben Franklin Hotel on Chestnut Street, and it was there that we got to know each other well, so well that he invited me to patrol with him from time to time on the nights when Car One was stalking the streets of the city.

Car One was the code name for the black, unmarked Ford sedan, driven by officer John Devine, that transported Rizzo through the heart of the city. I sat in the back, watching Rizzo riding shotgun with a nightstick by his side and a pistol concealed in a side holster beneath his suit. It was usually a Friday night when I rode with him, and on the police radio were the sounds of police life, including quite often the most dreaded call from a dispatcher: "Stand by—Twenty-sixth and Dauphin, assist officer, police by radio." An "assist officer" request means that a cop needs help instantly. An "assist officer, civilian by phone" is the most feared message, usually meaning that the officer has been incapacitated or is in some other deep trouble, making it necessary for a civilian to place the call.

One Friday night, Car One—my moving classroom—showed up in West Philadelphia, where an officer had called for help. A large man with a knife was holding the officer and threatening to hurt him. Without hesitation, Frank Rizzo walked calmly through the crowd of officers. He walked right up to the perp, as they called the perpetrator. "I'm Frank Rizzo, police commissioner of Philadelphia," he said. "Drop the knife, or I'll rip you to pieces." The perp, a robbery suspect, looked at Rizzo, dropped his head, and released his grasp, letting the knife and the officer go. By his mere hulking, threatening presence, the top badge had cleaned up a crime scene. It was arrest by fear, plain and simple.

The master of Car One was not a grandstanding egotist, although some observers would disagree with me on that. But he was a stickler for military-style precision and rules. Late one night, Car One was moving west on Cottman Avenue in Northeast Philadelphia when Rizzo spotted a red police car (the color of the city's cars then) parked in the lot of the Country Club Diner, a popular spot just a block from Northeast High School that was famed for its cheesecake. There was no one inside the car. Rizzo was curious. His chin up, his chest protruding in that suck-in-the-stomach pose he often took on, he went inside with me beside him, and we were treated to a quiet booth. Alongside was another booth, where two police officers were having steak and eggs. The officers' faces flushed, turning the color of a heart beating fast and a mind in the hold of fear and paralysis. It is standard practice that police officers, especially the two-man patrols of that day, never leave a car unmanned. Rizzo glared at the officers, not saying a word, just piercing them like a dagger with his eyes. We had some coffee and pastry. The check came. Rizzo walked over to their booth, picked up their check, and said, "If I ever catch you like that again, you'll be suspended, terminated, never heard from again." He paid both bills and, grinning, walked out to Car One, where, in perfect form and according to regulations, Officer Devine was sitting and listening to the police radio.

Perhaps the most interesting part of seeing Rizzo up close was learning about the operations of a nine-thousand-man police department. But in a reporter's life, the small, special moments provide the most glistening memories. The memory of one cold winter day when I traveled with Rizzo sticks and sticks hard. We were somewhere in Olney, in the northern section of the city. The car was cruising along rather quietly when we spotted two girls, about eleven or twelve years old, walking along the street with their arms wrapped around each other for warmth. Their coats were ripped, relics of an earlier life, hardly the stuff to keep you warm. Rizzo said, "Follow them." The path took us to a small row home, dilapidated to say the least. Rizzo emerged from the car, passed the girls on the steps, and rang the doorbell. When the mother answered, he said, "Listen, do me a favor. Here's a couple hundred bucks. Would you buy them some winter coats, please? I'm Frank Rizzo. Give me a call at this number. I don't want them to freeze." She said, "Thank you, sir." The gesture was followed by a phone call and a district car surveillance that confirmed that the sisters were indeed wearing new coats. Rizzo said to me, "If you tell anyone about that, I'll kill ya."

Rizzo had his bad moments, his fits of anger and discord, but the untold stories of his life tell you more about Car One's passenger than any public blunders. For example, as commissioner and mayor, he had an obsession with living things. His favorite book was Rachel Carson's *Silent Spring*. He stunned the community when he waded into the shallow waters of the Schuylkill River along with environmentalists to save Canadian geese threatened by an oil spill.

But first and foremost, Rizzo was a cop, which made his decision in January 1971 bittersweet. It was then that Frank Rizzo traded in Car One for a privately owned vehicle. He left the Roundhouse, the police headquarters, resigning so that he could run for mayor of Philadelphia. During his transition from private citizen to mayor, he held court at an office on Walnut Street, greeting supporters, doling out jobs, framing his administration. When my father, Jack Kane, was visiting from Miami, he asked to meet Rizzo. My father-in-law, Irv Jarrett, joined us.

Rizzo stood up and greeted my father and Irv with that powerful handshake that once, at an awards dinner, sent Donna's engagement ring hard into the flesh of one of her fingers. After the greetings, Rizzo inquired about his visitors. "What do you do, Jack?" he asked. My dad said, "I'm an electrical contractor." Then Rizzo looked at my father-in-law and said, "Whattayoudo for a living?" Irv replied, "I have a women's clothing store on Point Breeze Avenue." The mayor smiled and, with that big Santa Claus grin, looked him in the eye and said, "Irv, tough neighborhood. You have to be careful. So here's what I want you to do. Next Saturday, meet me at the Police Academy and we're goin' to teach you how to fire a gun."

Irv replied, "I don't want a gun." Rizzo countered, "You have to have one. And here's what you do. You hide the loaded gun in a drawer. When the thugs come in, you give 'em everything you got, all the money, everything. Then, Irv, when they turn around to walk out, you grab the gun and shoot 'em in the back, shoot them dead. That's what I call law and order." My dad, an avid marksman, walked away duly impressed.

The election of Frank L. Rizzo in November 1971 was a turning point in Philadelphia history. Rizzo was the first mayor to represent the interests of middle- and lower-income Philadelphians who didn't have the economic power to move to the suburbs. His rise to power was a holding action for them. Rizzo viewed it as his calling to preserve the neighborhoods—those in North, Northeast, and South Philadelphia that suffered from abandoned housing, severe unemployment, and neglect from government. Rizzo also used law and order as a political weapon, and his enemies equated law and order with racism. But his election was clearly a victory for the individuals of all races and backgrounds who wanted to keep Philadelphia neighborhoods vibrant. Rizzo, in the seventies, provided two strengths through government: clean streets and safe streets. He did for the neighborhoods in the seventies what Ed Rendell did for Center City in the nineties. Despite that, the accomplishments of the Rizzo administration were often overshadowed by Rizzo himself. His accomplishments bear a closer look.

One of those accomplishments changed the region forever. When Rizzo proposed a tunnel linking Reading Terminal on Market Street with Suburban Station, the idea was lambasted as a boondoggle designed to create nothing but thousands of construction jobs. That it did. But the tunnel also linked every rail line in the area together. Soon, there was no place in the five-county Pennsylvania region that you couldn't reach by rail. It was a masterpiece of urban planning.

Frank Rizzo was a genuine person, saying in public what many politicians only thought in private. He was a rebel with a cause, a man who shunned travel and vacations, preferring to stay in Philadelphia. Rizzo hated flying, but he loved driving through the streets of his city at night, checking on the police, looking for uncleaned streets, enjoying the sights and smells of the city he adored. He was often the target of writers who resented his appeal and viewed him as a right-wing fanatic. Rizzo was neither right wing nor fanatical, but he was bigger than life. More than anything, he was the most loyal politician I've ever met.

Mayor Rizzo was a reporter's delight, providing quotes and headlines sure to become the talk of the town. From 1968 to his death in 1991, I had a unique relationship with Rizzo, a relationship that was rewarding, challenging, and at times troublesome. Rizzo once said to me, "Watch out, Kane. People think I've got you in my hip pocket. They'll make trouble for you, because of me." He was right. Over the years, newspaper writers and others blasted me for alleged bias. In truth, Rizzo and I had a great and honest relationship. He wanted and expected positive coverage, but he didn't always get it. He knew I would report the news as I saw it, and I received many late-night phone calls from an angry Rizzo, who would say such choice things as, "Kane, I'm goin' to rip you a new asshole tonight." This would be followed by a ranting, screaming attack, which I basically ignored—unless, of course, there was merit to the criticism. I learned early on that, when it came to covering Frank Rizzo, you couldn't win. His friends thought you were too harsh, and his enemies condemned you for being a jellyfish. Rizzo was a man I respected and challenged, but there was always the insinuation that we were lobbing softballs at him. This was bogus, but considering what happened on election night 1971, I can understand why people felt that way.

Throughout the long campaign of 1971, his first bid for mayor, Frank Rizzo made and repeated a promise: he would appear first with me on election night. Realizing the pressures of a hectic election environment, there were doubts in the newsroom that Rizzo would really make this happen. First, of course, he had to win, and as election night approached, my anxiety rose. This was a decisive night in Philadelphia life: it was important that our coverage be the best. I told Rizzo to be in our studios for an appearance at 11:01 sharp.

The returns trickled in slowly at first, but by 9:20 P.M. there was no doubt that Frank Rizzo would become the mayor. He was well ahead of the popular Republican, Thacher Longstreth. At 10:00 P.M., Rizzo appeared in the ballroom of the Bellevue Stratford Hotel and declared victory. All the stations carried his speech live, which made what he was about to say even more remarkable. "I want to let you know that I'll return here for the party later tonight," he said, "but I promised Larry Kane that I would join him on *Action News* at 11:01 sharp for a live interview." My jaw dropped. There he was, on all the stations, letting everyone know he was going to be with us. The mind could envision the reactions of other news directors, who were probably livid that he had used their broadcast to promote ours. Up next was the challenge of getting him to the station.

At 10:53 P.M., News Director Mel Kampmann was in the place called panicville, a place where you're sure things are going to blow up. Paranoia is the heart of a news director's intuition. Peering into his office, I said, "Mel, don't worry. He'll show up." But as I descended the stairs to the studio, my feet were shaky. By 10:59, with ninety seconds to go until broadcast, hope seemed lost. The theme music started. I said, "Good evening." Then the big wide doors opened, photographers and aides ran in, and after them came Rizzo, big as a tiger, getting set to make a run for it. After tripping over a studio wire, Rizzo got up and emerged onto the set, whispering to me, "That fucking expressway—goddamit." At that moment, I introduced the mayor-elect, and we scored an enviable coup on a big story.

Unfortunately, members of the media and Rizzo's enemies saw his appearance as further proof that Rizzo and I were a team, in cahoots, part of some conspiracy to portray him in the best light. Of course, few will remember that, on the morning after Wilson Goode's victory in 1983, I had a breakfast exclusive with the entire Goode family, or that Bob Casey gave me the first interview after his election as governor in

1986. Getting exclusives was the name of my game, and it was upsetting that other reporters used my ability to get information from Rizzo as an excuse to portray my work as biased.

Frank Rizzo had a candid and warm relationship with me, but sometimes the candor overwhelmed the warmth. After a live special on Philadelphia's juvenile gang problem during which Rizzo offered some odd solutions, the mayor dressed me down in the station's hallway and wouldn't return my calls for weeks. Later, when we had made peace again, I reminded him, "Mayor, it was not I who said on TV that all the gang members should be locked inside JFK Stadium and allowed to fight it out with knives and guns, or that people should buy baseball bats to threaten the gang members." I continued, "You said it, didn't you?" But Rizzo, angry at himself for his usual "being Frank" frank talk, blamed me for the program. In reality, the broadcast was a straightforward assessment of the problem. Rizzo was disappointed at his performance and took it out on me.

As the Rizzo years began, the TV stations and newspapers had a field day covering Rizzo. His pledge to improve city services was fulfilled, and he added manpower to the police department. Philadelphia felt safe. And the media felt assured that, from Frank Rizzo, there would always be a great quote. A sampling: On law and order, "I'm gonna make Attila the Hun look like a faggot." On a convicted killer, "Put him in the chair, and I'll pull the switch." Those were the extremes, but, extreme or not, most of what Rizzo said rang true in the minds of many Philadelphians, especially his comments about criminals and con artists paying the price. Rizzo also delighted some people with his outrage and sense of humor. After his hemorrhoid surgery, he appeared at a news conference dressed only in a bathrobe and chided the reporters, "You guys have been trying to get me in the rear for years. Like I said, you're all a pain in the ass."

Rizzo's enemies salivated the day he flunked a lie detector test loaded with questions about deal-making with the Democratic city chairman, Pete Camiel. A few days later, Rizzo called, as he was prone to do. He vented. He raged. He said, "Larry Kane, I told the truth. Till the day I die, I'll know that I told the truth. It was rigged." For years, Rizzo denied that he lied. And that episode, coupled with a burgeoning city budget, failed to dampen his popularity.

In 1975, Rizzo defeated Independent Charles Bowser for a second term as mayor. Republican Tom Foglietta, now U.S. ambassador to Italy, finished third. On the night before his victory, I paid a visit to Rizzo's room at Hahnemann Hospital. A few weeks earlier, he had broken his hip at the scene of a huge refinery fire when his bodyguard, Tony Fulwood, fell on top of him. Rizzo looked like a wounded puppy, but he basked in victory and hoped he could be mayor for life. Those hopes were dimmed when a charter change that would have allowed unlimited mayoral terms was soundly defeated in 1978.

People have asked me for years what Frank L. Rizzo was really like. I've said a lot above, but there's always more to tell. The man who ran three times for mayor in the eighties and nineties was in love with power and the city. Privately, he was a sensitive man who acted as a mentor to many young politicians, belying the image of the arbitrary disciplinarian that the press created for him. Loyalty was the nerve center of his own morality, but it had to work both ways. He was leery of supporters who wavered and suspect of hangers-on. As far as race was concerned, I never heard Rizzo say a negative word about people of color, and these ears heard a lot of negative words from Rizzo. In person, Rizzo was Mr. Charisma. Even the people who hated his guts walked away feeling special. If he had one great failing, it was his failure to surround himself with more men and women of independent views. For a long while, Rizzo was right for the time, but his tenure was over when the times changed.

Rizzo's family was central to his life. He loved, respected, and feared his wife, Carmella. His daughter, Joanna, and son, Frank, Jr. (Frannie), were the loves of his life. His brother Joe was appointed fire commissioner, a mild form of nepotism compared to JFK's appointment of his brother Robert as attorney general of the United States. Today, Joe remains one of the most popular and respected members of the Rizzo family.

After leaving office following his two-term limit, Frank Rizzo continued to be a major force in Philadelphia, quietly pulling strings in the police department and eventually hosting his own radio show, a daily dose of the world according to Rizzo—law and order, triumph over evil, and love for Philadelphia. In his final run for mayor in 1991, he was victorious in the GOP primary. His heart was in the battle ahead, but it gave out before he had a chance to take on Ed Rendell in November.

Rizzo's death was not the first shocker of 1991 for me. April 4, 1991, was a sunny spring day. My friend Al Friedman and I were playing a few holes of golf at the Twining Valley Golf Club, a public course run by the Reillys, a famous family of golf professionals. Around noon-time, my heart started pounding. It was one of those many times when I sensed that something big was happening. As we drove home, I turned on the radio and heard the report that two aircraft had collided in midair in Merion with debris crashing to the ground of the Merion Elementary School. My foot got heavier on the gas pedal. I dropped Al off and raced home, where I grabbed a tie and my shaving stuff and drove quickly to the station. There, on the set and on the air, my unscripted words told the story. "John Heinz," I said, "has died, along with the copilots of his small aircraft, two crew members of the helicopter, and two first-grade girls on the ground." The collision between the aircraft and the heli-copter had scarred seven families, and soon it would change the politi-cal landscape in Pennsylvania.

Senator Heinz had been an amazing man, a growing force in the U.S. Senate who was determined to make his mark in spite of his bil-lionaire status. Heinz could have taken the easy road and run the fam-ily business, but he enjoyed the concept of public service. Privately, he was aloof and sometimes hard to reach, but there was no question about his zeal for serving the needs of his constituents. His final election in 1988 to a third term had been an illustration of power. His opponent, Allegheny County coroner Cyril Wecht, was running at the behest of desperate Democrats who were empty-handed in this statewide elec-tion. I moderated their only debate and, for the first time, I saw the only Achilles heel of the Heinz personality—his wealth.

Wecht lobbed one cheap shot after another at Heinz about his inherited wealth, and Heinz began to sweat, his lips pursing in anger. Finally, scowling, Wecht said, "When you're born with a silver spoon, it's easy not to understand the needs of people." Heinz did not directly respond, but from that point on, his voice was halting, his delivery hes-itant. Cyril Wecht had gotten to the most popular political personality in Pennsylvania. That was the first and only time I saw anger on the face of John Heinz, the Republican who defied party labels and who went on to hand the spirited Mr. Wecht a humiliating defeat in November. Heinz won by a million votes, a Pennsylvania record. His tragic death brought the appointment of Harris Wofford to the U.S. Senate.

In a year of political earthquakes came another aftershock of epic proportions. William Gray was one of my favorite politicians. Soft-spoken but cunning, he was always accessible and entertainingly quotable. His was a career of success—he had started out a minister, then become a Democratic congressman and House majority whip. He was on track to become Speaker of the House. In June 1991, he was the highest-ranking elected African American in the U.S. government.

Almost two years earlier, fireworks had exploded for Bill Gray. CBS News reported that Gray was the target of a federal corruption investigation. "High-level" Justice Department sources were quoted. Gray was shattered. I decided to work the story hard, making daily phone calls to Gray and his press chief, Jerome Mondesire, and to my sources at the Justice Department. There were reports that the so-called investigation was a vendetta by U.S. Attorney General Dick Thornburgh, a longtime political enemy of Gray's. Information was slow in coming out, but I made calls daily for two weeks. Then, on a hot summer night, I received a tip that the Justice Department was ready to back away. Sure enough, through Gray and my Justice Department sources, we confirmed that there was no criminal investigation of Bill Gray. The story was so big we broke into prime-time coverage. The next day, CBS News ran an item saying Gray had not been a target of unfair investigation. But for years I've wondered what happened there and whether the media was manipulated to target an innocent man.

With Congressman Gray fully cleared, it was even more of a shock to learn of his resignation in June 1991 to become head of the United Negro College Fund. Since that time, Gray has served with distinction, joined corporate boards, and refrained from all politics. I don't know why this talented man gave up his position of power, but his exit once again changed the political power game. Lucien Blackwell was elected to Congress to fill Gray's position, only to be defeated by young state lawmaker Chakah Fattah months later.

Nineteen ninety-one was a year of dramatic change. The Blue Route Interstate (476) and Vine Street Expressway opened. Suddenly, getting there was easier. The long-awaited Pennsylvania Convention Center opened, prompting a boom in new hotels. Buddy Ryan was fired as coach of the Eagles, a sad note to sports fans who enjoyed his blustery temperament. It was also a year of tragedy for the people who protect us. On the evening of February 23 and into the morning of February 24, a twelve-alarm fire ravaged the One Meridian Plaza building, an office building directly across from City Hall. Three firefighters—Captain David Holcombe, Phyllis McAllister, and James A. Chappell—died of smoke inhalation. The fire struck just as the ground war began in the Persian Gulf. Throughout the year, it seemed the earth was rumbling all around us, with the news flashing in bursts of progress and tragedy. When it was over, Philadelphia and the region were changed forever. So was my career.

When Ed Rendell took the oath of office in 1992, the new mayor launched a broad initiative to get Philadelphia on its feet. It was an exciting prospect—a presidential election and a new Philadelphia administration in the same year. I was looking forward to covering the developments. As the year got underway, I had no idea it would be my last at WCAU TV.

The troubles began in December 1990. Eugene Lothery had been general manager for about a year. Lothery came from CBS, where he had served as a radio manager, corporate vice president, and adviser. He was a tall and handsome man who looked younger than his forty-nine years, a well-dressed and smooth executive who traveled with so many ties that he had a special traveling bag for them. If Gene Lothery had needed an extra job, *GQ* would have hired him in a nanosecond.

Lothery had been wary of me from the beginning. The reason is still unclear, but he appeared to be uneasy about my leadership role at the station. True, I had been advising general managers and putting out fires for years, but there is a difference between influence and power. I had influence; Gene Lothery had power. I was and continue to be an outspoken broadcaster, but I have never threatened anyone. Nevertheless, for the first eleven months of 1990, our relationship was polite and cordial. That was before December 4.

Returning from a street assignment, I arrived in Lothery's office to offer some ideas about coverage of the pending war in the Persian Gulf. I talked, he listened, and then, without warning, he started screaming. "I don't give a shit who you are," he yelled. "Stop trying to kick sand. I'm the boss here, you little piece of shit. Don't patronize me, got it?" Then he got up from his chair, screaming something unintelligible and looking physically menacing. His temper had become a legend in the building by then, but I never expected him to try to verbally rip me apart. Finally, he went to his office door, opened it, and—glaring again—said, "Get out."

The shock of realizing that I was working for a person who was out of control set in as I arrived in the news director's office and went into emotional meltdown. The news director, Paul Gluck, was comforting to me and angry about the incident, but it didn't help me much. I was hurting badly. After I had cooled off a bit, Station Manager Carl

Wenhold (the number two manager) offered to drive me home. Wenhold was a tough former Marine who was the financial genius at the CBS TV Stations. On the way home, he tried to calm me down. It was an act of human kindness on his part to get me home, one I will never forget. A month later, Carl Wenhold was fired without cause.

Through 1991, Lothery and I rarely talked, but his actions spoke louder than words. One Friday in April, Lothery ordered News Director Drew Berry to end my "Political Notebook," a fifteen-year staple in Philadelphia television news that looked candidly at the inside of politics. More stories on politics were broken during the "Political Notebook" than anywhere else in Philadelphia TV. But Lothery cut it off, realizing that this would stab my creative heart. I was told about the decision the day before our daughter Alexandra's bat mitzvah. Lothery's timing and his mind-screwing ability were perfect.

When all the big stories erupted in 1991, News Director Berry had relied heavily on my expertise. Nevertheless, he had two jobs—cover the news and, on Lothery's orders, make my daily life miserable. That he tried to achieve, but Drew Berry did a bad job of playing with my head. First of all, he liked me. Second, evil wasn't in his nature.

It was a difficult time, but I got help. At home, Donna was a rock of support. I also received great moral support from my two co-anchors, Diane Allen and Jane Robelot. Ironically, their own fortunes were intertwined. Allen, a broadcast veteran, was replaced by Robelot on the eleven o'clock program. After losing the show and largely being ignored in the newsroom, Allen filed a complaint with the federal government, charging age bias, among other things. After proving retaliation against her by the Lothery regime, she walked out of the station a much richer woman three years later. Robelot, a sensitive woman and a Lothery favorite, became a close newsroom friend of mine and lived daily with my trials and tribulations. I owe them both deep gratitude for keeping me sane on the job. After her stint at WCAU TV, Robelot anchored CBS's *This Morning* for two years and is now working in Atlanta. Allen is a popular state senator in New Jersey, with some politicos predicting a future run for governor.

In April 1992, Alfred Geller, my professional representative, and I sat in a private room at the 21 Club in New York with Lothery's boss, Johnathan Rodgers, president of the CBS TV Stations. Rodgers completely shrugged off the behavior of his Philadelphia general manager. In a three-hour conversation, he blamed most of my problems on my relationship ten years earlier with Rodgers' good friend Jay Feldman, the general manager during the Mayor Bill Green episode. Feldman was the man who had pushed for the story to be broadcast and then, conveniently, let me take the public hits. Feldman was bitter about his firing and blamed me. He poisoned Johnathan Rodgers' mind, and by the time we met, it was obvious that Johnathan Rodgers was not interested in keeping peace at WCAU TV.

The final straw came one night in June 1992. Lothery had Drew Berry deliver a letter to me advising, in effect, that in return for a contract extension, he wanted my salary lowered. The letter was delivered moments before I was to emcee a gala dinner inaugurating the new Picasso exhibit at the Philadelphia Museum of Art, where Lothery and I would share master-of-ceremony duties. It was an intentionally cruel move, and I knew it. The following day, I called Rodgers and asked for help. His reply: "I don't care what happens. I don't care if you work for us or not." Three days later Donna and I drove to the upstate New York home of Alfred Geller, my representative and adviser. Without any guaranteed job at another station, I made the decision to leave WCAU.

Paul Gluck, the news director, had opted to leave before I made this decision. Gluck was disturbed over my encounter with Lothery, but the main reason for his sudden resignation never came out. Perhaps it was because Gluck was not ready to execute Lothery's plans to fire much of the staff. Independent and angry, Gluck resigned and showed up two weeks later at KYW TV. Would I follow him some day? The thought of jumping to another station was not a pleasant one until I met Jonathan Klein, the general manager of KYW, in a secret lunch at the Mandarin Garden restaurant in the suburb of Willow Grove. That was the beginning of a series of contacts and calls by negotiator Geller that resulted in an agreement that I would join KYW to anchor and produce a prime-time news magazine. I was nervous, but in mid-November 1992, the *Daily News* headline read, "KANE MUTINY." The die was cast: I was headed to my third Philadelphia station, becoming the only lead anchor in America to work at all three major network operations in a major market.

Over time, I've realized what lay behind the Lothery saga. Lothery's anger and unkind behavior, of course, was one factor. But my bitterness over that disappeared in a few months. The real problem lay within the corporate structure: the lack of courage and morality on the part of the leadership during the crisis. Johnathan Rodgers remained invisible. Howard Stringer, the CBS network chief, stood silent. And despite letters and appeals, Lawrence Tisch, then CEO of CBS, offered nothing to lessen the conflict. Months earlier, in 1992, I had attended the wedding of Tisch's son Andy. Despite that and a heartfelt letter to Tisch, his only reaction to the difficulties was silence. In broadcasting, as in all businesses, people will go to excess and abuse their power, but only if they are not held accountable. Executives who operate with total autonomy, without having to answer for their actions, become dangerous people. The people who let them run amok share the responsibility for their abuses.

At the end of 1992, my life had become as turbulent as Philadelphia politics. But that all changed when I headed downtown to Fifth and Market Streets, the headquarters of KYW TV, where my career would flourish in the shadow of the Liberty Bell.

Fifth and Market

On January 3, 1993, I finished my version of the trifecta, the gambling phenomenon of hitting all three numbers. I'd worked at Channels 6 and 10, and now I was beginning at 3. Walking into KYW TV was an unusual feeling because I had never been there before, but the welcome there was warm and open. Working in Center City was also special, giving me a chance to enjoy the combination of historic and modern architecture and to celebrate the access to the city's attractions, along with the bustle and the high-energy people on the streets.

Most people who've been at Channel 3 will tell you that KYW TV has the most pleasant working environment of any station in Philadelphia. Although its success had been spotty to that date, the station is known to have the closest thing to a family feeling in Philadelphia broadcasting.

My release by WCAU TV prohibited me from being an anchor for six months, so KYW assigned me the work I love best—reporting. Within days, I was off to Washington for the swearing-in of the new Congress and the inauguration of Bill Clinton. What a joy it was to be back on the street and reporting.

Two months later, I was on my way to Los Angeles for the second trial of the officers in the Rodney King episode. Since Willie Williams, former top cop in Philadelphia, was now running the Los Angeles Police Department (LAPD), the trial was a natural story for us. I spent a tense week in Los Angeles awaiting the verdict, a week that provided me a clear glimpse of the vagaries of broadcast journalism in the nineties.

The Los Angeles assignment was loaded with danger. A year after the big riots, the people of Los Angeles were buying firearms at an alarming rate for fear that another riot would erupt if the defendants were declared innocent again. The situation was so bad that, on each day of deliberation, many workers were sent home early, just in case. Mass paranoia had enveloped Los Angeles County.

On Good Friday 1993, the federal judge called a recess. To take advantage of the recess, a special event was scheduled for Good Friday morning at the West Angeles Evangelical Church of God, where the entire community would rally for calm and peace. The Los Angeles media had been informed of the event through regular channels. I was informed the night before by Willie Williams.

Our car pulled up to the church in time to make the big prayer breakfast. The crowd was extraordinary in scope: it included the mayor of Los Angeles, the police chief, the governor of California, the archbishop, rabbis, movie stars the likes of Jane Fonda and Denzel Washington, representatives of every ethnic group in the area. A message was being sent in a big way: peace would be kept because of the positive energy of the people. That message was obviously important, but there was still a problem. The only TV crew covering the rally was from KYW TV in Philadelphia. The story would be broadcast three thousand miles away, hardly the stuff of peacekeeping in Los Angeles.

That night, my lead story from the federal courthouse in Los Angeles was about the peace rally held at the church. During the report, I mentioned the failure of the L.A. stations to cover the event. They were so focused on the potential for violence that they had blown an opportunity to be of service to their community. After the broadcast, dispatched via satellite, producers from local stations begged us for the tape of the prayer breakfast. We gave copies away freely. After all, it was important that the local stations let the community know the extent of the movement away from violence.

What I witnessed in Los Angeles that day was a total disregard by the local electronic media for genuine public service. The L.A. reporters were fascinated with the culture of violence—bars on the windows, padlocked front doors, firearms training. They wouldn't give peace a chance. Our field producer, Kevin Harry, was dumbfounded. "Why," he asked, "would anybody blow off a story that is so important?"

The episode in Los Angeles was a picture postcard of what would happen to local TV in the nineties. Suddenly journalism was turning sour, and Philadelphia would feel it close up. When KYW and WCAU switched ownership in 1995, the new WCAU, known as NBC 10, became infamous for the term "breaking news," code words for frightening the viewer. When was "breaking news" really breaking, and when was it just a stunt to give an impression of aggressive reporting? Stations WPVI and our own KYW resisted the temptation to do copycat television, but occasionally we fell into the same trap. In the nineties, it was apparent from ratings and talk on the street that alarmist journalism was being rejected by viewers.

When I returned to Philadelphia from Los Angeles, the first order of business was assembling a team for the *Bulletin*, the new prime-time magazine I would host. Along with News Director Scott Herman and Executive Editor Paul Gluck, I searched hard for a winning format and a winning producer.

"The Bulletin"

The sun was shining brightly through the picture windows of Founders Restaurant atop the Bellevue Hotel in Center City Philadelphia when I asked the question and heard the words. I asked my interviewee, "Did you have uh . . . uh . . . you know . . . were you fulfilled?" She said, "Larry, it was wonderful. Everything came together. It was all worthwhile." Her reference was to her first sexual union after sex change surgery.

For a man who has grilled politicians and personalities, that was a tough question to ask. I gulped at the answer. The interview subject was Rachel Harlow, once a teenage boy in South Philadelphia, now a gorgeous woman. Harlow had never felt comfortable being a boy, and eventually he had a sex change operation. When Harlow became a woman in the seventies, she dominated the Philadelphia social scene with her beauty and grace. She opened a nightclub, and she became the stuff of legends. Harlow claimed that her first lover was the late city councilman Jack Kelly, Olympic hero and brother of Princess Grace.

Unfortunately, Kelly, an Olympic rowing champion, was not around to challenge Harlow's story. He died of a heart attack while jogging in 1986. Friends of Kelly dispute Harlow's claim, saying only that the two were close friends. Harlow's life was all glamour, but it included financial trouble, a divorce, and a return to work as a cosmetics specialist. Hers was a great Philadelphia story. My interview with Rachel Harlow was one of the first on the new program, the *Bulletin*. The program's name had been recommended by KYW general manager Tony Vincequerra. The actual *Bulletin* newspaper, once a staple of Philadelphia journalism, had folded in the early eighties, and Vincequerra felt the name was appropriate for a news program. Others in the station argued that, if the show was canceled, the press would say, "The *Bulletin* Dies Again." Their argument was prophetic, because in February 1996, the *Bulletin* died again. The cancellation came because Westinghouse, the owner of KYW, had purchased CBS. They felt it was inappropriate for a CBS-Westinghouse station to preempt its own network's prime-time programming. The *Bulletin* had pre-empted NBC programming, but with the corporate change, a prime-time slot was out of the question. Prior to the purchase of the network, KYW was an NBC affiliate. Now it was wholly owned by CBS.

During its life—104 shows over thirty-two months—the *Bulletin* set new standards for local broadcasting. The program was a home-grown hour based solely on the Philadelphia region. It gave me a new format—our average story length was much longer, about ten to twelve minutes—as well as a chance to show a more personal side. Even more, the program provided exposure to some of the most interesting people of our time, along with special moments.

Donald Trump was one of those moments. He always is. In his New York offices, we talked about his battle against a woman who refused to give up her tiny home near a big Trump casino in Atlantic City. The interview was getting kind of hot and heavy when the lights went out in the room. That was odd, because the rest of the floor was all lit up. Trump told an aide, "Hey, check that out, will you?" Minutes later, KYW cameraman Jim Spering came back with the real story: somebody had pulled the plug in the fuse box to get Trump to his next appointment. What a creative way to end an interview.

The interview with the late Gene Hart, voice of the Flyers hockey team, was a seemingly endless treat. We sat in the empty Spectrum arena while Hart told stories about his work on the stage and at the opera, his stint calling horse races, and finally, his role as the voice of the Flyers. The interview went on for two hours, but I could have listened to the man waxing poetic about the joy of life forever, especially about his first meeting with his wife, one of the riders of the famed "diving horses" in Atlantic City.

The trip to Bobby Rydell's house in Gladwynne was a trip down memory lane. Like me, Rydell had remained in this area for many years, raising a family and enjoying a real life with his high-school sweetheart. No controversy from Bobby Rydell, just a warmth that beamed right through the TV screen. Still a national star, Rydell had sustained the South Philly values that made him a star.

The interview with Jay Smith was a different story. Smith was the Upper Merion High School principal who was sent to death row in the early eighties for murdering teacher Susan Reinert and her two children. He was a free man in 1995, liberated by the courts because of prosecutorial misconduct. The location of the interview was a Center City law office. The interview was eerie. Smith had difficulty answering questions about the murders, his burglary of a store in the late seventies, and the disappearance of his own family members. His voice was halting, his hands shaking, when I asked him if he killed the Reinerts. His denial was less than convincing, but his willingness to speak out was unusual. To this day, the Jay Smith story haunts me. Was I talking to a killer or to an eccentric man whose odd behavior was the perfect setup for a framing?

Perhaps the most unusual *Bulletin* interview was the profile on Lenny Dykstra, the hard-living, tobacco-chewing Phillies centerfielder. Dykstra had agreed to the interview during spring training in Clearwater in 1994, and I could never have imagined what he would do.

He and I sat in folding chairs on the Phillies' practice field. Cameraman Jim Spering was ready to go. Dykstra had turned up shirtless. After we shook hands, he lobbed a large load of tobacco juice from his mouth to the ground, but the juice fell instead on my brand new Adidas sneakers—not a pretty sight. He said, "Hey man, sorry." I asked him to put on a shirt. He replied, "Why? Just put the damn microphone on my chest, and attach it to my hair." Indignant, I said, "Lenny, it's a bad image." He didn't reply to that, but he did say, "Who's going to see this report?" I answered, "The people in Philadelphia, and maybe the network will pick it up." "Oh. Good," he said. I added, "One other person will see it. Your mother, who gave us baby pictures, asked me to send her a copy."

At that point, he got up from the chair, spit some more tobacco juice, and ran to the clubhouse, where he grabbed a shirt and put it on. He returned and sat down again for the interview. Lenny was known for his insulting behavior, but even a bad boy doesn't want to embarrass his mother.

There were many other interviews: Bill Cosby on the set of the Cosby mysteries, Bruce Willis at Planet Hollywood in San Antonio, Ed Rendell, Thacher Longstreth, city planner Ed Bacon, and a profile on mayoral chief of staff David L. Cohen that got him in trouble. Cohen's fabled rise to power was accompanied by an interview we did with his mother in North Jersey. Proud of David, a lawyer and the prime motivator of Rendell's success, she still took the opportunity to blast him, suggesting that he needed to spend more time with his family. "It would be nice if he called his mother once in a while," she said. That was a great TV moment.

I also interviewed the Philadelphia-based musical stars of Boyz II Men on the set of Will Smith's show, *The Fresh Prince of Bel-Air*, in Burbank, California. I also caught up with the Boyz during a dramatic moment: their 1995 performance at a mass celebrated by the pope at Camden Yards in Baltimore.

The *Bulletin's* success was directed by Jo Ann Caplin. Scott Herman, Paul Gluck, and I interviewed her in New York when we were looking for an executive producer for the new show, and she was an instant hit. Caplin's talent was her ability to push the producers to a new level of clarity and understanding. This veteran of twenty-seven years in network TV produced a prime-time magazine with a staff of thirteen, a tiny staff in comparison to the hourly network magazine's. Don Hewitt, the legendary *60 Minutes* boss, marveled at the consistently high quality of the *Bulletin*. Caplin's editor was the ever-present Paul Gluck, who quietly shepherded the program along. Caplin reported to Gluck, and Gluck, the kid from Northeast Philly, made sure the *Bulletin* reported to the needs and interests of the people.

In February 1996, General Manager Jerry Eaton informed me that the *Bulletin* would be no more. That was a difficult day, but I understood. The *Bulletin* had perished again, but the memories of the stories still linger, along with the talent that produced them. Several of the young people who worked on the show are now producers at major networks. If I could bring one thing back in my career, it would be the *Bulletin*. But who can complain about having had the opportunity to do its 104 shows in the first place?

Back to the Anchor Chair

After I had worked for thirteen months at KYW, management decided to have me act as solo anchor for the eleven o'clock news. The show had reasonable early success, which was then tempered by the network switch prompted by Westinghouse's purchase of CBS. In 1995, WCAU, one of our direct competitors, became an NBC-owned station, while KYW became a part of CBS. This alphabet soup was confusing to viewers. NBC used the occasion to pour hundreds of thousands of advertising dollars into WCAU. Our management failed to answer in kind. The result in 1996 and 1997 was a diminishing audience, a slide further aggravated by several new anchor pairings and changes at KYW that completely mixed up viewers. Finally, in 1999, I returned to the solo anchor chair at eleven o'clock, and General Manager Marcellus Alexander and Station Manager Joel Cheatwood gave the station new momentum with stable anchor pairings on the other news shows.

Away from the hot local competition, the nineties was a period of bizarre developments, surprises that sometimes rocked the senses: the O. J. Simpson trial; the Aimee Willard murder case; the accidental deaths of John Kennedy, Jr., and Princess Diana; and of course the scandal involving President Clinton and White House intern Monica Lewinsky. Delaware, rarely the place of sensational news, was home to two odd cases—the murder of Governor Tom Carper's secretary, Anne Marie Fahey, by Tom Capano, a prominent lawyer and former state prosecutor, and the death of an infant, with charges filed against the parents, two college students. And back in Philadelphia, Mayor Ed Rendell continued pursuing a better city right to the end of his term in January 2000.

Two local stories stood out during that period, both testing the limits of love and hate. The first, the death of Eddie Polec, was more than just a murder; it exposed the potential for human violence, reminding us of how fragile life can be. Eddie Polec, a teenager, was chased down railroad tracks and beaten to death on the steps of his church. The reason was a neighborhood feud, but there was no rhyme or reason to the death of Eddie Polec. That the murder happened in a middle-class Philadelphia neighborhood was a shock to the establishment. Fox Chase is a neighborhood where bad things aren't supposed to happen. But the fact remained: bad things were happening to good people all over the region, and the Polec death was a grim reminder that no neighborhood is exempt from wanton killing.

The killing was a blow to the Philadelphia 911 emergency system as well, which responded so poorly that its performance forced a renovation of the entire unit. Through nationwide broadcasts, Philadelphia was embarrassed by the voices of the 911 operators, who appeared much less than helpful when responding to desperate calls from witnesses seeking to save Eddie.

The Polec case also led to a low moment for reporters. A few of the suspects were former or suspended students from Abington High School in Abington, a township near Fox Chase. Immediately, all students at Abington were slandered by this association. The *Philadelphia Daily News* ran a "clever" banner headline, "MURDER HIGH," that was hurtful in its insinuations. Abington High itself had nothing to do with the killing of Eddie Polec. Neither did the majority of young people from the Fox Chase and Abington neighborhoods. But many news organizations incorrectly reported the murder as an offshoot of inter-community tensions.

For me, it was a deeply depressing story. The vision of the Polec family enduring this tragedy will never fade from my mind. As parents, my wife and I grieved for the family. The fact that the murder had occurred near our neighborhood was also troubling. Our daughter was a senior at Abington High. And to this day, every time I drive through the area of Oxford and Rhawn, near where the murder occurred, I think of Eddie Polec and his family. Sometimes I drive on Oxford Avenue and glance over at the railroad tracks, picturing his attackers chasing after Eddie and reaching him on the steps of his church. I've run into the Polecs here and there. I am rarely at a loss for words, but with them I don't know what to say. It's been years now, but to me the story always feels like it just happened. Outside of the Move confrontation, no one story has ever affected me as profoundly as the murder of Eddie Polec.

But there was good news, as well. In the spring of 1997, Old City Philadelphia bloomed with the Volunteer Summit, a coalition involving thousands of organizations from around the country. Oprah Winfrey hosted the main events, but the star of the show was General Colin Powell, whose energy and drive had guaranteed the success of this first-ever exposition about helping others. Prior to the event he had organized, Colin Powell joined me on a park bench in the rear of Independence Hall for an interview. That was the second time we had met. With General Powell, an interview was more than an encounter; it was a treat. Powell is affable, outgoing, and inspiring. When he speaks, you hear the voice of honesty and assurance. Powell was aided in his effort to draw so many volunteer groups together by President Clinton and former presidents Bush, Carter, and Ford, along with former first lady Nancy Reagan. The Philadelphia gathering was a star-studded show and only a nonpartisan leader like Colin Powell could have made it happen. The purpose was to energize Americans to sacrifice their time to help others.

KYW broadcast hours of the event live, giving me another day of goose bumps. From a makeshift studio on the ninth floor of the Rohm and Haas building on Independence Mall, I worked as anchor throughout our coverage. What a view! After a cloudy morning, the sun slowly emerged, its rays glistening over the treetops on Independence Mall. President Clinton and his official entourage took their places on a wooden stage in front of Independence Hall, the building where the Declaration of Independence was signed. Thousands watched from the mall as a band played the Star Spangled Banner. Oprah Winfrey was the host. The summit lasted two days. Volunteerism was in the spotlight, but it will be years before we know the true impact of this event.

Joy of Competition

Sometimes, news coverage requires more than the usual innovation and creativity, especially when you're aiming to get the story before your competition does. In June 1985, newlywed Blake Synnestvedt of Bryn Athyn was among the Beirut hostages returning from their ordeal to a U.S. Air Force Base in Frankfurt, Germany. Before my departure, his wife gave me a tiny wad of paper, folded over several times, with a letter inside. She said, "You may see him first. Please give this to him."

Once in Germany, as we prepared for the arrival of the released hostages, the WCAU cameraman, Frank Goldstein, had an idea. Frank went to a nearby market, where he purchased a huge sheet of cardboard and a Magic Marker. On the cardboard, he wrote in bold letters, "BLAKE, COME OVER TO THE FENCE, LARRY KANE HAS A NOTE FROM YOUR WIFE."

When the C-141 Starlifter arrived, hundreds of news people lined the airport fence, including our competition. The pressure was intense to land an interview with Blake. As the hostages came down the steps, I held the sign high, and in moments, the Bryn Athyn man made eye contact with it. He came over to our position, took the note, and we talked for several minutes about his captivity. WPVI's Marc Howard glanced over, his jaw dropping. Howard is an aggressive reporter who will stop at nothing to get a story. Now he knew he'd be playing catch-up.

Scoring exclusives is a part of the job, an exciting part. Nothing is more gratifying than being first—except, of course, being accurate. And getting first access to stories comes in part from years of developing relationships with newsmakers, current and potential—not just the well known policymakers and movers and shakers, but the individuals who make their marks quietly and forcefully. This unique perspective, as you're about to learn, is the stuff of legends, lore, and a newsman's memories.

Part Four

Politics, Personality, and the Future of TV

If you want to cover news, you have to know people. The more people you know, the better chance you have of getting exclusive information. Along the way, you develop relationships with people in power and learn more about them. The people I've covered have been famous, controversial, and never uninteresting. Spend an evening with Ed Rendell, and you'll discover what drives the former mayor. Politics is addictive. Power is seductive. Watch Senator Arlen Specter up close, and you'll find a perfectionist who is the most difficult and the most brilliant U.S. senator.

In the following pages, you'll meet some of the more powerful people of our era—in government, in jail, in boardrooms and backrooms. But, as I've learned, the most interesting people may not be in public life. As you read their stories, beautiful stories of courage and love, you may come to see that not all newsmakers are rich and famous.

In this section you will also meet some of the news "takers," those unscrupulous managers who are more concerned with drama than fact, the broadcasters who damage the credibility of everyone in the industry and threaten the future of television news.

My Super Bowl

For this reporter, election night has always been the World Series and the Super Bowl wrapped into one glorious night, the night when average citizens make the news. Despite attempts to stifle my pursuit of political news, my instincts for politics and lengthy list of sources have remained intact, cemented by decades of personal and phone contact. In 1991, when WCAU general manager Gene Lothery killed my long-running news segment, "Political Notebook," through guile and some cunning, political news still managed to make its way to the air through other reports during the news hour. It was hard at times, but I managed to get my inside political news to broadcast.

I love covering the political scene in this region, especially because of the people I've encountered over the years, the people who tried, the losers and the winners. Losers are very important. In area politics, losing gracefully can be a critical virtue for those who refuse to quit. Bob Casey, Milton Shapp, Arlen Specter, Bill Green, Jim Florio, and many others were losers before they became winners. Losing gave them humility, respect for the voters, and knowledge of their own weaknesses. When you learn your soft spots, you are ready for battle. Politics is a blood sport. No one understood that more than Frank L. Rizzo, whom we've already visited, but others have also stood out and, sadly, stood down. First, of course, there is Edward G. Rendell.

Rendell

Rizzo's sudden death in 1991 cleared the way for Ed Rendell to become mayor of Philadelphia. The Republicans put up a fine public servant named Joe Egan, but he didn't have a chance against Rendell. Frank Rizzo called Edward G. Rendell "fast Eddie," implying that Rendell was swift and tricky. Rendell was swift, but the only political trick he had was a talent for raising money and getting elected. Rizzo reserved his most caustic invective for those he feared most, and he feared Rendell because the man had charm, charisma, and a self-deprecating style that even his enemies envied.

It's true that all four of Ed Rendell's victorious city elections, two for district attorney and two for mayor, were against weak Republican foes. But he deserved to win them. For Rendell, losing had been a lesson, and in the late eighties, Ed Rendell was branded a loser—finished, the pols said, by his primary defeats in races for governor and mayor. Conventional wisdom had him labeled damaged goods. But in the combat zone of Philadelphia politics, conventional wisdom is often shot to pieces.

Publicly, Rendell is a smooth, confident executive whose power of personality has transformed the image of Philadelphia. Privately, he has the uncontrolled temper of a man who wants his way and is determined to get it. His bouts of temper, rarely seen, are not uncommon among people who work eighteen-hour days and are constantly sleep deprived. In his eight years as mayor, Rendell's public appearance schedule was the most rigorous in city history. Rendell appeared to be everywhere because he was. One week in May 1998, he and I appeared three times together: at an Arts and Business Council of Philadelphia lunch, at the MS Walk, and at Philadelphia's Fiftieth Anniversary Celebration for Israel at Penn's Landing. His has been a life of service and untiring devotion.

All people have frailties, and Rendell's weakness is a private contempt for the media, odd as that may seem, since he's had a media honeymoon for many years. He is not bashful in bashing the media, especially when we dare to report crime. Rendell took it personally when serious crime happened on his watch, and he did not hesitate to blame the media for accenting crime coverage. He also has a tendency to speak before thinking. That can be dangerous. During the massive snowstorm of 1996, veteran KYW 3 journalist Robin Mackintosh asked Rendell why his own street had been plowed first. Rendell went off on Mackintosh, at times appearing physically threatening, at one point gripping his arm. This was all caught on tape and appeared on that night's news. At the Democratic convention in Chicago, the mayor held an impromptu press conference to talk about the Dick Morris scandal. The Clinton adviser had been linked to prostitutes. Looking at me with exasperation, he said, "You guys are always looking for personal stuff to embarrass people. It's an out-of-control media." Brinn Friedman, a reporter for WTXF, badgered him: "Mr. Mayor, don't you think the personal life of a public official is important?" I don't recall his words, but his face turned deep red, his voice raised, sweat beaded on his forehead, and he proceeded to rip her to pieces verbally while his press chief, Kevin Feeley, counted the seconds until the end of the get-together.

If temper and contempt for the media are parts of the Rendell repertoire, so be it. His accomplishments far outweigh his peculiarities. But it would be wise for Rendell to shake off his obsession with the media, at least in public. Pawning off frustration on the media has been a part of American politics for decades. For a man of Ed Rendell's brilliance, it's an unnecessary exercise.

My own relationship with Rendell has been exemplary, and it was further strengthened when the mayor and his wife, Midge, came to my rescue in June 1985. The return of the TWA hostages to Germany after their ordeal in Beirut coincided with a major event at the Torah Academy, a private school in Merion. The academy had decided to honor me, but there I was, off to Germany to cover the hostages' return, which was especially important to our region because one of the hostages was a newlywed from Bryn Athyn. I was concerned about the affair back home. I placed a phone call to the district attorney. I said, "Ed, no big deal, but could you fill in? If not, I totally understand." Rendell replied, "I think we can do it. It would be an honor. You take care of yourself in Germany." Ed and Midge appeared at the dinner, escorting my wife, Donna, and our children, Michael and Alexandra. He sang songs, charmed the crowd, and filled in for me with his usual gusto. Ed and Midge stayed up late that Sunday night to save the day with an act of kindness and generosity.

Over the years, covering Rendell has been a pleasure, although there have been a few close calls. In 1982, Rendell decided not to run for governor, a fateful decision that would cause him seven years of anxiety and eight years of success. I invited Rendell to join me as analyst on election night. Rendell spent most of the night wanting to kick himself in the butt for having decided not to run. Republican Dick Thornburgh narrowly defeated a little-known congressman named Alan Ertel. Rendell said to me, "Lar, I could have won it." He said it to me more than once.

Rendell was busy reading returns, so he had to rush to the news set to appear with me at eleven. I noticed with alarm when he appeared on the set that his fly was down. Dick Thornburgh had easily won election, we were getting ready for the eleven o'clock newscast, and the district attorney's zipper was an open book. Since I was already talking, it was impossible for me to tell him. I pointed my finger at his zipper, and he looked at me with a sly grin that said, "What the hell is this about?" To make matters worse, he was due to stand up at an electric tote board.

I gestured with my left hand and then with my right. At the moment when I said, "Joining us for analysis of returns is Philadelphia D.A. Ed Rendell," something happened. In a split second, Rendell reached for his zipper and pulled it up. As his hand was moving, he continued that movement by turning to the tote board and pointing at numbers. I was impressed with his speed.

Rendell's analysis was fabulous, but he appeared grim and flushed with bitter anger, mostly at himself for not having gotten into the fray. When the newscast was over, we both laughed at his near brush with exposure. The election night of 1982 may have been a defining moment in Rendell's career. Realizing that he could have beaten Dick Thornburgh after all, Rendell seemed to take a new tack, a more aggressive approach. As his friend Bill Clinton taught the other Democrats in 1992, you can't win unless you have the guts to run for office.

Rendell finished his second term as district attorney in early 1986. Next he ran for governor and mayor and lost both races. Rendell languished in loser land for five years, with political insiders declaring him deader than dead. But he pressed on. I would see him at luncheons, dinners, charity walks, and civic functions, a politician without portfolio, familiar to the crowd but with no power base, a lonely figure needing the political fix that keeps all these candidates going— a win. Most politicians would have given up after two big losses, but Edward G. Rendell campaigned for years, championing the good causes, fighting against the enemies of the city, maturing as a leader, and, eventually, like the city he helped transform, coming to life in a position of power.

Specter

"He's younger, he's tougher, and nobody owns him." The brilliant political image-maker Elliot Curson had crafted that slogan for Arlen Specter's successful campaign for a second term as Philadelphia district attorney in 1969. Stung by his razor-thin defeat in the mayoral election in 1967, Specter rebounded with big numbers in 1969, only to be shattered by defeat in 1973. He ran for office twice again, then captured a U.S. Senate seat in 1980. Today, Arlen Specter is the only senator in Pennsylvania history to serve a fourth term in office.

Specter's rise, fall, and rise offer a brilliant example of the pursuit of power and the American dream, a portrait of the determination and willpower it takes to rise above setbacks and defeats. Many had written his political obituary in the late 1970s, but those who covered him knew that he wouldn't be gone long.

When I first encountered Arlen Specter in late 1966, he appeared to be the most media-savvy politician in the city. A blue drape covered the back wall of his conference room, a splendid color for television. The setting was ideal, but the words were even better. Specter had that uncanny ability to form his words in thirty-second increments, shaping his thoughts gracefully and intelligently. Arlen Specter was king of sound bites (the TV expression for short, focused comments), capable of making a broadcast at a moment's notice. He was and is a master communicator.

Specter took a liking to me right away. During a basketball game at the Palestra (the University of Pennsylvania's basketball arena) in 1967, he waved me over and said, "Kane, you do a hell of a job. You could own this town." Since he was stroking my ego, Specter was an instant hit for me. As the years progressed, he would remind me repeatedly that he had been an early handicapper of my career potential.

The senator could also be biting and ornery, leaving little room for incompetence in his world. In the early nineties, appearing on a live town forum at KYW TV, the senator leaned over to me and said, "Where the hell is my chart?" I whispered back, "What are you talking about?" He replied, "My chart on the Clinton health care fiasco." Incredulous, I answered, "We don't have a chart." He said, "Then I'm leaving." I added, "If you want to leave in the middle of the program, fine. We've got hot, live microphones here, so go if you want to go." This entire conversation took place in between questions from the audience. As Specter left the building, he was still yelling at aides, asking for his chart.

Today, that chart, blown up to cover an entire wall, is the primary artwork in the conference room of his Washington office. The chart provides a clear schematic of the bureaucracy that would have been caused by the Bill and Hillary health plan—a plan that evaporated, many believe, because of Specter's research and his beloved chart.

Specter's demand for excellence, in joy or anger, is unquestioned in Washington, where he is a genuine power, a Republican with moderate credentials who is the "go to" man on key legislation. Nowhere is his talent more visible than in his prosecutor's ability to go for the jugular. In 1986, I was asked to moderate a debate between Specter and his Senate challenger, Democratic congressman Bob Edgar. The studio was at WTAJ in Altoona. In the afternoon hours, I prepped for the live broadcast, set to begin at 7:00 P.M. and to be broadcast statewide.

At 6:50, Bob Edgar arrived and began getting comfortable at his podium, joking with the press, and conversing with his aides and family. Edgar seemed relaxed, sanguine, ready for battle. At 6:55, Edgar stood alone; Specter was not to be seen. Sixty seconds before air, Edgar was fidgeting, Specter still invisible. A grin started forming on my lips as I realized that Specter was doing a psych job on the challenger. At exactly thirty seconds to broadcast, Specter walked into the room, turned his microphone on, and said, "Let's do it." Edgar was visibly shaken, and in the next hour, Specter left Edgar in the dust, which was what the Edgar campaign had turned to by election day.

Specter is blessed with real talent and a supportive family. His wife, Joan, has been his lifeline in a career of highs and lows. His son, Shanin, is his most trusted adviser, an advocate of political compromise. Shanin, a successful lawyer, has wisely decided to stay out of elective politics for now. Specter has one other ability that I admire intensely. In a society where people continue to walk away from their ethnic and religious heritages for political reasons, Specter defends, celebrates, and publicly praises his Jewish heritage. His very being and that of his family is rooted in that legacy, from his days as a child in Russell, Kansas, to his rise to power in the corridors of the U.S. Senate.

Lady Law

The justice establishment has had its heroes and goats over the years. Federal judge Norma Shapiro, for instance, was vilified for her court-ordered release of criminals, her solution to prison overcrowding. Other judges have been forced to resign for taking payments from the roofer's union. Despite the bad marks, however, the system has its champions, including Lady Law—or, in the words of Frank L. Rizzo, "one tough cookie."

Lynne Abraham and Frank Rizzo had a love-hate relationship that lasted for two decades. Abraham always managed to tee off Rizzo. But despite her willingness to stand up to the big guy, Rizzo always had a soft spot for Abraham.

Abraham was a successful young prosecutor, the director of the Philadelphia Redevelopment Authority, a common pleas court judge, and eventually district attorney. In her first election, Abraham was so enormously popular that she was supported by both the Democratic and Republican parties. Today she is the pre-eminent woman in Pennsylvania Democratic politics.

I first met Abraham in the late sixties, when Rizzo was eying her for a future slot in the government he hoped to run. She was a liberal Democrat who was an archconservative when it came to the prosecution of criminals. After Rizzo took office, Abraham was appointed director of redevelopment. But she didn't like patronage or being muscled by Rizzo. Eventually he fired Abraham, labeling her "one tough cookie." That label has stayed with her through the years and is a popular theme for her election campaigns.

I'll never forget the day Abraham called to give me the news that she had been axed. She said, "Lar, the shithead canned me. Can you believe it?" I asked, "Why?" She jumped in quickly: "Because I wouldn't play ball." I called Rizzo, who said, "Listen, Larry Kane, that woman is one tough cookie. She can go to hell as far as I'm concerned. You can quote me." I didn't use the "go to hell" quote on the news that night, but I couldn't resist the cookie line. Little did Lynne Abraham know that Frank Rizzo had helped seal her political fate with those remarks. She used the words "one tough cookie" on campaign commercials and billboards throughout Philadelphia.

Today, Abraham is a force to be reckoned with. She can occasionally shoot from the hip, but she is a powerful advocate for victims of crime, and she still has a link to Frank Rizzo. Tony Fulwood, the tall bodyguard who served Rizzo for decades, is her chief of security, and a week doesn't go by when Lynne and Tony don't reminisce about hizzonner.

Abraham is a fascinating personality surrounded by a complex mystique. The district attorney's office is piled high with feminine comforts, such as soft pillows and colorful cloths. She is especially fond of cats. And in a courtroom, Lynne Abraham becomes a different kind of cat—a tiger whose hunger is not satisfied until its prey, the criminal, gets the max.

When I first met Abraham in 1969, her views on justice were already clear: criminals should pay for their crimes. Although her critics charge that her punitive personality is merely political bluster, nothing could be further from the truth. Her sentiments about justice are real, rooted in her compassion for victims. She was one tough cookie way before Frank Rizzo said so.

The Man Who Got Tony Boyle

He's a short, soft-spoken, slight man who may on first glance look powerless, but when you pause and look at his face, you see the eyes of a tiger. In a town of legal giants, Dick Sprague is the most feared and respected lawyer of his time.

Sprague was the first assistant district attorney under District Attorney Arlen Specter in the sixties and early seventies, which meant that he was the operations manager, selecting priority cases and assigning lawyers. Sprague's style of fighting crime was simple—find the perpetrators, jail them, and keep them away forever. He was such a great prosecutor that he was drafted to get the killer of Jock Yablonski, the United Mine Workers dissident. Sprague pursued the case fearlessly, convinced that Mine Workers president Tony Boyle was the mastermind of the murders of Yablonski and members of his family. It took years, but Sprague, arguing the case himself, got the murder conviction. As he was led away from the Delaware County Courthouse in Media, a handcuffed Boyle, once a titan of labor leaders, looked over at Sprague and spit at him. I watched Sprague. As Boyle glared at him, a smile emerged on Sprague's face, a look of gratification. The long, hard battle was over.

In Philadelphia, the mere mention of Dick Sprague's name has lawyers running for cover. During my Philadelphia career, I have had a policy of avoiding any professional association outside the news context with the people I cover. But in late 1992, trying to extricate myself cleanly from my contract at WCAU TV, I asked Sprague, then a private lawyer, to represent me. Leery of Eugene Lothery's game-playing and with KYW offering me a deal to anchor a prime-time news magazine, I needed Sprague. The mere mention of his name got the attention of Lothery and the CBS legal team. Within days, a separation agreement with CBS was inked, and I was free to go.

Jim Florio and Beware the Pollster

Jim Florio was the governor of New Jersey from 1990 to early 1994, but he had almost been elected in November 1981. That's the night we broke Jim Florio's heart.

Florio, a former amateur boxer, a lawyer, an assemblyman, and a veteran congressman, had long dreamed of becoming governor. He was a tenacious, street-fighter politician, with a take-no-prisoners attitude and a Boy Scout's intensity about good destroying evil. His touch can be felt today in the cleanup of toxic dumps, the national passenger rail system, and the vigorous grassroots campaign against the sale of assault weapons. Florio was that rare politician who called it like it is and rarely fudged his philosophy when talking to the media. Personally, Florio was tight and humorless. Yet as he grew to middle age, Jim Florio let his guard down, allowing voters to see a wee bit of his insides.

The night we wounded his psyche was election night 1981, the face-off between Florio and Republican legend Tom Kean. Kean and Florio were locked in a razor-close race, too close to call, as the fearless pollsters said. I anticipated the night with the glee of a kid waiting for holiday gifts. To me, an election is an epic political battle in which the American system shines its most beautiful light. The people decide, and that's how power is acquired in the land of the free. The powerful, the rich, and the mighty answer to the voters.

Our broadcast on the night of the Florio-Kean encounter was a joint effort with WCBS TV, our sister station in New York City, which was also covering the race. We had access to an exit poll. Exit polls are rarely wrong, because the interviews are conducted after respondents have voted. A little after 8:00 P.M., we received word that, when all the votes were counted, Jim Florio would be elected governor of New Jersey. Celebrations erupted at Florio's headquarters at the Cherry Hill Inn. The polling results had made the state and national news wires. Florio, though, decided to remain in his hotel suite until the actual raw vote certified his victory.

At 9:00 P.M., we received a phone call from WCBS advising us that the race was in fact "too close to call." At 9:15, word came down that the initial survey report had been wrong. By 9:45, Tom Kean had pulled slightly ahead. And when the night was over, Kean had won by a handful of votes. The subsequent recount lasted for weeks, and the final victory carved out by Tom Kean was based on just seventeen hundred votes.

Pollsters can be more than dangerous to your mental health; they can be dangerous to your reputation. On election night in 1987, respected pollster Steve Teichner delivered his exit poll to WCAU news director Jay Newman. The poll showed Wilson Goode with 68 percent of the votes, Frank Rizzo with 32. Newman said, "Larry, would you go with it?" I replied, "No way. Are you kidding?" Even Teichner seemed shocked by the unexpected results. The eventual outcome was a much smaller margin of victory by Goode, a mere two points, proving that in elections where race is a factor, voters often lie to pollsters, lest they be branded as racists. What they say and what they actually do may differ. My advice to reporters and news directors: respect, examine, and trust your instincts, but in the end, beware the pollster, especially in exit polling, because the bad news could be yours.

Over the years, I've tried to imagine what the roller coaster must have been like for Jim Florio and his family. First elation, then anxiety, and finally bitter disappointment. But Florio never expressed his frustrations to me or the voters. Weeks later, when the recount was over, I visited Florio in his Runnemede office. He seemed resigned to wait for another day. That day came in 1989, when he was elected governor.

Florio's first and only term was a time for courage. He raised taxes mightily and banned assault weapons. Even though, in retrospect, the tax increase kept New Jersey solvent, voters reacted severely. The Democrats lost the legislature, and Florio lost his bid for a second term to Christine Whitman.

A week before the election, New York reporter Gabe Pressman and I hosted a debate between Florio and Whitman at the NBC studios in New York. In the dressing room, I watched as Jim Carville, a Florio consultant, urged him to go for Whitman's jugular. Carville said, "You make mincemeat of her phony baloney tax-reduction plan. Ask her why she wants to legalize assault weapons. Go for it, man. Eat her alive." Florio didn't take Carville's advice. He acted like a statesman, while Whitman went for the jugular, branding him as the tax man cometh personified. She won the debate—and the election.

Jim Florio recovered from that debacle to practice law. The Kennedy family honored him with the Profile in Courage award for his battle to keep weapons out of dangerous hands. I was at the Kennedy Library to watch the luminaries: JFK, Jr.; Jackie Kennedy; Ted; Ethel; and Caroline. In the early morning, I interviewed Caroline Kennedy about the award. "Why Jim Florio?" I asked. Caroline responded,

"Because this award in honor of my father is given to a person who has the courage of their convictions, regardless of the consequences. Jim Florio is a man of principle in a sea of political mediocrity. That's why we honor him."

In politics, winning isn't everything. Being true to your beliefs can make you a winner, even if your heart is broken by a TV news operation on election night.

Bob Casey, the Real Bob Casey

Perseverance is an important attribute, and Robert Patrick Casey apparently learned that early on. He ran for governor of Pennsylvania five times. His last run in 1986 was the lucky charm.

Casey ran on several key planks. He was pro-death penalty and vigorously antiabortion. Ironically, he never sent one person to his or her execution during his eight years in office, and despite numerous advances in education and business development, Casey is remembered mostly for his crusade against abortion, which he carried on after office.

They called Bob Casey the Real Bob Casey, because other politicians with the same name had found the name was magic when it came to securing votes. But the Real Bob Casey has never been exposed to the public. Until now, of course.

Casey, who died in June of 2000, was a handsome and powerful figure, charming and down to earth, much like his home in Scranton and exactly like his wife, Ellen, a woman who had enough charisma to run for and win public office herself. Casey was also one of the most loyal people on earth. When he made a promise, he became the original promise keeper. The promise he made to me in November 1986 was for an exclusive breakfast interview at his Scranton home the morning after the election.

Bob Casey defeated Bill Scranton, Jr., on November 4, 1986, and at daybreak I took a plane to Scranton for some pancakes and conversation with the governor-elect. There I ran into James Carville, who would become one of the most famous political gurus of his time. Carville was one of the inner circle of Arkansas governor Bill Clinton in the 1992 campaign. But before Clinton, he worked for Bob Casey and underwent a vicious encounter with an anchorman from Philadelphia.

When I arrived at the Casey home, other reporters were waiting outside. They were clearly upset by my presence, but a deal was a deal, and that's why I was there. I entered the home and proceeded to the kitchen, where Ellen Casey and one of her daughters greeted me with coffee. In the archway, the man known as the raging Cajun began yelling, "Get him the hell out of there! We don't need this fuckin' trouble! Goddamit, I call the shots here." I answered, "Cut the language, okay? Mr. Casey invited me here, and. . . ." Before I could finish, Carville, in that condescending way of his, shouted, "I don't care who the hell you are. Get out!" I replied, "Fine."

I began to leave the house, but Bob and Ellen Casey stopped me. And then the Real Bob Casey stepped forward. So it was on a snowy November morning that James Carville was taken to the woodshed by the future governor. Casey put his arm around Carville and led him to the foyer, where he said a few words. Carville, a tall and wiry man, seemed to slump in dejection, but Carville wasn't finished yet. Ellen Casey, with a worried look on her face and still embarrassed by the bad language, watched anxiously as Carville and an entourage asked me to go down to the basement.

The Casey basement was like a college dormitory, with beds sitting side by side, a reminder of what it's like to rear eight children in a small house. As I sat on one of the beds, Carville started screaming again. "You have no goddamn right to mess up the governor's morning." I replied, "I think you're the one who's messed up the morning. Isn't that right, Jim? Are you screwing up your client's morning?" Bill Batoff, Casey's fund-raiser, tried gingerly to intervene, but it was a standoff until the raging Cajun and I reached a negotiated compromise. I would wait around till the dust settled and do the interview after lunch, when the news herds would have departed. It was an acceptable deal, but my stomach was in a knot from the degrading way Jim Carville had tried to rain on my exclusive. The exclusive interview was conducted four hours later, and no one else interviewed one-on-one that day.

They say you can judge a person by the company he keeps. That would not apply to Bob Casey. Casey and Carville were joined in a campaign of political faith, but beyond that they had no real connection. I remember vividly sitting next to Casey at the 1992 Democratic National Convention in Madison Square Garden and watching the governor fume bitterly after the Clinton forces, led by Carville, refused to allow him a mere three minutes to express his pro-life views. He felt betrayed, but he shouldn't have. In politics, hired hands like Carville rarely offer solace and support when they're off the clock.

Bob Casey's eight years in office were good for Philadelphia. He visited the city often and felt a connection with the people, especially the downtrodden. Casey would tremble when he walked through the minefields of the Eighth and Butler drug zone. His administration was generous in its care of the poor, and he was genuinely touched by those who had little to enjoy in life.

Personally, Casey faced challenges. A heart-liver transplant saved his life. A few months after the operation he invited me to the Governor's House for his first interview since the surgery. The Governor's House has an elevator to its second floor. Casey was so weak that he needed the elevator to reach the ground floor, where we had our interview. During that conversation, he talked about the gift of life and began a diatribe against abortion. With Casey, the topic always turned to the abortion issue, an issue that has blurred the real accomplishments of his administration—luring businesses to Pennsylvania and enhancing social services.

It was the subject of abortion that brought Bob Casey to the 1996 Democratic National Convention in Chicago. Casey, by then a former governor, was not a delegate, but he made more news than most of the people who had come for the second nomination of Bill Clinton. Casey came for one purpose—to chastise the Democratic party for its pro-choice platform plank. He was an irritant to the Clintonians, and he knew it. Striking back for his snub in 1992, the Real Bob Casey came out of the gate swinging in a news conference at the Chicago Loop. Casey was brilliant. He knew there wasn't much controversy in the preordained convention, and he filled the gap. He delivered some comments about "baby killers" and suggested he might vote Republican in November. As usual, the family was with him—son Bob, who was running for auditor general, and his wife, Ellen. After the news conference, Casey retreated to a small office, where he rested and got caught up with me. "Why do you do it?" I asked. Casey replied, "Larry, I have no other choice. They are killing babies, snuffing out life." I retorted, "But why expend such energy and get so aggravated?" Casey said, "It's what I have to do."

Politicians change with the polls and the winds, just like the seasons, but Casey never wavered. Many Pennsylvania voters were adamantly pro-choice, but they elected Bob Casey to two terms in office, the second time by a landslide.

Power

Some Philadelphians are addicted to power. For them, there is no chance of rehabilitation, no way to ever kick the habit. People like Ed Rendell and Frank Rizzo savored power for the opportunities it gave them to govern and influence people. Others play a different role in the power game, but once they've tasted it, there is no retreat.

In order to win in politics, though, you have to be able to raise money. Raising political money is an art form. No one has practiced that art as consistently well as Herb Barness and Bill Batoff. Barness, at the time of his death in 1998, was the most respected Republican power broker in Pennsylvania. Batoff has been the Democrats' most potent behind-the-scenes influence for two decades. Both have demonstrated political prowess when it comes to picking winners. Herb Barness gave me advance notice in 1992 that a little-known congressman from Erie would be governor of Pennsylvania. Tom Ridge won two terms in office, by large margins. In his second run, Ridge was so impressive that even the Democrat Batoff supported him.

Few men can pick up a phone and get through to a president, but Herb Barness could do that with Ronald Reagan and George Bush, and Bill Batoff had a direct line to Jimmy Carter. Barness helped elect three governors, two presidents, and the senator with the longest tenure in Pennsylvania history, Arlen Specter. Batoff was involved in the elections of Frank Rizzo, Bill Green, Wilson Goode, and Ed Rendell. In his shining moment, Batoff financed and coordinated the victory of Robert P. Casey as governor of Pennsylvania. The records of both men in influencing local politics have never been matched.

Power is fleeting—unless you know how to work the crowd, develop contacts, and most of all, never betray your loyalties. Two things matter most in area politics: early support for a candidate and absolute loyalty. Both men could write textbooks on those attributes.

Others, too, deserve notice for their background power. Background power is different from elected power. Ron Rubin, the successful developer, has quietly influenced major city elections, with barely a few words written about him. Rubin knows that good, progressive politics is good business. Another developer, Willard Rouse, has carefully walked the political minefields while creating his high-rise empire. Steve Cozen, a Philadelphia superlawyer, is becoming an extraordinary influence on the political scene. Lew Katz, a South Jersey businessman, is a background power with money and influence that helped elect Governor Florio in New Jersey and Mayor Rendell in Philadelphia. Campaign finance guru Bob Feldman was the architect of John Street's election as Philadelphia mayor. Tom Leonard, the former city controller, and his brother-in-law Marty Weinberg, a candidate for mayor in 1999, comprise a power duo that sends chills up the spines of potential political opponents. Charles Sexton, the Republican leader of Springfield, Delaware County, is one of the most powerful Republican leaders in the United States.

Bill Miller is power personified. The former deputy register of wills and current owner of a communications company, he was the architect of Wilson Goode's successful run for Philadelphia mayor in 1993. Miller is a brilliant political operative who practically invented the Philadelphia politics of inclusion. No one has built coalitions better than Bill Miller.

A new generation of power has arrived for Philadelphia's twenty-first century. Charles Pizzi, leader of the Chamber of Commerce, has been the town's classiest operative, creating the environment business needs to thrive. Fred DiBona, the Blue Cross chief, is a rock-solid leader who places no limits on his time for philanthropy. Both are strong possibilities for elective office. City Councilman Jim Kenney of Philadelphia will someday be mayor. Kenney has a mixture of street savvy and brilliant political intuition. Another councilman, Michael Nutter, demonstrates a rare independence in the debates of City Council, showing himself to be a free spirit who understands the limits of power. The young Democratic councilman is a rare bird in the political sky, a man who votes his conscience. And Democratic Congressman Chakah Fattah is a fast-rising star in Washington. In the suburbs, all eyes are on Delaware County district attorney Pat Meehan. The Republican is a lock for higher office.

In New Jersey, the Andrews era is well underway, as in Congressman Rob Andrews. The First District Democrat is emerging as a powerful force, reaching out to Republicans and independents with independence and a savvy style. Andrews has never been afraid to buck his own party on a vote of conscience. The Andrews factor includes a trait that few politicians acquire—the ability to listen. Andrews is a great listener and a rare, independent voice in Congress.

In the world of power, there is a separate category that one man occupies, a man who has ascended to a level that no one else has ever reached. The name of that man is Fumo, as in Vincent Fumo.

Some twenty years ago, I sat on a couch in a row home in South Philadelphia, staring at the tears rolling down the cheeks of Vincent Fumo. Fumo was facing prison after his conviction on charges of padding payroll with ghost employees. At that moment, Fumo was shattered, emotionally drained by the experience that would bring pain to his family and that he knew could eventually diminish the most important aspect of his career—power.

Vince Fumo was and is a master of the political game. I've followed his career since 1966, the year I arrived in Philadelphia. And there has never been a dull moment. My first in-person contact with Fumo was in 1971, when he served as the commissioner of Professional and Occupational Affairs in Pennsylvania. At the age of twenty-seven, he was heading a major state agency and exposing mail-order prescription ripoffs. Years later, he helped unravel the scandal at Farview State Hospital, where patient cruelty was the order of the day.

Even before his election to the state senate in 1978, Fumo emerged as a power in Philadelphia politics. Controversy was never far away. Fumo had an incredible duality in his personality—charm and gut-wrenching chutzpah. He held up the construction of a section of I-95 for years to protect the interests of his constituents. Newspapers call him arrogant. I understand what people say about the ego and the power quest, but pound for pound, there is no finer legislator in Pennsylvania.

Why does a man like Vincent Fumo prevail? I once asked him, "What are you all about?" He replied, "Brains and balls." He speaks the truth. Fumo maintains an encyclopedic knowledge of government and has the inner strength to use that knowledge as a seed, growing power base upon power base.

Fumo has come a long way from that dark moment after he was found guilty in 1980. The federal court threw the case out months after the 1980 verdict. That night, Vince Fumo, accompanied by every major Democratic politician in the city, had a celebration party. Appearing live with me, he said, "Lar, I was never guilty, just persecuted. Now it's time to look ahead."

David L. Cohen has been looking ahead most of his life. The former chief of staff to Mayor Rendell, Cohen was a driving force in major historical events in Philadelphia: Ed Rendell's election, Ed Rendell's re-election, the acquisition of the 2000 Republican National Convention, and the election of John Street as mayor. But don't think for a minute that David L. Cohen is solely a figment of Ed Rendell's reputation. Cohen is the brightest mind to make the Philadelphia scene since I've been here. Cohen has all the qualities for success: a way with people, a fine intellect accompanied by a keen perception of what is attainable, and a self-deprecating personality that charms and motivates. My advice to future leaders: study him, emulate him, follow in his footsteps. No one personality has ever been more truly honest with me than Cohen, who always returns my calls with candor.

Drew Lewis ran for governor of Pennsylvania in 1974 and lost to Milton Shapp. Lewis was the most respected Republican public servant in Pennsylvania, and power was always waiting for him. He became U.S. transportation secretary in the first administration of President Reagan and will always be remembered as the man who fired the striking air traffic controllers. In 1980, Drew Lewis was a quiet kingmaker at the Republican National Convention at the Joe Louis Arena in Detroit, where he served as a top adviser to Reagan. Throughout the convention, my friendship with Lewis served me well. I got inside information and access.

But the untold story is how Drew Lewis, Republican giant, captain of industry, almost let the career of George Bush slip down the toilet. On the third night of the convention, the Reagan forces were debating a choice for vice president. Would it be Gerald Ford or George Bush? The nominee and his staff debated for hours. Finally, they chose George Bush. Governor Reagan had given Drew Lewis Bush's private number. But in the frenzy of the day, Lewis had accidentally tossed the scrap of paper into a toilet bowl. When Reagan asked to speak to Bush, a terrified Lewis raced into the bathroom, looked into the bowl, and somehow retrieved the slip of paper.

Lewis shared that story with our viewers one day in 1980. He also told me how foolish he felt when he realized where the phone number was. Yes, Reagan would have found the number anyway, but for a few fleeting moments, the future of George Bush was floating in a bowl of water, submerged and sinking, until rescued by a die-hard Republican from Schwenksville, Pennsylvania.

In the exercise of power, there are lessons to be learned. John Street nearly blew the 1999 mayor's campaign by failing to reach out to his political adversaries. Burned in this contest, Street has learned to change his style. Republican businessman Sam Katz came close to upsetting the veteran Democrat, an impressive accomplishment based mainly on Katz's ability to look beyond the internal shell of his own campaign and ignite the passion of city voters. Katz campaign manager Bob Barnett was always ready to answer questions. Street's press chief, Ken Snyder, was as good as it gets, but he had a hard time getting his candidate to be available to the media. Reaching out is an art that has been defined by Pennsylvania governor Tom Ridge and Mayor Ed Rendell. The 1999 mayoral campaign in Philadelphia is textbook material for future candidates.

The 1999 election was also proof positive that, in America, dreams live, despite awesome obstacles. John Street's rise to become mayor of Philadelphia was one of the most unpredictable happenings in the city's history. Street grew up on a farm near Norristown, settled in as a street vendor in Philadelphia with his sparky brother, Milton, and eventually graduated from Temple Law School. From there, he was elected to City Council and was chosen by his peers as council president. To many, John Street is a mystery. In fact, few journalists know him well. But in 1999, I ventured into uncharted territory: Street's house.

Street may be the most private of Philadelphia's public people. In early 1999, I set up a series of interviews for the eleven o'clock news with all of the candidates for mayor. But this was a different kind of series, one designed to reveal the candidates in a more personal way. Former city council member Happy Fernandez was taped playing tennis. John White, Jr., was cooking dinner for his son. State Representative Dwight Evans, bookworm that he is, joined me for coffee at Borders bookstore in Chestnut Hill. Lawyer Marty Weinberg had a family party. Sam Katz was taped at dinner with his family. And John Street? He was hard to get. After weeks of phone calls, Street finally consented to an interview inside his home and with his wife, Naomi, present. His press secretary, Ken Snyder, said Street would do it "because it was me."

When I walked into the house, I realized that Naomi Post, Street's wife, was petrified. My first job was to make her feel relaxed enough, and that was hard, considering that prior to this no television camera had ever entered her home. While the cameraman set up, Street gorged himself on a few hotdogs, a gourmet meal for a candidate on the run. Naomi sat there, looking stricken. I imagined what she was thinking. I assured her that this was not going to be a probing, tabloid-style expose, but rather a profile of their life together.

For a half hour, I questioned John Street and Naomi on their life away from work. Both were reserved and cautious with their answers.

I didn't want the pat interview, so I decided to look for passion, which I found in their attitudes about their work. When Naomi started talking about her work to keep children safe, her eyes lit up, and she began to smile beautifully and naturally. Even John Street noticed the difference. By this point, she was really talking, while he was posturing. How, I thought, could I reach inside this master of municipal affairs, the man of intensity who never opened up? So I tried a new tack. "John," I said, "what's your most exciting moment of the day?" He paused, then replied, "Larry, my most exciting moment is getting up at five, heading downstairs to brew some rich coffee, and then returning to Naomi's side of the bed, where I bring the coffee and set it down next to her. It's a beautiful way to start the day, isn't it?" While he was talking, Naomi Post was beaming with delight.

For John Street, it was a tender moment. Later, after the broadcast, viewers told me how surprised they were at the sensitivity of his remarks. John was indeed full of feeling, even if only for that moment.

Driving away from their home, my thoughts turned to Street's place in life. Once feared for his rhetoric and temper, Street was months away from becoming the chief executive of a great city. Like his Republican challenger, Sam Katz, Street was committed to Philadelphia. How proud he must be, I thought, that he has traveled so far. As a reporter, you look for human qualities along with leadership ability. People view Street as a cold fish, a man with no feeling. But they are wrong. Street's passion for achieving overwhelms his ability to let his guard down. What you see is what you get. And after an extraordinary campaign, scores of debates, and a focus on the issues, John Street narrowly pulled off his victory, and Philadelphians got a new mayor, one improved by the heat of the campaign and tested by years of overcoming the challenges of poverty, education, and elective politics.

Not all of the powerful people run for office. Temple University president Peter Liacouras transformed North Broad Street with an ambitious expansion, tackling community concerns and security questions along the way. Today, the grounds of Temple University appear safer than the sprawling campus of its Ivy League rival across town, the University of Pennsylvania, where the administration is more guarded in its dealings with the media.

Whether one is a university president, an elected official, or a corporate chief, avoiding the media is a recipe for trouble. In the most difficult media relations jobs in the area, Neil McDermott and Mike Wood of PECO Energy have made a career out of dealing directly with problems. Those in the public eye should also follow the model of David L. Cohen: return phone calls, be honest, and by all means don't hide behind your power.

Away from press considerations, the power arena in Philadelphia is more than a lunch at the Palm. It is a carefully crafted world that relies on two things—loyalty and truth. Through four decades, powerful lawyer Marty Weinberg has marched through the bloody terrain of Philadelphia politics and maintained his integrity and respect, in victory and defeat. That's because Weinberg stays true to his friends. Weinberg never gets good press, but his reputation endures. Philadelphia council president Anna Verna, a woman whose power has often been underestimated, maintains a cadre of loyal professionals because of her loyalty. Much the same respect is afforded the courageous John White, Jr. White broke ranks with his fellow Democrats in 1999 to endorse Republican Sam Katz. The respect and admiration of his contemporaries continues for White today, even though his candidate lost.

Unions are another key power source. Rich Costello, president of the Fraternal Order of Police, uses his broad verbal skills to argue the case of the individual police officer. Costello's power rests on the fact that police officers know he will never compromise their values. Many people in power, like Costello, maintain their political muscle through a fierce sense of loyalty to the people they serve. In power politics, "you" and "we" are much more important words than "me."

Endurance—the ability to survive in the power game—is truly admirable. Thacher Longstreth lost two elections for mayor, in 1955 and 1971. Despite those setbacks, the veteran city councilman endures into his ninth decade of life as a man who can only be described as Mr. Philadelphia. Lanky and long, distinguished and bow tied, Longstreth is so loved that Mayor Rendell endorsed the Republican in his 1999 re-election bid for City Council, an extraordinary move considering that Rendell had just been appointed Democratic national chairman. Longstreth has the usual political ambition and ego, but both traits are offset by an uncommon dedication to the needs of people.

Thacher and I have a common bond—MS. His wife, Nancy, and her lifetime of MS prompted Thacher to help organize the national effort to battle MS back in the fifties, the same decade that MS first visited my mother. Over the years, I have seen Longstreth fall off bicycles, lift heavy weights, run marathons, and cry his eyes out while inspiring people challenged by MS. Thacher was the chairman of the MS board while I was vice chairman. I can say with deep respect that having Mr. Philadelphia as my boss of sorts has been an honor.

Underdogs: Winning Isn't Everything

In Philadelphia politics, the troubled and those on the losing end are often the most interesting to cover. Winners glow in the joy of victory; losers, in their hours of defeat, tell you much about their character. In his unsuccessful years, Ed Rendell was a good loser, cheerful and determined to move on.

The best loser I have ever encountered is a real winner. His name is A. Charles Peruto. Peruto was one of the great criminal defense attorneys of his time, a beguiling man who caressed juries with his soft-spoken words and a body language that seemed to embrace jury members.

In 1969, Peruto ran for district attorney and lost. His campaign was aggressive and direct, a precursor of the Rizzo law-and-order era. Prior to election night, as was my practice, I called all the candidates, inviting them to join us live at Channel 6 after the votes were counted. To Peruto I said, "I want you here, win or lose."

When he was soundly defeated, a proud Peruto showed up at our door, much to the shock of the news executives. News director Pat Polillo said, "What are we going to do?" I replied, "Put him on television." The Peruto appearance was the most unusual political interview. The attorney, using strong and emotional words, said, "I didn't do it tonight, but I fought the good cause for a better society. I may have let a lot of people down, but in my heart, I know that running was the best thing, the only thing. This is such a great city. It would be wonderful to serve it. But I got my you-know-what handed to me, so onward and upward." Peruto said more, but what really sticks with me is a vision of him walking out of the studio. He glanced over at me, winked, and said, "I told you I'd be here, win or lose." A class act, that Peruto, in person and in the courtroom. Peruto's Democratic opponent, David Berger, was soundly defeated by Arlen Specter in the November election.

For Bob Brady, the son of a policeman, rising to the top was a rough, rugged road. He has served as committeeman, ward leader, Democratic city chairman, and congressman of the First District. The

First District is loaded with irony and history. Congressman Bill Barrett ruled the district for thirty-five years, flying home every day from Washington. Congressman Ozzie Myers, a political veteran of the South Philly wars, was forced to quit after Abscam. Tom Foglietta took Myers' place, serving with distinction. Bob Brady replaced Foglietta when Foglietta became ambassador to Italy. Brady is big in size and stature and is respected by most Democratic politicians. But his rise to power was not without bumps and bruises.

In 1991, Ron Castille, the popular incumbent D.A., had resigned to run for mayor, and the Democrats were looking for a replacement. Brady, an irrepressible joker, remarked in a leadership meeting that there would be too many Jews in office if Lynne Abraham got the nod, a reference to the fact that both mayoral candidate Ed Rendell and Controller Jon Saidel were Jewish. Brady's remark was greeted with raised eyebrows. It sparked a firestorm of controversy, but those who know Brady could understand the context of his ill-timed remark because they knew Brady didn't have a hateful bone in his body. In the back rooms of Philadelphia politics, for better or for worse, it is common for whites, blacks, Jews, Italians, and Irish to joke about their own and other people's ethnic groups.

Realizing that Brady was disturbed by the outburst in response to his remark and looking to clarify the story, I called him at his Democratic chairman's office on Walnut Street. I said, "Bob, you're upsetting all of my friends. What gives?" He answered, "No way, you know me. It wasn't like that at all." I said, "Bob, meet me at the station. You can explain whatever you want."

The interview revealed that Brady was remorseful and clearly embarrassed. His explanation, that it had all been political joking around, seemed plausible. The report that night helped people understand that Bob Brady was not a bigot. For that, he was forever grateful, especially given that the man doing the interview was Jewish. For Brady, the furor was a small detour on the way to Congress and power. For me, the unusual interview cemented an already strong relationship.

Part of the art of news-gathering is the ability to improvise and surprise. I've always enjoyed calling election losers, consoling them and offering my analysis. The usual result is that I get their stories first down the road. But the call I made to Joe Biden in the late summer of 1987 was not enjoyable.

Joe Biden had just withdrawn from the race for president after accusations that he had plagiarized from a speech given by a noted British political leader. In retrospect, considering the excessive scandals of the nineties, Biden's alleged impropriety pales by comparison. But in 1987, it was a big deal.

Two months earlier, I had joined Biden on his whirlwind trip through America to announce his candidacy. We began at the Wilmington train station, traveled to the U.S. Senate, and then on to Des Moines, Boston, and three cities in New Hampshire in an exciting and uplifting exhibition of political prowess. Joe Biden was and is the real thing. If he had stayed in the race, I'm positive he would have been the Democratic nominee in 1988. Biden was a charismatic, eloquent, and seasoned Senate veteran. During his stops on the announcement tour, ordinary people were turned on by his direct style and his appeal for sanity in government.

Earlier that year, Biden and I had dinner at Mara's, a popular Italian eatery on Passyunk Avenue. There, over pizza and pasta, Joe Biden, the youngest man ever elected to the U.S. Senate, offered his strategy on winning. He said, "Larry, I can win. I can reach the middle and secure the left, and I can beat Bush." His only problem was Mario Cuomo, but the New York governor, as he was prone to do, decided not to run. That left Dukakis, who was fairly weak.

But Biden never got the chance to show his stuff. That was a blessing. On the night of the 1988 New Hampshire primary, walking in a snowdrift with our producer, I got the word that Joe Biden had an aneurysm that had almost killed him and that brain surgery had saved his life. What if Joe Biden had labored on the campaign trail with no chance to pause for a checkup?

Biden remains one of the most powerful senators in Washington, a man who has made his small state proud. Quite often, when I look at the cast of characters on the national scene, I wonder what might have followed if that colorful campaign in the summer of 1987 had been allowed to survive.

Jailbirds

Allenwood Federal Prison in central Pennsylvania has a reputation as a country-club prison, an image fueled by the municipal golf course that runs alongside the minimum security facility. In reality, Allenwood is a prison of dormitories where prisoners are on a routine—up at five o'clock, work at seven o'clock, lights out at nine o'clock. It is a prison—no question about it.

One chilly morning at 6:00 A.M., Henry Cianfrani emerged from Allenwood. Buddy, as he's known in Philadelphia, had served longer than anyone convicted in Watergate, a full twenty-seven months in prison. Cianfrani was once the chairman of the Senate Appropriations Committee in Pennsylvania. He knew the path to the money and had the keys to the kingdom known as the capital of political influence. Often, during his imprisonment, he had been placed in shackles and brought to an office, where he was given an offer. The Feds, he told me, said, "Buddy, give us Rizzo and you're out of here." Cianfrani told me, "Rizzo was clean. I don't know what they were talking about."

Cianfrani had agreed to meet me for an exclusive interview on the day of his release. The man who faced me that morning was changed. Gone was the cheerfulness that had marked his public image. Buddy Cianfrani, the pride of Philadelphia politics, seemed angry and bitter—relieved to be out, but tired and beaten.

Cianfrani, a Democrat, had been convicted in a federal court of mail fraud and obstruction of justice. Many insiders, including prosecutors, felt that Cianfrani was punished as an example to other state legislators because he knew where the skeletons were, or so the government thought. If there were indeed skeletons, no one ever found them, because Cianfrani was the stealth prisoner, serving his time in poised and controlled silence.

Buddy Cianfrani was one of my first and most powerful news contacts, a practical man who taught me more about street politics than anyone in Philadelphia. He taught me about WAM—"walking around money," or the casual cash distributed by the legislature to lawmakers routinely for "special projects" in their districts. Cianfrani also taught me about the power of ward leaders. If you wanted to win citywide, you had to pass Cianfrani before you reached the end of the rainbow. He was the ultimate ward leader.

When the senator went to Allenwood, he lost his power, but not his allure. Cianfrani received so much mail that he asked people to stop writing. In the years since his imprisonment, he has consulted for almost every major candidate for office. Several years ago, Cianfrani's seventieth birthday was marked by a gala party. The celebrants included mayors, senators, the district attorney of Philadelphia, most members of City Council, and dozens of legislators. Buddy was near tears. The man dis-

graced in the prime of his career was feted by his most important constituents—his peers—in a vindication of sorts, an expression of respect
for a life of giving.

Cianfrani was a high-profile prisoner, but he wasn't alone. In a
period of a few years, more than a fourth of my political contacts were
gone from the scene. Corruption investigations savaged the career of
Congressman Josh Eilberg, who had once sat in judgment of Richard
Nixon in the House Watergate investigation. Pennsylvania house
speaker Herbert Fineman went away for a while. Abscam, the bribery
trap launched by agents posing as Arab businessmen, sent New Jersey
senator Harrison Williams to jail and forced Congressman Ozzie Myers
from office. Other Abscam felons included Congressman Ray Lederer;
George X. Schwartz, president of Philadelphia City Council; Councilman Harry Jannotti; and the popular mayor of Camden, Angelo
Errichetti.

But the arrests and disgrace didn't stop at Abscam. Philadelphia
councilman Leland Beloff went to federal prison on bribery charges.
Pennsylvania attorney general Ernie Preate was also a corruption victim and headed off to prison. Preate, a gubernatorial hopeful and the
state's top law officer, was stunned and saddened. Statewide, State
Treasurer Budd Dwyer shot and killed himself before a news conference rather than face jail for his conviction.

There were others, their paths strewn with broken dreams. One
of those ill-fated dreamers was the man who invented downtown block
parties in Philadelphia, a colorful politician with a flair for the dramatic.
His charisma followed him all the way to jail.

When I arrived at the Schuylkill Federal Correctional Facility near
Pottsville, the prison publicist outlined the rules: I could spend one
hour with the prisoner, no more. Walking through a corridor, I glanced
in at an inmates' meeting and saw evidence of the demographics of
white-collar crime. Most of the heads were graying; many were bald. It
was a sight both startling and pitiful: men in the autumn of their lives
wearing prison green, aging in incarceration, a lifestyle they had created by their own actions.

Jimmy Tayoun walked in, surrounded by prison officials. Tayoun
was grinning broadly. It had been years since our last meeting, just
before he was sentenced in a bribery and racketeering case. Tayoun,
the extroverted, hard-driving Philadelphia city councilman, has been a
man to reckon with. Tayoun owned the Middle East restaurant on the

east end of Chestnut Street. In between hummus and belly dancing, he managed to rebuild the image of Old City Philadelphia, with annual street fairs and block parties that enlivened the neighborhood and attracted new businesses. He was a promoter's promoter, and when Jim headed to the federal prison for abusing his political position, the neighborhood around Front and Chestnut was never quite the same.

A week earlier, I had interviewed Delores Tayoun in the couple's South Philadelphia home, learning of her difficulties while the love of her life was in prison. Delores kept referring to Tayoun as "my Jimmy," and it seemed that, more than any financial hardship or public embarrassment, she suffered from missing him terribly. When Tayoun greeted me at prison, he asked, "How's Delores? How is she doing?" I said, "Fine, and how are you?" He replied, "Let me tell you about my life here."

Tayoun looked fit and trim, though his hair was no longer jet black, but more salt and pepper. In the conference room, two other inmates were mopping a linoleum floor. Tayoun said, "Look at them, Larry. They mop that floor every day for hours. That's what they do, mop the same floor over and over again. What a waste." I said, "Jim, what's your job?" Tayoun replied, "I keep the books for the food here and tinker with the computers. I also counsel younger prisoners about life on the outside. I'm also writing a book to prepare convicted felons for life in prison."

Then, much to my surprise, the interview turned around, with Tayoun pleading with me to give him a complete fill-in on the political landscape of 1995. The man was in prison for his extracurricular political activities, but politics was still running through his nervous system. He was addicted.

The interview on his life in prison lasted for over an hour, followed by a walking tour of the facility. In the hallways and on the grounds, Jim was treated as a respected elder, a star, with his boundless energy and knowledge of the art of getting things done appreciated in jail as much as it had been on the streets. After the camera was put away, a middle-aged man in a business suit walked over to Jim and embraced him. It was the warden, who extolled the virtues of having a man like Mr. Tayoun in the federal prison system.

I was impressed. Facing his punishment, the King of Lower Chestnut Street had emerged as the handshaking, energized, unofficial mayor of the Schuylkill Federal Correctional Facility, with enough time left to write a book and mediate prisoner disputes.

Tayoun was remorseful about his crimes and concerned that the folks back home would forget him and the positive side of his public service. He was also devilish in his art of dropping pieces of information here and there, little teases of questionable knowledge. Before our departure, Jim shook my hand and said, "I have a tip for you. Watch out for Delores. She may run for my old seat." I said, "Gimme a break." He said, "Larry Kane, my word is my word. Don't bank on it, but Delores might make a run for it." He was tickling my political funny bone. That fiendish look in his eyes told me everything I needed to know.

Delores Tayoun never ran for political office. Jim Tayoun came back to town, closed up the Middle East, his restaurant, and acted as adviser for several political candidates. His book was a best-seller among the handful of convicts able to buy it. Today, his audience is broader. Tayoun is the publisher of a weekly newspaper covering politics and government.

The fates of others I've mentioned here have varied. Buddy Cianfrani continues to serve electoral hopefuls with advice for the ages. He remains a Philadelphia political legend. The other people in my coverage circle who went to jail emerged to different lives, mostly obscure, far from the crowds that ran to them like magnets at the height of their victories. The lives of these men serve as proof that, in Philadelphia and its region, power is fleeting, and abuse of it can take you from top gun to songbird to jailbird in a few easy steps.

Toys in the Attic

The Governor's House sits on the banks of the Susquehanna River in Harrisburg. The house is more like a museum, with its walls lined with Revolutionary War–era paintings, and antique curtains draped around its beautiful windows. The house was nearly destroyed during the 1972 floods of Tropical Storm Agnes, but money was found to rebuild it.

Since early 1979, the Governor's House has been fully occupied by three governors and their families—the Thornburghs, the Caseys, and the Ridges. Milton Shapp, the governor from 1970 to 1978, rarely stayed overnight there, preferring to shuttle back to his Merion home. The Casey family seemed awed by the building. Tom Ridge and his wife had

two young children to care for, as the basketball court set up in the driveway attested.

Dick and Ginny Thornburgh enjoyed the big building, entertaining
with flourish and relishing the chance to walk the halls of history. The
Thornburgh house was formal and proper, very old-line Republican,
almost a Union League west. But it contained a secret place, and I was
taken to it on the Thornburghs' final day in the Governor's House. The
governor had granted me an exclusive look at his eight years in office.
He seemed sad and sentimental as we walked through the halls of the
family quarters. Then the governor said, "Larry, I want to take you to a
special place." He opened a small door, we climbed a few steps, and
there in the attic was the private world of Richard Thornburgh—a play-
room, an escape, "his room," as he described it. Thornburgh said, "I
needed a place to wind down, cool off, and just be a normal, disheveled
person." Indeed, in front of us sat a clutter of books, stacks of paper,
enough newspaper to fill a recycling center, and hundreds of letters. The
governor of Pennsylvania, at times a stoic, extremely conservative man,
had his private hideaway, his own tool shop of words.

Thornburgh served as attorney general of the United States in the
Reagan and Bush administrations. He ran unsuccessfully for the U.S.
Senate, served at the United Nations, and then went into practice as a
private lawyer.

Guest at the White House

I never slept in the Lincoln Bedroom, but I have visited the White
House a dozen times. Those visits were tantalizing in their revelations
of the moods and characters of presidents.

In June 1972, Donna and I met Richard and Pat Nixon. We were
invited to a White House briefing session, followed by cocktails with the
first family. It was just days after our son, Michael, was born, and Channel 6, recognizing Donna's delicate situation, sent us down in a car.

The briefing featured John Ehrlichman and Bob Haldeman, two
Nixon advisers who would later fall as a result of Watergate. The most
interesting briefer was National Security Adviser Henry Kissinger, who
forecast that Communism would fall by 1990. We thought he had lost
his mind.

In the White House, we stood on a receiving line to meet the president and first lady. Nixon, who had been briefed ahead of time, said, "Mr. and Mrs. Kane, I understand you have a baby boy. Do you want him to be president?" Donna spoke for us both when she answered, "I hope he'll have a lot of options." Then Nixon started talking about Frank Rizzo and urged me to send his regards. Later that night, I called Rizzo with the message, but he did me one better. "After your little visit," Rizzo told me, "the president called me to say hello." I asked, "What did he say?" Rizzo replied, "That we have to get together and shoot the breeze. Great man, isn't he?" Rizzo was smitten with the presidential attention.

My most revealing White House visit was a similar briefing offered by the Reagan administration in the fall of 1981, months after Ronald Reagan had been shot and wounded. Somehow, I managed to wind up at the president's table at lunch. Reagan looked healthy. But he was obsessed with the food and wine on the table, urging us to try the Napa Valley wines. "Nancy picked out the wines and the dessert cookies," he said. "Everybody, take one. You'll love it." At one point, I asked Reagan about his tax cut plan, but he kept pointing to the cookies. And then came a moment I will never forget. Throughout the meal, he kept directing questions to one of his press aides, who had been with him for years. Her name was Carla, but he kept calling her Karen and even addressed her as Karen in an impromptu speech. She was near tears. When Reagan left the room, I asked her what was wrong. She explained, "You know, sometimes he just forgets."

The Press

The rivalry between the printed press and the broadcast media has been alive and well since the days when John Cameron Swayze pioneered the first national newscast in the fifties. Philadelphia's newspapers have produced brilliant journalism, and during my early years here, it was common for TV news reporters to scour the newspapers for stories. Today, the opposite may be true. TV newsrooms, sophisticated in the art of pursuing local news, are often first on important stories. Not one newspaper newsroom in the Philadelphia area doesn't monitor local newscasts regularly.

In my time, I've run into some impressive journalists and witnessed some extraordinary efforts in the print arena. The *Inquirer*'s investigative reports on police corruption changed the scope of the Philadelphia Police Department. The *Daily News* is a power in its own right, with longtime editor Zach Stalberg leading the way. But the real story lies in the effort by print journalists to get the facts, whatever it takes. There are two types of journalists in this town: the crafty information gatherers and those who intentionally or inadvertently become assassins in print. First, the good news.

Paul Taylor is one of Philadelphia's major contributions to American journalism. A political reporter at the *Inquirer* and the *Washington Post*, Taylor chronicled the rise of Frank Rizzo with a sharp pen and an even sharper eye for analysis. Taylor is now the leading activist fighting for free air time for national political candidates. Buzz Bissinger, who covered the Wilson Goode contests and recently published a book on Ed Rendell and city, may be the best political writer I've ever read. Columnists have also made their mark. The finest of this generation was the late Tom Fox, a *Daily News* and *Inquirer* columnist who pinned the moniker "big bambino" on Frank Rizzo. Fox wrote of the city's people—their passions, their dreams, and their lives on area streets. Stu Bykofsky has left his mark with his lively and news-breaking column at the *Philadelphia Daily News*. *Inquirer* columnist and editor Acel Moore was a pioneer in urban reporting. Howard Shapiro, one of Philadelphia's greatest government reporters, is the most multifaceted journalist in Philadelphia, covering just about everything—politics, the arts, and now travel.

My experiences with local journalists have been mostly pleasant. TV writers Rex Polier and Harry Harris chronicled the growth spurt of local TV news. Neal Zoren has continued their tradition at the *Delaware County Times* and other suburban papers. Ellen Gray of the *Daily News* is a media-savvy writer who generates wonderful reader response. At the *Jewish Exponent*, Mike Elkin makes his mark as one of the most knowledgeable and talented entertainment writers in the nation. But for the last eighteen years, Gail Shister has been the premier TV columnist in this region.

If Gail Shister were an investigative reporter, I would put political and government leaders on red alert. She is one of the most unstoppable, unrelenting reporters in this business, so much so that little information about the business of television escapes her grasp. Shister began her TV beat in 1982, after three years of Philadelphia sports reporting. She was the *Inquirer*'s first woman sports journalist. She is a friend, but friendship will never get in the way of her reporting. Her *Inquirer* column has become a "must read" for network executives. She is rarely off base, but if she is, she'll hear from me first. The mark of a first-rate reporter is the willingness to have a thick skin when it comes to criticism. Shister has that, but not everybody does.

Chuck Stone was a veteran columnist for the *Philadelphia Daily News*. Stone was a brilliant writer who motivated people to think, and sometimes he was a person with a rage and a passion that were excessive and uninhibited. In his zest for justice for all, Stone was such a respected crusader that he holds a Philadelphia record for suspect and fugitive surrenders. It was commonplace for those sought by the law to give themselves up to Stone.

Stone had one problem: sometimes his columns bordered on race-baiting and character assassination. A favorite target was Congressman Bill Gray. Stone skewered Gray, suggesting personal improprieties and a lack of integrity. Gray, at the time, was on a fast track to leadership in Congress and was personally enraged at Stone's campaign against him. But it didn't stop. Stone never did. For the *Daily News*, Stone was a big attraction. But sometimes he indulged in the kind of the excessive journalism that can give our industry a bad name. And Chuck Stone, the man whose attacks would sting and hurt others, was also one of the most thin-skinned people in Philadelphia journalism.

The former *Daily News* columnist had never really been comfortable around me. In fact, Chuck Stone disliked me—especially on the night of May 13, 1985, when he went way too far, almost igniting the city. The Move neighborhood was burning, and our distinguished reporter Harvey Clark was interviewing Stone live on TV. Stone started insinuating that the bombing was racially motivated and suggested that the problem might spread citywide. He began a monologue on the events of the night that was inflammatory and irresponsible. Troubled, I cut him off. Just said thank you and moved on. Wrong. He later crucified me in speeches. But he was playing with fire on the night of the Move confrontation, and there was no way I was going to let him do that. If I could change one thing about that night, I would have cut him off sooner.

Let's Break for Sports

Sports has always been a necessary diversion from the news, providing us with excitement and drama. In Philadelphia and its surrounding areas, big league sports is a way of life, and the people who run the teams are among the community's most fascinating characters.

Eagles owner Leonard Tose is the forgotten man of Philadelphia sports. Even when embroiled in an unsuccessful court battle over his gambling debts, the former trucking-company millionaire was one of the most generous people in public life. During the Italian earthquake, Eagles general manager Jim Murray presented me privately with a check for $25,000 to take to a devastated community. It was vintage Tose—supreme generosity, no need for publicity. Tose's years of running the Eagles were memorable years of class and accomplishment. It's a shame that his living the high life erased all of that, but many still remember his small and large acts of generosity.

Norman Braman owned the Eagles and sold the Eagles, but he made one mistake. As I had during my two-city broadcasting jaunt in 1977, Braman lived in Miami and commuted to games. Philadelphians don't like that. But I liked Braman a lot. During a profile for the *Bulletin* program, Braman took me to a Holocaust memorial in Miami Beach that he had almost single-handedly pushed to completion. He was a man on a mission, a man who was clearly a humanitarian, even though he may have been dismissed by the fans as a carpetbagger.

Ed Snider, the owner of the Flyers, and Pat Croce, chief of the Sixers, are two awesome Philadelphians. Snider will spare no expense to fund a winner. Croce brought the fans back into the Sixers' mix. Both men embody the best in sportsmanship and community spirit, giving their time and money for a variety of causes.

And when it comes to the Sixers, let's not forget Charles Barkley. Barkley came here from Alabama. In the mid-eighties, they dubbed him "the round mound of rebound," a not-so-delicate reference to his heavyweight physique. In two years, Charles would slim down for the Philadelphia 76ers basketball team and emerge as one of the All Stars of his generation.

My experiences with Barkley were, in a word, fantastic. During a taping of the adoption special, "Thursday's Child," Barkley entertained an eight-year-old foster child with wit and compassion. In those days, he called me "Mr. Kane." He was usually polite, but sometimes another side emerged. In 1990, at my annual charity golf classic at Twining Valley in Upper Dublin, Charles participated and left a special impression. On the thirteenth hole, Barkley, intense and defiant in golf as in round-ball, smashed a 270-foot drive that hooked perilously toward oncoming cars. The ball bounced on the pavement, landing in a front yard. Charles launched into a sentence of a hundred profanities, cursing and screaming so loudly that I could hear him at the clubhouse. Next to him, an admiring young boy looked up in shock. Barkley went over to the youngster and said, "Now, son, if I ever hear you repeating what I just said, one word of it, son, I will get mad. What I did was bad, you hear me—bad! If you ever repeat those words, young man, I will crush you."

In 1997, I conducted an all-day interview and a lifestyle shoot with Charles at his home in Houston, where he was playing for the Rockets. The two of us spent the day watching TV, joking about life, and engaging in some serious talk. Charles was trying to convince me that he, the wild and outspoken conscience of the NBA, had matured—that he was going to avoid abusive fans in bars, calm down his language, and grow up. He was believable. The next week, back in Philadelphia, the news wires reported that Charles, insulted by a rowdy man in an Orlando bar, took the man with both hands and threw him through a plate glass window.

The Charles Barkley basketball era ended with an injury in December 1999. The game, ironically, was being played against the Sixers in Philadelphia. He returned later in the season to play one more game and retire in style.

In sports as in life, it's hard to find heroes. But there are a few. Temple basketball coach John Chaney is a man who puts the cause of people before winning, and this makes him a winner. Ditto for former Eagles coach Dick Vermeil. And my all-time favorite Philadelphia sports figure is Bob Clarke. For over three decades, Clarke has been part of the Flyers' picture as player, general manager, and president. In all of that time, Bob Clarke has retained the same values as the nineteen-year-old who arrived at the old Spectrum in the late sixties. Through it all, winning and losing, he came back to Philadelphia.

Which leads me to an interesting observation. Most of the original Flyers champs stayed here, far from their homes in Canada. Eagles stars—including Mike Quick, Ron Jaworski, Bill Bergey, Harold Carmichael, and a host of others—remain here. Even Dick Vermeil, who coached in St. Louis, maintains a home in our town. Some athletes have spent their whole lives in this community, such as Joe Frazier, the heavyweight champion of the world. Joe was a hero to me, a Philadelphia man who, through hard work and grit, became a boxing legend. Like Chaney and Clarke, Joe is always there for the community and always available when you need him. What makes these people stick here, while a star like Mike Schmidt lives elsewhere? It's simple. Philadelphians know when people really love them. The affection our town displays for sports heroes goes beyond their accomplishments. It's all about the attitudes, not the platitudes. That's why Julius Erving, Larry Bowa, and Pete Rose, wherever they live, will always be able to view Philadelphia as home sweet home.

Doing some sports reporting has always been a fantasy of mine. Can you imagine a job where almost everything is scheduled, where work is a ticket to a sporting event? And what about the studio work? Three minutes a night, and you can wear a polo shirt to work. No crime, just lots of stats, stories about egomaniacal players, and dramatic, last-minute finishes. Beasley Reece knows that if he ever falters, if the voice is stopped by a cold and a cough, I will be ready to step in. But does he worry? I'm afraid not. In terms of my creative ability to fill the vacuum of a man like Beasley, the former star NFL player who does the sports reporting on KYW TV has absolutely nothing to worry about.

Personalities: "Unknown"

Ask any reporter. It's the small stories you remember, the small stories you recall with smiles and sometimes embarrassment. The dates and times of these events may have faded away, the names may be unknown, but the incidents are unforgettable.

The Philadelphia narcotics squad is one of the nation's best. During the taping of a special report, I accompanied the narcs on an evening of drug busting that took us to a most unlikely place, a row home in Oxford Circle occupied by two young women, both professionals. When no one answered the door, the axe went to work, along with the hammer. As we walked into the living room, we heard the sounds of a toilet flushing and voices screaming in the back of the house. Two women in nightgowns were running through the rooms. Once caught, they were handcuffed. Lying on their stomachs, they moaned and spit at any leg they could find. One of them said, "You ugly pig pricks, bastards!" Then she looked at me and exclaimed, "Larry Kane! I watch you all the time. Never miss you." In a flash, the look of surprise faded away and she added, "Kane, you are a bastard. What the hell are you doing here? You're a real shit." I felt badly about the intrusion, although that feeling went away when the two were convicted of distributing cocaine.

Another crackerjack unit of the Philadelphia Police Department is the stakeout squad, designed to handle terrorism and civil unrest. The squad quite often travels in disguise to capture drug dealers. The late George Fencl, the famed police mediator who supervised the department's civil disobedience unit, once urged me to ride with stakeout and to take a look at their mastery of disguise.

So I did. The first order of business was to take me to an abandoned school, where I received a makeover—a blond wig, a blond moustache, some pancake makeup—to guarantee my anonymity. When I looked in the mirror, I was stunned by the makeover job. I was confident that even Donna wouldn't have recognized me.

Our first job was to arrest a mugger on Lehigh Avenue. Knowing that I could walk the streets anonymously, I strolled up to the wagon where the suspect was sitting, handcuffed and scowling. He looked up and said, "Lar, are you crazy? What are you doin' with that bad rug and the blond hair. Have you lost it, Lar?" It's moments like that that a newsperson never forgets.

A Philadelphia Story: Almost Murder on Bustleton Avenue

Sometimes, the most memorable stories are the ones you hear told by real people, not reporters. Joseph Donahue has been cutting my hair for thirty years. Joe is a man of talent. His hairstyles are famous, along with his stories about life in Philadelphia. One tale he tells evokes true passion in him: an instructive story about the Philadelphia mob wars in the eighties.

Bustleton Avenue and Magee is an intersection off of Roosevelt Boulevard in the heart of the Northeast. The neighborhood is filled with

thank Mayor Ed Rendell, one of the keynote speakers at an Ad Club function mark-ing my thirtieth year in Philadelphia broadcasting. (Photo courtesy of Liz Wuillermin)

U.S. Senator Arlen Specter joins me for a live town meeting in the studios of KYW TV (Photo courtesy of Liz Wuillermin)

The city's chief law officer meets the nation's chief law officer. Lynne Abraham, the Philadelphia district attorney, hands U.S. Attorney General Janet Reno a care package of food during Reno's 1998 trip to Philadelphia. (Photo courtesy of Lynne Abraham)

epublican National Committeeman Herbert Barness pauses to talk with me on the oor of the 1996 Republican National Convention in San Diego. (Photo courtesy of 1argaret M. Cronan)

I take a walk with former Philadelphia councilman Jim Tayoun at the Schuylkill Federal Prison near Pottsville in the winter of 1995. (Photo courtesy of Andrea Korff, KYW-TV photographer)

Pennsylvania state senatorial power Vincent Fumo huddles with Governor Bob Casey, plotting legislative strategy, in early 1992. (Photo courtesy of Senator Fumo)

At the Governor's House in Harrisburg in 1995, I get ready for a profile of Governor and Mrs. Ridge during the governor's first year in office. (Photo courtesy of Jim Spering, KYW TV)

President Richard Nixon greets me during a 1972 reception at the White House. (Photo courtesy of the Nixon Project/National Archives)

I watch pensively as President Reagan addresses a group of editors and reporters at a luncheon six months after the attempt on the president's life in 1981. (Photo courtesy of the Ronald Reagan Library)

Philadelphia 76ers star Charles Barkley joins golf pro Will Reilly and me at the 1988 Twining Valley Charity Golf Classic, which I have chaired for thirteen years. (Photo courtesy of Hugh P. Reilly)

Joe Frazier, heavyweight champion of the world, and I pose outside the WPVI studios in 1974. (Photo courtesy of Donna Jarrett-Kane)

During a 1968 union banquet at Palumbo's, Emil Capobianco gathers with his family. Capobianco is seated third from the right-hand end of the first table, facing the viewer. The young man to his left is his son, Emilio Capobianco, Jr., who is seated next to Emil's niece, Patricia Picariello. The first three people nearest the viewer are (right to left) Emil's niece Elizabeth (Lisa) Picariello, his sister Elizabeth (Betty) Picariello, and his girlfriend, Margaret Mahoney. (Photo courtesy of Patricia Picariello VanGilder)

Camille Lucci visits me on the set of Eyewitness News at KYW 3 in February 2000. (Photo courtesy of Camille Lucci and Donna Jarrett-Kane)

Walt Hunter at work. Hunter is famous for his broadcast exclusives. I consider him the greatest Philadelphia reporter of his era. (Photo courtesy of Walt Hunter)

Before the 1988 election, I host a debate between the two surviving Democratic candidates, Jesse Jackson and Michael Dukakis. (Photo © David M. Warren/GSP)

post–World War II row homes, baseball fields, synagogues, and churches. It is relatively safe, with its wide streets and easy commerce. Before he moved to Jenkintown, Joseph Donahue's barber shop was located there. It was late 1983 when disaster almost struck.

Joe has told this story for years in his Jenkintown salon, and it never gets old. He says: "So, it's a nice morning and three guys come in that I've seen before. Two of them are part of some hit man gang, a branch of the old Bruno mob. The third is an ex-FBI agent who advises them. They're waiting for a haircut, smoking, just talking, when out on the sidewalk, they see a tall man wearing a trench coat, a hat covering his face, looking kind of scary to them. The man in the coat makes a left turn and [comes] down the steps into my shop. He walks confidently, with a sort of a bounce. As he enters the door, they go crazy. Both of them reach under their coats and pull out 357 magnums, the safeties off, and they take direct aim at the mystery man in the coat. I look over and scream, 'No, don't! Don't!' They are about to pull the triggers when the man, frozen with fright, takes his hat off. The man is a customer, a well-known guy in the community, a rabbi. No kidding, a rabbi, just walking in for a Thursday morning haircut. The men calmly put the guns away. The rabbi, realizing that his life was saved in a second, sits in the waiting area. Later, I apologized to the rabbi, gave him a haircut, and he left. I never saw him again. Can you blame him?"

Putting a Face on the Names

Not every memorable personality is well known or the stuff of celebrity. Some offer stories that take you to a higher understanding of events and people you might have covered in the abstract, stories that contribute to your knowledge in invaluable ways.

When you write about the perils and misery of individual people for a living, you can become numb to their pain. Night after night, you read names, and for most journalists, the names have no faces. Some prefer it that way. What you can't see won't hurt you. But if you don't feel the news as you tell it, you risk becoming jaded.

When it comes to remembering news stories, your memory doesn't always think the biggest stories are the most important. Sometimes you forget the details of those big stories, but you remember the specifics of stories that the public has long forgotten. That's because these stories have faces along with the names.

Very few people knew Emil Capobianco in the fall of 1968. But Emil's courage in the face of adversity may have saved hundreds of lives. His life may not be the stuff of legends, but to this reporter, he will always be a hero, and his plight, an unforgettable story.

Emil was one of six children born to Italian immigrants and raised in Philadelphia. At the age of fifteen, he joined the navy. His military career was eventful, earning him a purple heart, a silver star, and most of all, the respect of his fellow crew members aboard a landing craft that dropped off soldiers in Italy. It was on that craft that the trouble began. As the landing craft returned to pick up more soldiers, Emil heard a whistling sound in the air, and the officer next to him disappeared, blown away by a shell fired from German strongholds on the beaches. The episode traumatized him so much that, upon his return to the United States, he received psychiatric treatment for six months.

After that episode, Capobianco's heart began to weaken. In the summer of 1968, two cardiac surgery teams at Hahnemann Hospital had a turf war over who would perform the hospital's first heart transplant. Time was running out for Emil Capobianco, and he knew it. The carpenter from Northeast Philadelphia, oblivious to the risks of this dramatic new surgery, decided against both Hahnemann teams and flew to Houston, Texas, to a scheduled surgery with one of the transplant pioneers, Dr. Michael DeBakey.

I'd been working on the story for several weeks and hoped to follow it through. When Emil flew down to Houston, I joined him. We talked incessantly, mostly about his life. Capobianco had once been a boxer, the light heavyweight champion at navy boot camp. If he felt fear about his upcoming operation, I didn't see it. His only visible emotion was a determination to live. For three hours on the plane, a doomed man whose only chance was a heart transplant talked about his hopes for the future and his life in Philadelphia—the joy of living in a neighborhood of row homes, a failed marriage, a girlfriend, a son. His sister, Betty Picariello, joined us in Houston, where we said our farewells at the huge medical center. Two days later, the surgery was performed, and he only survived six hours after it. But in death, he gave others a better chance at life. His transplanted heart had come from a woman who was brain dead. For Emil's surgery, the doctors had kept her heart pumping artificially. The surgery's failure benefited future heart recipients, because surgeons learned that they could not transplant a heart that had been sustained by a pump. That was the first story I had done one on one with a person whose life was at risk. It gave me a face and a voice behind the name. Emil Capobianco died on October 24, 1968. He was forty-one. I will never forget his face or his courage.

The faces I remember from the night of November 17, 1974, were covered with bandages. The bodies were mainly in casts, the limbs in traction. The night before, I had received an urgent phone call to Channel 6 from Jack Essig, business manager of WPVI's rival, WCAU TV. Jack's family was closely associated with Country Day School of the Sacred Heart, located on Haverford Avenue just off City Line. On November 8, tragedy struck the small school. A station wagon carrying members of the field hockey team was en route to a game with Notre Dame Academy, their last game of the season. The late autumn sun was shining brilliantly, perhaps blinding the driver. The wagon struck an oak tree. One girl, only thirteen years old, died. The other nine suffered serious injuries. Country Day School of the Sacred Heart was enduring a tragedy. The suffering of the community was enormous, and the school administration was giving the devastated students love and support. Representing the school, Jack Essig called to tell me that one of the more seriously injured students hoped I would come and visit.

When I walked into Camille Lucci's room at Bryn Mawr Hospital, the sixteen-year-old was surrounded by a circle of family and friends. Camille's body was wrapped in traction, healing a fractured left arm, left wrist, and pelvis. After the accident, she was listed in poor condition. Yet that evening, her eyes beaming, her broad smile lighting up the room, Camille was in stable condition and deeply appreciative of my visit. When I leaned over to shake her hand, she gave me a polite kiss on the cheek. Excited, she said, "I'm so thrilled you came. This is such a bad time." We talked for a while, and then I was escorted downstairs to visit to another accident victim, a girl who was still in a coma.

When I returned to Camille Lucci's room, a visibly nervous Camille asked me, "Mr. Kane, it would mean so much to me if you could speak at our graduation. It would help everybody. Please." So in June 1975, I was commencement speaker at Country Day School of the Sacred Heart. It was a day packed with emotion and memory, tributes and praise. All graduation ceremonies are celebratory, but this event was also a prayerful remembrance of one child who couldn't be there and of nine others who cheated death. When Camille introduced me, there wasn't a dry eye in the courtyard.

In the twenty-five years since the Country Day School of the Sacred Heart tragedy, much has changed. The school moved to Bryn Mawr, where it regularly commemorates the tragedy. A policy now forbids students to drive themselves to take part in sporting events. Camille Lucci graduated from Beaver College, then earned master's degrees from Bryn Mawr and Rosemont. The one-time sports editor of the Sacred Heart newspaper has worked as a writer, teacher, and pension specialist for a major company. And every October 21, for the past twenty-five years, I have received a birthday card from Camille, along with a personal note. We have exchanged phone calls and visits, and during trying times, she has offered solace and sympathy.

Camille talks of my kindness. I appreciate her thoughts, but her plight and courage have served me as a priceless lesson, a reminder that we in the business of news are talking about real people. Camille Lucci, in her suffering, recovery, and friendship, put a human face on a tragic news story. Over the years, recalling Camille's plight and the plight of her friends in the Class of '75 has reminded me of how superficially we sometimes look at the challenges people face. Sometimes, regrettably, we forget that we are real human beings. Sometimes, in my business and in my Philadelphia, we forget our purpose and our calling, to serve people and to report on the challenges of life that confront them.

TV News: Hypocrisy, Reality, and the Future

As of this writing, local television news is at a critical juncture. Our credibility is at stake. Audiences are declining. Quality is not always job one. Listen to the analysis of two super professionals to get a deeper sense of what's at stake.

Veteran news director and current PBS executive Paul Gluck says, "We've underestimated the viewers so far that I hope that we'll still be able to serve them with the most important news—news that touches their lives. We've cultivated the blood lust of viewers. I only hope they can recognize the kind of service they deserve once news organizations go back to providing it."

CBS Stations News Vice President Joel Cheatwood sees peril ahead. Cheatwood says, "We'll become extinct unless we stay in touch and understand the visceral needs of viewers. We've got to plug into issues that stand out for people, especially local issues. Local news must become more niche-oriented. No longer can all the news stations have the sameness they do today. We must continue to provide alternatives. For me, the question is simple: Can local TV news provide enough fresh and special material to offset the immediacy of the Internet and cable?"

The warnings and caution flags are a sign of the damage done by some news executives. If local stations hesitate to act, they may become irrelevant. First, I would like to clear up some misconceptions.

In recent years, news organizations have received much criticism for moving toward "soft" news—stories about lifestyles and trends and away from the hard news of the day. This criticism has been lobbed mainly at television, but newspapers and magazines have drifted even further away than local television news from hard news—stories of government, crime, housing, legislation, and controversy. Yet newspapers are rarely criticized for their magazine-style coverage. Since the newspapers do much of the critiquing, it's no surprise that the newspaper trend toward feature news has rarely been spotlighted. This kind of hypocrisy runs rampant in the circle of national TV critics, who blast local TV news for its superficiality, but ignore the shortcomings of their own newspapers.

But it is true that TV news has moved toward "softer" stories. This move is a direct result of changing viewer appetites. But there's another change underway, and this one is for the better. Crime, the main staple of news in Philadelphia, is no longer the king of the airwaves. Crime is easy to cover, and it's a cheap way to fill newscasts. It's easier to cover a shooting than to examine the roots of crime, the social structure that foments it. In my early days at *Action News,* most of the newscasts were crime blotters. Covering crime stories of high impact is still important, but the days of petty crime reporting are over. Still, there are some news operations that would rather show pools of blood on a street corner than a high-school seminar against violence. And there are some news directors who, in the words of Frank Rizzo, "could screw up a two car funeral." For them, being first is more important than being right. The tabloid trend—the tendency to cover sensational stories with few or little facts—is causing blurred vision. The lines between truth and tabloid are hard to define—except, of course, when a sensational report is just plain false. In 1997, for instance, a Philadelphia television station reported the death of a New Jersey state trooper. The trooper never died, but the station hadn't checked out the facts. Such bad news practices cause a diminishing respect for television operations. This must stop or audience erosion will continue. The contest today is not one between "hard" and "soft" news, but one between the ratings-dominated quest for immediacy versus the need to be ethical and accurate.

There are some hopeful trends, including a move toward renewing the role of beat reporters and accentuating coverage areas that have meaning, such as education, finance, labor, medicine, fitness, and criminal justice. And some reporters have never lost touch with what matters. In the arena of justice and the law, KYW's Walt Hunter is the most powerful reporter of his era. He works the crowd and gathers information, moving like a deer hunter on the first day of the season. Walt Hunter is the best at it, hands down.

Hunter has his own World Wide Web of information gathering. He works his sources of information carefully. When suspects are arrested for major crimes, Walt Hunter gets the story first, and he gets it right. During a major investigation in late 1999, I asked a detective, "Please, remember to get the info. to us first." He replied, "Don't worry. Walt Hunter will have it before *we* do!" Hunter works the phones day and night. And he has the classic form of the great investigators: he will never compromise a source. Information is power, and Hunter knows how to use it. Burn a source one time by releasing information prematurely, and the information faucet will run dry. There is no luck in beat reporting, just the results you get from painstaking work.

On the political beat, knowing who to trust is important. I can't count the number of times politicians or press secretaries have floated information to me that was incorrect. The "float" is the art of sending information to powerful reporters and hoping that the information will be broadcast as a trial balloon for a possible candidacy, for pending legislation, or for a controversial decision. Sometimes, in close political campaigns, politicians will float nasty rumors, hoping that reporters will fall for the bogus reports and actually help foster the growth of the rumor. My biggest-breaking political story of 1999 was the report that Democrat John White, Jr., would endorse Republican Sam Katz for mayor. I confirmed the story at 10:56 P.M. When I broadcast it on KYW TV, I had no qualms whatsoever. I trusted my two sources, a trust built on years of conversation and dialogue. Exclusive reports usually come through years of establishing contacts.

Besides Walt and me, there are some other beat reporters left in TV journalism. Vernon Odom of WPVI has a good beat on government news. Dave Schratweiser of WTXF is a good investigator. I hope the move toward more compartmentalized news will foster the growth of reporters with similar talents.

The biggest shortcoming of local news lies in its coverage of the area I love most, politics. The fact is that politics is the bastard stepchild of local television. Tell most news directors to accent political coverage, and they will suggest you send a resume to public television.

But since I joined a television news team thirty-four years ago, politicians have been my game. Covering them has been exciting. And as I've mentioned above, for me, any election is a majestic happening. Free and without interference, voters make their choices, empowering politicians in victory, humbling them in defeat. Election day has always brought me butterflies—not the nervous performer's type, but the type you get when satisfying a wondrous and nervous fascination.

On every election day, I've traveled to polling locations and watched the people in line. And because of my supercharged election mood, on election night I always endure constant humor and ribbing. When the food is delivered for the staff covering the results, I generally pass. Election night brings me a state of anxiety unlike any other. But when all the results are in, I get a peaceful feeling. Driving home, I glance at the bright lights shining on Independence Hall, and in the dark of the night, pride at our freedom fills my mind and body. Yes, it's true. Politics is tarnished by money, lies, and betrayal. But it's also a force of change. That peace I feel is not about the state of politics, nor about the quality of politicians. Instead, it is a profound respect for the fact that, once again, the real root of power, the people, have had their way.

Many broadcast journalists consider politics boring. But government and the electoral process can alter our lives. Politics is taxes, schools, speed limits, abortion, crime fighting, license fees, military recruitment, zoning laws, freedom of speech, the drugs you take, the retirement you'll have, restrictions on behavior, limits on litigation, the stop sign in your neighborhood, and your freedom of action. Politics is insurance, criminal justice, the draft, food safety, consumer products, and the prices of what you buy. Does that cover just about every aspect of living?

There are two reasons for the distaste some journalists have for political news: an impression that no one in the audience cares and an awareness that it takes some hard work—the grinding pursuit of information—to cover politics well. Political coverage requires knowledge and sources.

Politicians often complain to me about the scarcity of political coverage. They are right on target, but they try to connect coverage with another issue. They seek free time during campaigns, an effort to separate access to huge amounts of money from political results. Other democratic nations require licensed stations to provide free time to candidates. We do not. Members of Congress voted to deregulate the broadcast industry, so they have themselves to blame. Deregulation has been a financial boon to my business, but it has also lowered government expectations for public service and community-based coverage. Deregulation is what freedom is all about—but politicians have to accept the new reality—that without regulation, stations are free to be what they want to be. My advice to Congress: if you give away the candy store, don't expect free candy.

And then we have another challenge: the exaggeration factor. Selected news directors, worried about the next rating book, the audience measurement standard, have lowered their guard and their values. WCAU TV in Philadelphia has made an art out of deceptive headlines and so-called "breaking news." All of us are guilty of overhype, but there should be a limit to the gross excesses of newspeople who never allow unconfirmed information to get in the way of a breaking story.

Credibility is built in two places—on air and behind the scenes. Producers who put news programs together are often not well read and are fascinated more with video than with information. They often overlook judgments about content. To my mind, the real superstar producers are the ones who understand what's important to people. These producers stay close to real people and real issues. I've been fortunate to work with many of them. But good journalism starts at the top. Nowhere is the trickle-down effect more important than in a TV news organization. If management commands that credibility is job one, than it usually results in a respectable product.

Some reporters and anchors in the current era are also not well equipped. It's refreshing to see anchors who are truly working journalists. They study. They learn. They understand ethical challenges. But many others wallow in ego, pinned to a desk and refusing to hit the street. They are the new TV deejays—desk jockeys. Desk jockeys do not flourish. They do not grow in stature with viewers. They really *are* anchors, anchored to their desks.

Another genuine challenge is the cult of personality in the TV news business. Paul Moriarty, the consumer reporter at KYW, is a definable personality, but he also delivers the goods: reports that are both educational and interesting. But local news has created a generation of "lookers" who trade on their raw appeal to compensate for knowledge and credibility. I have no quarrel with good looks. The combination of a good appearance, an inviting voice, and credibility is rarely a loser in local news. A local professor asked me, "Have you ever seen an ugly anchor?" Ugliness, like beauty, is in the eye of the beholder. But yes, I have seen successful broadcasters whose faces would never grace the cover of *GQ* or *Vogue*. What keeps all reporters and anchors successful is hard work and knowing the news.

Knowing your region and its newsmakers is another vital aspect of being a good broadcast journalist. Several years back, a writer asked me, "Tom Ridge is a Democrat, isn't he?" (The governor of Pennsylvania is a Republican.) The question revealed his lack of knowledge, but at least he asked. Many young producers and anchors will write first and pay later.

Along with knowledge, the "R" word comes into play: responsibility. As an anchor with years of experience, I've had the opportunity to make the newsroom a classroom for ethics. It has worked. Watching young people grow and learn in the newsroom environment has been one of the most gratifying parts of my career. In 1998, a murder happened in Montgomery County. We knew the victim's name, but the next of kin had not been notified. Before I could utter a word, a producer who was barely thirty years old screamed out to the writers, "Don't release that name. Under any circumstances. You'll be looking for work if you do."

These are the challenges facing television news: maintaining credibility, upholding responsibility (including ethical practices), developing broadcasters who are both journalists and captivating personalities, enhancing coverage of politics and government, and keeping the viewers' trust by taking care of their needs, information that will take them through the rigors of everyday life.

Here's what I see as the bottom line: providing information to the public is a dangerous business. Philadelphians and their neighbors are demanding viewers. Cross them, deceive them, give them false information, and you are toast. Work hard to give them unbiased, accurate news, and even when you screw up occasionally, they'll forgive and forget, though not before letting you have a piece of their minds. A long time ago, while I was walking down Market Street, a construction worker ran up to me. The man shook my hand, stared into my face, and said, "Lar, you're a no-bullshit guy. You give it to me straight, and that's the way I want my news." I replied, "Well, we try real hard." He roared back, "Well, Lar, that's what you have to do, because if you screw up, I'll grab that remote and click you out of my life. Have a great day, Lar."

Epilogue

Before I Say Good Night

The city of Philadelphia still shines brilliantly in the night for me, its skyline taller and its lights glowing in the tree-lined neighborhoods, reminding me that Philadelphia is the greenest city in the world, even at night.

My life has taken me to all of the beautiful big cities of the world: Paris, Prague, London, Rome, Barcelona, Chicago, and others. Philadelphia's beauty is still unmatched, with the meadows of South Jersey and the lush countryside of Delaware, all of its secret hideaways and treats for the eyes. In my fourth decade here, it still takes my breath away to see the Ben Franklin Parkway at night.

At the turn of the century, this beautiful city and its surrounding areas face challenges that seem insurmountable. The racial divide is still problematic. Regional cooperation is invisible. Efforts for improvement in these areas must be enhanced and fostered. Without its communities working together, Philadelphia will become like other big cities, strapped financially and trapped in its own legacy of provincialism, unable to find partners in the suburbs to keep it whole. But the area has survived past many crises and continued to flourish. What is emerging now is a Philadelphia region dominated by the suburbs but still dependent on the city for its emotional and spiritual drive.

Personally, my career in journalism is at a crossroads. My zest for news and broadcasting is stronger than it was when I started. I must admit that being a veteran has its advantages, automatically earning you respect. Once I was the kid anchor, and now I'm the so-called dean. Today, as I look around the newsroom, I see ever-present reminders of my years in broadcasting. Consumer reporter Paul Moriarty at KYW was once a production assistant for me at WCAU. Tracey Russell-Greene, our former assignment manager, was also a production aide, along with David Rogers, the successful meteorologist at KYW, now at WKYC in Cleveland. Watching people like them grow and develop in this business has been gratifying, but witnessing their growth firsthand is a reminder that I am suddenly becoming a senior rather than a junior anchor.

The viewers also tell you about age. Ten years ago, viewers would say, "Mr. Kane, I grew up watching you." Now their children are saying the same thing. Soon I'll be hearing from the grandchildren.

When I look back at my experience, at the length of time, the multitude of experiences, a realization sets in. Like Philadelphia, a timeless city retaining the same attitudes and traits, I really never changed in personality or in outlook. But, like the city and the region, for me reinvention was the key. With the help of family and friends, I kept reinventing and learning, probing and discovering, turning failure into a fearless time to move on and grow. It hasn't been easy, but neither are the growing pains of a great region.

Philadelphia's skyline grew higher as its spirits sank lower in the eighties, only to find hope and resurrection in the nineties. My time has had highs and lows, too, with few valleys of quiet in between. The other factor in staying power is the pact you make with people never to compromise your ideals, never to compromise their faith.

It's been a great run. Often, those brave enough ask, "Larry, what's next?" That's always the mystery, isn't it? What's next? What surprise or challenge is just around the corner? Obviously, no one can really see tomorrow, but I do know this: I will always be involved in news and in the life of this community. When the day comes to throw out the makeup (yes, I do my own), turn off the computer, and leave the newsroom, other pursuits of information and service will be waiting for me. Sure, I'll miss the drama, excitement, and challenge of telling the truth to people, but I'll find ways to be heard and to serve.

In the meantime, the wait continues. The phone rings, a bulletin arrives on the wires, sirens blare on the streets of the city, City Hall buzzes with speculation, lives are saved and lost, people are elected and thrown out of office, electronic journalism changes every day, and I wait for the next story, the big one. Will we get it first? Even more important, will we get it right? In the end, the only things that sustain you as a reporter, the only things that count, are your reliability, credibility, and capability to tell people the truth.

Thanks

Ron Tindiglia died on November 10, 1997, after a brutal battle with lung cancer. He was my best friend. We met in the newsroom at Channel 6 in 1966, where he started as a production assistant, rising quickly to writer and producer. We were buddies and soul mates who talked every night on the phone for thirty-two years, sharing our thoughts on TV and life, the pursuit of which was at times frustrating and challenging. Ron grew up in Yeadon, Delaware County, and came of age in the corridors of broadcast power, but he never forgot his roots or his family. Ron's kindness, caring, and focused brilliance touched the lives of hundreds of broadcasters. He was the ultimate people person, a problem solver with a passion for his business. We talked incessantly from the fall of 1966 to November 8, 1997, two days before his death. When Ron died, his going left a hole in my being, a vacuum where there had been a vital friendship that was central to my life. I think of him every day, and his pursuit of ethical and exciting journalism reverberates in my reporting, writing, and outlook on covering news.

Real friends are a rarity in television. Most people are professional acquaintances. But a few others also stand out. Rick Friedman, a Philadelphia native, worked with me for thirty years in various capacities. Rick, an amazing producer, has also been a great friend. In 1988, I hosted a live presidential debate between Michael Dukakis and Jesse Jackson. As airtime approached, Jesse Jackson was a no-show, an empty chair signifying my dilemma. Seconds before airtime, I asked the floor manager to find out what I should do. Suddenly, in the earpiece, a voice roared out, the voice of Rick Friedman from the control room. Rick said, "Lar . . . hmm . . . Lar . . . rock on!" Rock on I did, and when Jackson showed up five minutes later, I managed to bring him into the broadcast smoothly. Later I asked Rick, "What the hell did you mean when you said 'rock on'?" "Lar," he replied, "I didn't have a clue about what to do!"

Paul Anthony Gluck is a real Philadelphian, a kid from the Northeast with extraordinary talent and a mouth and a sense of humor to match. Gluck, now a high-ranking executive in public TV, was my news director twice, at WCAU TV and at KYW TV. Gluck is a strong journalist with an understanding of Philadelphia life, his mind a road map of the city's streets and themes. Paul did have one career problem—he never held his feelings in. His candor with two general managers cost him dearly. But in the end, Gluck was true to himself, and truth, to Paul Gluck, is more important than playing the political game.

Orien Reid was and is a Philadelphia star. A consumer reporter extraordinaire, Orien retired to devote her life to Alzheimer's research. We've been friends for over twenty years, and we share a birthday.

Merrill Reese is one of my heroes. The voice of the Eagles should be the subject of a book entitled, *When Good Things Happen to Good People.* Merrill's abilities are well known, and his record as one of the great guys of broadcasting is unmatched.

Bill Lawlor of WUSA in Washington and a former news director at WCAU is one of my professional mentors.

Many others offered me guidance and solace through the years. Steve Cohen, a graduate of Northeast High and Penn State, served as my general manager at WCAU TV. Jay Newman, a seasoned broadcast executive, was news director twice at WCAU. Jay is a man of enormous talent and is now a general manager in Baltimore. Scott Herman, now a key executive for Infinity Broadcasting, played a major role in making my transition to KYW TV so pleasurable, presiding as well over the launch of the *Bulletin* magazine. Jo Ann Caplin, executive producer of the *Bulletin,* taught me so much about magazine journalism. Her gang at the *Bulletin* sent a message to the industry: quality programming still counts. Joanne Calabria, communications director at KYW TV, sets the standard for press relations in our business. She remains the heart and soul of Channel 3.

It is true that my career and daily life have been enriched by the people behind the scenes, talented producers and technicians whose names are not known to you. The producers and writers, camera people and video editors are the lifeline of a news operation. I have worked with so many extraordinary people that it would be virtually impossible to name them all.

At KYW, the technical staff is led by two very talented people, crew chief Chris Brady and editing coordinator Charlene Horne. In their names, I salute the men and women of KYW TV, who work so hard to make the product great. You know who you are.

During the writing of this book, several people at KYW offered invaluable assistance and support. I want to thank General Manager

Marcellus Alexander; former station manager Joel Cheatwood; our current news director, Melissa Klinzing; and executives John Bell and Joanne Pallotta for their help and patience. Mike Quinn, our senior writer, offered invaluable help, along with Jane Matheson, whose experience in this community really enhanced the information in this book. Dave Harris, KYW information systems manager, gave me advice and shared his expertise, which was critical to the book.

There are so many people I've worked with on the air. It would be impossible to name all of them. People come and go, but some leave an indelible impression, mostly because of their friendship and kindness. I judge my fellow broadcasters on the content of their characters, not just on the level of their abilities.

Former on-air partners David Rogers, now a weatherman in Cleveland; Anchor Alan Frio, currently in San Diego; and Joe Pellegrino, still living here, where he is writing and doing sports radio, are among those special people. Orien Reid, as I have mentioned, is a magnificent friend. Harvey Clark, now in the public relations business, remains close.

My fellow anchors at KYW are a close-knit group. I hope I've given them as much support as they've given me.

The two men who sit by my side on *Eyewitness News* at eleven have made a real difference. When you see my eyes light up or my lips begin to curl into a smile, you can be sure that Weatherman John Stehlin and Sports Director Beasley Reece are brightening the night.

Alfred Geller, who has represented me for the past twelve years, understands the world of television and has helped me immeasurably. Geller is truly one of America's best. He stands out for one reason—his understanding of news and people. Alfred proves a point to all of his clients: you can never stop learning.

Behind the scenes, Lew Klein has made a major difference in my career. Klein is a retired broadcast executive who has helped hundreds of people aspire to greatness in this community. Klein, even in retirement, shapes the careers of many executives. All the broadcast world eventually returns to Lew Klein.

One of the pleasures of working at Fifth and Market Streets is the proximity to two great stations. KYW Newsradio's Roy Shapiro, Steve Butler, Mark Helms, and Bill Roswell are always supportive. Tim Sabean and the folks at WYSP are a pleasure to be with. Having the rock station in our building keeps us forever youthful.

The National Multiple Sclerosis Society continues to inspire me and gives hope to eight thousand MS clients in this region. My mother would have been proud of the work of President Judi Cohen and Director John Scott. Thacher Longstreth's dream of a world without MS is getting closer. The people at the National Adoption Center, especially Carolyn Johnson and Gloria Hochman, who support our Sunday's Child program, have inspired greater understanding of the needs of children.

Donna and I owe a great debt to her parents, Irv and Norma Jarrett; her sister, Robin; my father, Jack; and my brothers, Bruce and Monte, and their families.

Writing this book has been a great learning experience. My thanks go to Temple University Press and my editor, Doris Braendel, who helped me become a better writer and was an initial advocate for this book. Doris went above and beyond the call of duty to make sure my writing style was as palatable to the eye as my broadcast style may be to the ear. I owe her a debt of gratitude for her guidance and passion for my story. My special thanks also go to Temple Press director Lois Patton, lawyer Fran Freedman, and a tireless and determined researcher, Sheri Herman-Carr.

Finally, as I did at the beginning, I end this work with a million thank yous to Donna, Michael, and Alexandra. There are no words adequate to describe my love and respect for them. There is no one like Donna in the world. What a mix—brilliance, talent, and beauty, inside and out. Her support and that of her company, Dynamic Images, has been key to this project. I cherish Michael's love as a son, along with his intuition and his extraordinary desire for quality television. Alexandra is a young woman with a passion for her family and for excellence. Her campaigns to fight bigotry make us proud. Donna, Michael, and Alexandra are simply the best.

Index